FRY

LORNA DOUNAEVA

ALSO BY LORNA DOUNAEVA

The McBride Vendetta

Angel Dust

Cold Bath Lane

The Wedding

May Queen Killers

The Perfect Girl

The Perfect Friend

Holiday Thrillers

The Christmas Party

Domestic Noir

The Girl in the Woods

For Denis

Thank you for believing in me and my dream. Thank you for the endless cups of coffee and homemade cakes. Thank you for the technical support when I wanted to throw a brick at the computer. Thank you for restraining me when it still didn't work.

ACKNOWLEDGMENTS

There are so many people I would like to thank but I'll do my best not to make it sound like a drunken Oscars speech. In particular I'd like to thank Margaret James, Rob Barker, Mimi Dendias, Rory Matheson, Nicola Welch, Greg Malcolm, Faye Malcolm, Virginia Malcolm and Clifford Malcolm.

Editor
Maria Dounaeva

Cover
Coverquill

Copyright © 2013 by Lorna Dounaeva

All rights reserved.

No part of this book may be reproduced in any form or by any electronic or mechanical means, including information storage and retrieval systems, without written permission from the author, except for the use of brief quotations in a book review.

FRY

1

"NO!"

I STAMP HARD on the brakes. She stares back at me, her eyes stricken with terror, but it's too late for me to do anything. We brace ourselves for the impact.

A tomato flies out of the grocery bag on the back seat and splatters brutally against the windscreen. Its juicy pulp oozes down the glass as my car shrieks to a halt, just inches from her porcelain face. She slides down to the ground.

"Oh my god!" I tear off my seat belt, and in my panic, I almost forget to apply the brake. I leap out and rush round to the front of the car. "Are you all right? Do you want me to call an ambulance?"

She looks up at me with strange, unblinking eyes. "Why would I need an ambulance?"

I laugh nervously. "I nearly ran you over."

Slowly, she sits up. "No…no, it's alright. I just need a minute."

I kneel down next to her. "I'm so sorry, I just didn't see you!"

I shake violently, my heart pounds in my chest. I feel guilt and shock and nausea in equal measure. "I just didn't see you."

I don't understand what happened. Can't understand it for the life of me. One moment she wasn't there and the next she was. She was like an apparition, materialising in the middle of my driveway. I shake my head. It's all too much. Maybe I should get my eyes tested.

"Would you like to come in?" The words force themselves from my trembling lips. "I…I'll make us some tea. If you're sure you don't want me to call an ambulance?"

She pauses for a moment, and then nods thoughtfully. "A cup of tea would be lovely."

I offer her my hand and she pulls herself up off the gravel driveway. I feel a surge of electricity as our fingers connect. She is very small and delicate, a woman in a child's body. And yet she has an iron grip.

The keys jangle as I unlock my front door. For some reason it brings to mind the image of a jailer, unlocking a cell door. But my cosy, one bedroom home is anything but a prison.

"Fluffy?" I call, but my cat has gone into hiding. "Here, make yourself at home." I clear a pile of laundry off the sofa so she can sit down. But she follows me into the kitchen, watches closely as I make the tea, as if she's never seen it done before.

"Do you have any sugar?"

"Here, help yourself."

She takes a spoonful and dumps it into her cup, then another and another. And another. It must be the shock.

"Come on, let's go and sit down." Nodding, she follows me back into the lounge, stopping to straighten a picture hanging on the wall. I couldn't even tell it was crooked. "I really am sorry about nearly knocking you over. Are you sure you're OK?"

"I'm fine, though I'm sure I'll have a bump the size of an egg tomorrow." She pats the back of her head and giggles.

Why's that funny? Hell, she'd better not be planning to sue!

"You hit your head?" I ask nervously.

"Only a little."

"Would you like some ice?"

"Oh no, it's fine." She strokes the soft velvet arm of the sofa, as if it was a cat. She's a bit younger than me, early twenties I'd guess. And waif-like in her long flowing skirt, her hair a tangle of wild black curls.

For a while, neither of us can find anything to say. She stirs her tea vigorously to fill the silence.

"What were you doing outside my house, anyway?" I finally ask.

"I was delivering leaflets." Her voice is very squeaky. It reminds me of Minnie Mouse.

"What sort of leaflets?"

"These ones are for pizza. It doesn't pay very well, but I've only just moved to Queensbeach and I haven't found a proper job yet."

"What kind of work are you looking for?"

"Whatever I can get. There doesn't seem to be much going at this time of year."

"Oh, well they need shelf stackers at Robertson's. That's where I work."

"That's that big supermarket, right?"

"Yeah. Why don't you pop in tomorrow? I'll talk to my manager. I'm sure I can get you an interview."

"Wow, that's very kind of you, thanks. I'm sorry, I don't even know your name?"

"Isabel."

"And I'm Alicia. Alicia McBride." I get the feeling she wants me to remember her name.

She looks down into the bottom of her empty cup for what seems like an inordinate amount of time.

"Would you like another cup of tea?"

"No thanks."

"Perhaps I should take you home then?" I don't mean to sound rude, but we don't seem to have any more to talk about.

"I don't want to be any trouble…"

"No, really. It's the least I can do." I grab my jacket.

"Where shall I drop you?" I ask, wiping the tomato pulp from my windscreen. I'm a little nervous about getting behind the wheel again, but I suppose it's best to get it over with. Alicia fiddles with her seat belt.

"The caravan park, down by the beach."

"The caravan park?"

"You know it?"

"Yeah, I just hadn't even realised anyone lived there out of season. I thought they were meant to be doing it up?"

"It's just temporary, till I find something better."

I am careful not to catch her eye.

The windscreen wipers screech noisily as I drive down the main Coast Road. It's raining only lightly, but the wind dumps handfuls of sand over the car, making it difficult to see.

The caravan park is even more dilapidated than I remember.

"Thanks for the lift," Alicia calls as she climbs out.

"No problem, and seriously – come over to Robertson's in the morning. I'm sure we can sort something out."

"You don't have to do that."

"It's the least I can do…" my voice trails off as I take in the boarded up doors and smashed windows, not to mention all the rubbish strewn around. What a tip! I watch as she walks up the steps of a guano-splattered caravan. There is no one else about. The place is completely silent, save for the shrill of the gulls and the whistle of the wind. I find it a bit eerie.

Alicia watches me from her broken window as I drive away. I feel guilty leaving her there but what else can I do? I don't want to invite her to stay with me – I need my own space. Besides, I've only got one bedroom.

I'm sure she'll be fine, I tell myself. She can move somewhere better once she gets a proper job.

I switch on the radio and sing along on the short drive back home, try to get Alicia and that ethereal smile of hers, out of my mind.

Mustafa's Restaurant and Coffee Bar - 8 PM

"I'll have a bottle of red please," I tell the waitress as I sit down at my usual table, a couple of hours later.

"Anything else?"

"Um, maybe some bread and olives."

"Coming right up," she says, scribbling this down on her notepad. "Hey, your necklace is undone. Would you like me to do it up for you?"

"Would you?"

I pull my hair up off the nape of my neck and she reaches round to refasten it. Her head is bent over mine as my friends walk in.

"Told you," says Deacon Frost, plopping down on the couch opposite. "Women, they're all into each other."

"If you say so." His brother Rhett carefully removes his designer jacket and hangs it on the coat stand.

"What are we having?" Deacon asks. "Red or white?"

"I've already ordered a bottle of red," I tell him.

"Red it is then."

Mustafa's serves a hundred different kinds of mezzeraki but only two types of wine, red or white. As for the beer, it's completely unpalatable to start with, but Deacon reckons it gets better, the more you drink. You're probably wondering right now why on earth we come here – but it's one of the few places in Queensbeach that stays open all year round, so we've come to get used to it.

"Where's Kate?" Deacon asks.

"She's meeting Julio," I say. "Apparently he called her, completely out of the blue."

Rhett looks concerned. "What does *he* want?"

I stare up at the ceiling, pretend to be fascinated by the odd collection of hanging lamps. "No idea. Nothing to do with me."

"He *is* your brother."

"Half-brother. Anyway, I haven't seen him in months, have I?"

The waitress brings the wine and I inhale mine in big, nervous gulps, without much regard for the bar-snacks. Deacon raises an eyebrow, but doesn't say anything. I don't mention the incident with Alicia. I'd rather just forget it ever happened.

"So what are we doing this weekend?" Rhett asks.

It's pelting it down outside, but all anyone can talk about is how this coming weekend is tipped to be one of the hottest of the year. In November. If the predictions turn out to be true, then global warming is even more messed up than I thought.

"We could have a barbecue," Deacon suggests.

"What if the weather people have got it wrong?"

"It'll be alright. We've got outdoor heaters and we can put up the gazebo if it's not too windy."

"I can make a potato salad," I offer, as this is about the limit of my culinary skills.

"OK, but make sure the potatoes are cooked this time," Deacon says wryly.

I blush. "That was a simple mistake. Could happen to anyone."

"I'll make cocktails!" Rhett cuts in, clapping his hands

together. Deacon rolls his eyes at me, but I'm with Rhett. I love cocktails.

"Yeah, and maybe you could invite some of your sexy doctor friends?" I suggest, batting my eyelashes at Deacon. He pulls an expression I can't quite read. I'm not sure if that's a yes or a no.

"Cool, a belly dancer," a man at the next table chirps.

Not cool. Shandy may look exotic, but I happen to know she's from Lewisham. Loud, jingly music starts to play, but she continues to sit at the bar, applying lipstick with a bored expression. Reluctantly, she climbs up onto a table and starts dancing. I have to admit she looks good, with her tanned skin and toned tummy. But within five minutes, she is bored. She leaps down and starts walking around, flanked on each side by two bartenders who act like her personal bodyguards. She's looking for a victim.

"Don't look up," Rhett hisses. But it's too late.

Shandy seizes me by the hand and propels me to my feet. Her henchmen surround me, tying a scarf around my waist and shouting words of encouragement. I am helpless but to join in or I'll look like a party pooper. My friends whoop and cheer as I begin circling my hips to imitate hers. She does things with her tummy muscles that no mortal should be able to do, but I twist and grind as best as I can to keep up.

I'm actually starting to enjoy myself when Deacon yells: "Up on the table!"

To my horror, the henchmen seem to like this suggestion and they hoist me up. Looking down at all those people, my inhibitions return with a thud. Plus, there is the very real danger that I might fall off. I gyrate awkwardly, wondering how much longer this bloody song's going to go on for. It doesn't seem to have a middle or an end and all this circling my hips is making me giddy. How does Shandy do it? Actually, where *is* Shandy? I haven't seen her since they lifted me up here.

I scan the room. I don't believe it – she's back at the bar, having a drink, while I dance on like an idiot. The cheek of it! She's the paid entertainer; I'm the customer, the entertainee! I give my hips one last wiggle and by some miracle of fate, the music comes to an end. I slink back to my table, to a smattering of applause.

"I'm going to kill you," I growl at Deacon, reaching for my wine. He leans forward and sticks a tenner into my waistband.

"Hey!" I retrieve it and tuck it into my purse. "Don't think you're getting that back."

"Worth every penny," he smiles sweetly.

I grab my bag. "Come on Rhett, I need a cigarette."

❄

It's half past eleven by the time we spill out onto the street. I've just missed the last bus, and there's not a cab in sight.

"I'll call you tomorrow," I tell Rhett and Deacon, as I turn to go.

"Wait, I'll walk you," Deacon says, even though they live on the other side of town.

"You don't have to do that."

"Yes, I do."

I'd argue some more, but Deacon's old-fashioned like that. So I say good night to Rhett and we trundle up the road, me slightly unsteady in my heels.

Deacon taps his foot with exaggerated impatience as I fumble for my keys outside my house.

"I don't know how you find anything in there," he says, in awe of my oversized handbag.

Triumphantly, I locate the keys but my cigarettes fall to the floor. He stoops down and retrieves them for me.

"You'd be better off without these."

That's Deacon for you, always ready with a lecture.

"Hmm…" I turn the key in the lock. As I open the door, a black and white fur ball shoots out.

"There you are, Fluffy."

I scoop him up in my arms and he purrs contentedly.

"Right, well I'd better be off before Mr Krinkle's curtains start twitching." Deacon says.

I giggle. Mr Krinkle is my extraordinarily nosey neighbour.

"OK, well thanks for seeing me home."

"Any time."

"Night."

I walk into the gloomy house. I forgot to leave the light on in the front room, so I have to fumble around in the darkness, with Fluffy running circles around me. I find the switch, and see that there's a red light on the answer phone, which means I have a message. I press play.

"Izzy, it's Mum. I just wanted to let you know that I've left you a message on your email."

I smile to myself. Mum's only recently got online and she's still getting the hang of it.

"I bought a lovely new tea cosy from Shopfitter95 on eBay – do you know her? Seems like a very nice woman…" I let her chatter on as I walk into the kitchen and open the window so that I can have one last fag before bed. I'm not really supposed to smoke in the house, but I was planning to give up when I moved in. I pour out a late night snack for Fluffy. I'm not supposed to have a pet either, but try telling him that.

Later, I snuggle down in bed with the latest issue of Marie Claire, but I can't help sensing that someone, or something, is watching me. Glancing up, I notice a filmy cobweb above my bed, with a big spider parachuting its way down towards me.

"Gah!"

I grab an empty glass and trap it before it reaches my pillow. I try to return to my Marie Claire, but it's impossible. I keep stealing glances at the nightstand, watching with morbid fascination as the spider taps at the sides of the glass with its delicate, spindly legs.

Now what?

I don't want to squash it, but I don't dare let it go. I know I should let it out the window but I can't face it right now. I put down my magazine and switch off the light. I'll deal with it in the morning.

2

All eyes are down, focused on the last ten minutes of the class. Early morning spin is not the place for making friends. My fellow cyclists and I barely exchange a nod as we sit down, stand up and pedal frantically - faster, faster, faster, pausing only to gulp down water and dab at our foreheads with already sodden towels. We are in competition - with each other, but most of all with ourselves.

Afterwards, I emerge from the shower, revived and alert. My body is no temple but I pride myself on being toned, if not trim. I allow myself a contented smile as I fasten the buttons on my charcoal grey suit. It was a deal breaker, I told them when I was offered my job. I'd wear my own clothes, or they could get someone else. I wouldn't be seen dead in the hideous uniform the rest of the staff have to wear; the clown red trousers, lime green shirts and hideous orange baseball caps that clash with my auburn hair. No job is worth that.

I smile to myself as I walk out to my car and toss my gym bag in the boot, but my good mood starts to evaporate as I see the queue of traffic heading out of town.

Monday morning gridlock; just what I need.

Even stuck behind all the traffic, I can see my place of

work. Robertson's Superstore is a bright yellow blot on the horizon. It spans ten football fields, topped by a giant 'R'. You can see if for miles around, in fact, I have a disconcerting view of it from my bedroom window.

Eventually, I pull into a space near the front of the store and sit there for a moment, window rolled down as I smoke a cigarette. I like the way the tobacco mingles with the salty seaweed scent of the air.

"Isabel?" My manager, Sonya, peers in at me.

"Morning." I give her a weary smile.

"Did you have a nice weekend?"

"I worked most of it," I remind her. Now that Robertson's is open 24-7, there are never enough staff to cover all the shifts.

"Yeah, me too," she says with a sigh. "Are you coming in? I want to get started."

"I'll be right with you."

But not till I finish this cigarette.

Robertson's is like a walled city, fortified with rows and rows of economy baked bean cans. We sell everything from groceries to washing machines and mobility buggies. Workers stream through the doors behind me, punching their time cards in unison and shuffling forward, like inmates in a chain gang. Fortunately for me, I am not one of the gang, though my job is only marginally better. As a junior manager, my days can be spent doing anything from dealing with customer complaints to operating the checkout. And since they sacked the cleaners last month, I could even find myself slopping out the toilets, if no one else is available. I haven't had to do this yet, but I plan to be *very* sick that day.

"Wide load!" someone bellows as I fall into step with Sonya.

We whirl round, but it's just Stu, our senior manager, making one of his rude jokes about the size of Sonya's bottom. He's so un-PC it's not even funny. Though for a man who sprays himself Day-Glo orange, he's on very shaky territory.

"Oh, there's a girl here for an interview," he says as an afterthought. "She's waiting in your office."

With that, he heads back to the warehouse, where I suspect he spends most of his time sharing sexist jokes and playing cards with the lads.

Sonya rolls her eyes. "This place would be so much better without him."

I can't help but agree. Stu is a bit of a pillock.

We step into the office. Alicia is sitting in the corner, looking like a bedraggled orphan. Her hair is all wet from the rain, and she has draped her coat over the radiator to dry. I can't help noticing that one of her shoes has a hole in it.

I force a smile onto my lips. "Hi, glad you came! Sonya, this is the girl I was telling you about."

"Good to meet you, Alicia. Isabel, why don't you tell her a bit about Robertson's?"

I lick my lips. "Well, as you probably know, this supermarket is the largest one in the area – or it was," I correct myself. "Until J.Filbert's opened last year."

"That's the place with the squirrel logo?"

"Yes."

"We primarily need shelf stackers at the moment," Sonya moves on, "but you'll probably find that you get to work in other areas of the supermarket too. Do you have any retail experience?"

"No, but I like shopping!"

"Me too!" I smile.

"And I'm very keen to learn," she adds quickly. "I'm a hard worker."

"That's good." Sonya glances at her watch. "Sorry, ladies, but I've just realised the time. I need to get to a meeting at Head Office. Let's cut to the chase, shall we? I suppose the next question, Alicia, is when can you start?"

Alicia beams. "I can start right now!"

"Wonderful," Sonya says. "I just need you to fill in some forms and we'll put you to work." She reaches up onto a shelf and pulls down a new starter booklet.

"Don't we need to check her references first?" I ask in a low voice, as Alicia fishes about in her handbag for a pen.

"That's OK – we'll do it later. Anyway - any friend of yours is OK by me."

I'm about to explain to Sonya that Alicia isn't exactly a friend when her phone rings.

What does it really matter anyway? I reason, as she takes the call. I nearly ran the poor girl over. I owe her. So what if I don't really know her? It's just a lousy shelf stacking job. What harm can it do?

"Isabel?" Sonya sets down the phone and looks at me apologetically.

"I hate to ask you this but someone's dropped a huge vat of Ribena in the soft drinks aisle and they're making a pig's ear of cleaning it up. Can I count on you to sort it out? I really have to get going."

"Of course," I smile. "No problem."

I leave Alicia to fill in her forms, and walk to the back of the shop, where I unlock the door to the cleaning cupboard. It stinks of bleach in there. I can see the mop standing against the wall but it's just out of reach so I step inside. As my hand closes around it, the door swings shut with a resounding bang. It sounds very final.

3

With the door shut, the room is plunged into darkness. I fumble for the handle. It's stuck. I grip it more tightly, but the damn thing won't budge.

"Very funny. Let me out!"

I bang furiously on the door, but there is no response – not a giggle, not a titter.

"Is there anybody there?"

Maybe there isn't anyone out there after all? Maybe the wind slammed the door and forced it shut. I hear the whir of the forklifts in the warehouse next door and someone shouting instructions as a new delivery arrives. No one can hear me. No one knows I'm here.

The walls edge closer together. I don't like confined spaces. I never have. No windows. No light. No air. I look up at the ceiling. No way out. I feel a prickly heat crawl up my back.

"Let me out!" I thunder at the door.

The stink of bleach tingles in my nostrils. My eyes start to smart. I tug at the door handle with all my might. I kick the door in frustration. It won't budge.

OK, don't panic.

I pound on the door again, shout even louder than before.
"Help! Somebody help me! Get me out!"
I punch the door until my knuckles are raw. I punch so loudly, I almost don't hear the reassuring voice on the other side.
"Calm down, love! I'll get you out."
My panic subsides. I know that voice. It's Jon the security man! There are a couple of short clicks, and the cupboard fills with light. The door's open! I practically throw my arms around his neck, then, seeing the crowd gathered behind him, I try to regain my composure.
"Thanks." My voice is little more than a whisper.
"Need a cigarette?" he asks.
"I'll just get someone else to mop up the Ribena," I say, shakily. "There's no way I'm going back in that cupboard."

The Beach House - Saturday

"You sure they won't mind me coming?" Alicia looks anxious as I lead her into Rhett and Deacon's place.
"Course not," I assure her. "It's a party."
Rhett is in the kitchen, arranging a tray of tequilas with a concentrated look on his face.
"Hi, I brought the potato salad."
"Great."
"Where's Deacon?"
"Out in the garden."
"I'll go and see if he needs a hand."
I turn to go, when Rhett calls after me: "Hey, Isabel?"
"What?"
"Who's your friend?"
"Oh, right!"
I look guiltily at Alicia, who is hovering behind me.
"This is Alicia."
He gives her an easy smile. "Hi."

Alicia mumbles something incomprehensible and blushes. Rhett raises his eyebrows at me. Wow, she is really shy around men! I dread to think how she's going to fare with Deacon.

"Come on, the garden's this way."

I adjust my sunglasses as we step outside again. The weather people were not wrong. They cannot agree on why, but the temperature is distinctly tropical. Charred autumn leaves litter the lawn, and horse chestnuts lie roasting in the sun. It's quite peculiar. I think this is the first time I've ever worn a sundress and sandals in November, though I brought my winter coat just in case.

Deacon has stripped down to his vest. His longish dark hair glistens with sweat and he hauls cast iron garden furniture around as if it weighed no more than paper. He is so engrossed in what he's doing, he doesn't notice us watching him.

"Hey, Deacon! I'm here!" I wave my arms to get his attention.

"Oh, hi." He sets down the chair he was carrying.

"This is Alicia. She brought beer."

"Ah, my kind of woman!"

"Want one?" Alicia asks, shyly.

"I wouldn't say no."

She breaks a can from the pack and tosses it in his direction. He catches it with ease and peels back the tab to take a long slug.

"You have a lovely house," she ventures, looking at him from under her long dark lashes.

Deacon beams. "I can give you a tour if you like, once I've got the barbecue going."

"That would be lovely."

He puts down his beer and begins setting up the barbecue, laying down charcoal and pouring on lighter fluid.

"Damn, I'm out of matches. Isabel, can I borrow your lighter?"

I poke around in my pocket. "Sorry - I must have left it at home."

He looks at Alicia. "You got one?"

She shakes her head. "Sorry."

"Never mind, I'll go and ask Rhett."

He walks back to the house, while Alicia looks at me inquisitively.

"Maybe we can help?" she suggests shyly.

"How?"

She walks over to the rock garden and digs around in the dirt.

I wrinkle up my nose. "What are you doing?"

She picks something up.

"What's that?"

"Flints."

I watch, half amused, half fascinated as she stands over the barbecue, rubbing them furiously together.

"Alicia, I don't think that's going to work,"

She is so determined, that for a moment, I almost believe that the barbecue has started to smoulder, that there are wisps of hot, grey smoke rising from the coals. I can almost sense it in my nostrils, though it can only be a trick of the light.

"You found a lighter then," says Deacon, when he comes back out.

"What?"

I glance back at the barbecue. It's undeniable now. There are actual flames. I go over and hold my hands over them, unable to believe that they are being warmed by something Alicia created so quickly, so craftily.

"Nice work."

"Alicia did it all herself!"

He looks at her approvingly, but I don't think he gets my meaning.

"Nice," he repeats. "Isabel, can you start setting out the food? Rhett's still fannying about with the cocktails."

People start to arrive. They are strangers, mostly; Rhett's mates from the rugby club, their work colleagues and neighbours. No sign of Kate yet.

"Anything I can do to help?" I ask Deacon, a little bored.

"Yeah – can you watch the barbecue for a few minutes?"

"OK – where are you off to?"

"I promised your friend a tour of the house, remember?"

Something gets caught in my throat.

"On second thoughts, maybe someone else should mind the barbecue – I'd hate to burn the burgers! Here," I pick up the tongs and hand them to the nearest man. "You can watch the barbecue for a bit, can't you?"

I don't even wait for his reply.

Deacon strides through the house, pointing out a window seat here and an antique dining table there. Alicia admires the baby grand piano in the sitting room and the grandfather clock in the hall. I know this house almost as well as I know my own, but I trail after them regardless, joining in with the oohs and aahs in the appropriate places. We explore various rooms on the first and second floors, and then head up the stairs to the third floor, Deacon's room, which smells of his own distinctive scent.

It's quite clean for a man's room, apart from the unmade bed. He doesn't seem the least bit concerned about this as he pushes open the French windows, through which there is a balcony that overlooks the water.

"I can't believe you live here!" gasps Alicia. Her face is flushed with excitement as she watches the waves crash against the rocks below. He has picked just the right moment for this view, just as the sun is melting into the horizon.

"You're so lucky," she breathes.

Deacon smiles. "Yes, I suppose I am."

She glances over at me. "Just imagine Isabel, to wake up every morning and see this incredible view."

"I know," I agree. "It's must be heavenly."

When we come back downstairs, I find Kate sitting by herself in the gazebo, sheltering from the heat. She holds a glass of wine in one hand and her wedding ring in the other.

"So what happened with Julio?" I ask softly.

"He wanted me to sign the divorce papers. He said he wanted to get married again – as soon as possible."

"Oh Kate!"

But a tiny part of me is actually glad, because maybe now Kate can move on with her life and stop wishing for a reconciliation that's never going to happen. I don't really know what to say to her. I have no wise words. I've never been married. Never been divorced. I haven't even been in a relationship for ages. What advice can I possibly give? The best thing I can think of is distraction. For the time being, at least.

"You're never going to believe this!"

"What?"

Hurriedly, I tell her how Alicia got the barbecue going.

"She did it just by rubbing two stones together," I exclaim. "I've never seen anything like it."

Kate shrugs. "Maybe she was in the Girl Guides."

"*I* was in the Girl Guides and I never learnt anything like that!"

But Kate seems more interested in the contents of her wine glass than in what I'm telling her.

"Talking of Alicia, I suppose I'd better see if she's OK. She doesn't know anyone here and she's kind of shy. Do you want to come and meet her?"

"No – you go and find her. I'll catch you up in a bit."

I find Alicia sitting by the barbecue with Deacon. Her shyness seems to have completely evaporated and she is quite animated as she hands him a bottle of suntan cream. I blanch slightly as he pours some into his hand and rubs it into her pale shoulders.

I can't see Rhett, or anyone else I recognise, so I go and stand on the edge of a throng of people. I stand there for a while, nodding and smiling as the others talk, but the only person who takes any notice of me is Deacon's boss, whose jokes are so highbrow that I've no idea what he's talking about.

I edge away, picking up a platter of party snacks to offer around. I usually find food to be a good ice-breaker.

"Thanks," says a guy with floppy brown hair, "I love olives."

"Me too."

He's not my type, but I smile back anyway, grateful to be acknowledged.

"So how do you know Rhett and Deacon?" I ask.

Before he can answer, a small, busty woman flounces over and wedges herself in between us. I give a resigned shrug and move along. Sometimes I forget the rules. As a single woman, I can't monopolise any man for longer than five seconds, lest his wife or girlfriend thinks I'm trying to steal him.

I venture further down the garden. There's some great music playing and I wouldn't mind a dance, but I can't find anyone to dance with. Who are all these people? Why did Rhett and Deacon have to invite them all?

Disheartened, I let myself out of the back gate and wander down to the beach, which is covered in sandwich wrappers and drink cans from the sudden influx of visitors. I glare, as the last of them climb back into their coach, singing and laughing as they drive off.

There is a refreshing breeze in the air now. I slip off my heels and pick my way along the cool, soft sand. I'm ruining my Armani tights, but I no longer care. This beach has a lost, desolate beauty that I've always found mesmerising. The noise of the party fades away as I listen to the rhythmic sound of the waves, lapping in and out.

"Isabel? What are you doing out here?"

I turn to find Deacon watching me with a bemused expression on his face.

"Oh, I don't know, just thinking."

"About what?"

I shrug. He slips an arm around me. "Come back to the party, it's getting cold out here."

I'm not sure what's changed – maybe it's the drop in temperature, but when we return to the party, it has a completely different vibe. Everyone seems to have mellowed, and there are a lot more people dancing. I wonder briefly if Rhett's slipped something into their cocktails.

"Are my eyes deceiving me, or is that Kate on the dance floor?" Deacon exclaims.

I look out and see her next to Alicia, laughing and dancing like she hasn't a care in the world.

"She's a little treasure, your friend," Rhett says, handing me a drink. "I don't know what she said to Kate, but it seems to have done the trick."

I shake my head in bewilderment, wondering what Alicia will do next.

When they emerge, giggling from the dance floor, they look more like old friends than two people who met not more than half an hour ago.

"You two look like you were having a good time," I comment.

"The best," Kate agrees, with a grin. "Alicia is *so* funny!"

She is?

"So what were you giggling at?"

She glances at Alicia. "Oh you know, just stuff."

What stuff? I want to ask, but I don't get the chance. There is a loud bang that makes us all jump. Someone is hammering on the door. Deacon rushes over to investigate. It's one of the guests who's just left the party.

"Quick, call the fire brigade!"

"Why? What's happened?"

"The caravan park is on fire!"

4

The sky is black with smoke. Bits of obliterated caravan float gracefully in the wind, spreading the fire to neighbouring trees and bushes.

"Keep back," Deacon warns, moving nonetheless closer to the blaze.

"Deacon!" I call after him, my eyes stinging from the fumes.

Two men stand on the sidelines, showering the flames with what looks like a garden hose. They might as well be sprinkling confetti for all the good it's doing.

"Is anybody hurt?" Deacon calls out to them.

"We don't know!" the older man yells back.

"There's a young woman staying here and nobody's seen her since the fire started." He looks back towards the coast road. "Where's the bloody fire brigade?"

Then his eyes fall on Alicia and he heaves a huge sigh of relief.

"Thank god! She's here, Dan! She's safe!"

Deacon looks uncertainly at Alicia.

"That's what I was trying to tell you," I hiss. "She lives here."

"*Lived* here," he corrects me, quick to recover his composure. "Look at that inferno! This place has had it."

Kate slips her arm around Alicia, who is staring, mesmerised by the flames.

"You OK?"

Alicia doesn't reply.

"She's probably in shock," Deacon whispers. "Take her back to the house – get her a cup of tea or something."

"Yeah, that's probably a good idea. Aren't you coming?"

"No, I think I'll stay until the fire brigade gets here."

"OK. Don't be a hero." I give him a wink, but deep down, I wish he would just come back to the house.

Back at the Beach House, I watch as Rhett and Kate fuss over Alicia, but I can't participate. Something is bothering me. I just can't put my finger on it.

We are all still up when Deacon returns a little later.

"Is it as bad as we thought?"

He nods. "There's not much left of the caravans, but they've managed to prevent it from spreading any further."

He looks across the table at Alicia. "You'll have to stay here tonight."

Alicia has gone all shy again. She looks down at her hands. "I don't want to impose."

"Nonsense, you've seen the place - we've got plenty of room. Now, do you need to call anyone?"

She shakes her head.

"Are you sure?"

"Quite."

She lets out a big yawn and covers her mouth and I'm not sure, but I think I see her smile through her hand.

My House - Sunday Morning

I am awoken by someone stomping about on my stomach. I push Fluffy off and sit up. In the cold light of day, my concerns about Alicia seem silly, laughable even. Obviously, what she did at the barbecue was some kind of stunt, a party trick. She's just an ordinary girl. She can't create fire out of nothing, no one can. The nearly getting run over, the fire at the caravan park – it must all just be some strange coincidence. After all, what reason would Alicia have for setting fire to the place where she's staying? And how could she, when she was at the party all evening?

Downstairs, I find the answer phone blinking. I press play and smile to myself as Mum's chirpy voice fills the room.

"Hello Izzy, are you there dear? Auntie Jean and I have booked ourselves on a fabulous Over 60's break to Morocco! Isn't that fun? It's over the Christmas holidays. I do hope you don't mind? Give me a ring, dear, and I'll tell you all about it… "

Once I'm showered and dressed, I drive over to Rhett and Deacon's to help with the post party clean-up, but to my delight, Rhett is putting the last of the dirty glasses into the dishwasher as I arrive. Deacon is still sweeping up in the garden, but I decide to leave him to it.

"Is Alicia up yet?" I ask Rhett. "I was hoping to have a word with her."

"Why don't you go and see?" he says, pouring some powder into the dishwasher. "She's upstairs in the White Room."

I head up the stairs to the first floor. The White Room is next to Rhett's. The door swings open before I even knock. Alicia greets me as if she's been expecting me. She is wearing the same gypsy skirt she had on yesterday plus a designer jumper of Rhett's which shrank in the wash.

"Hi. Mind if I come in?"

"Course not."

I plump myself down on the bed.

"This is a lovely room."

"Yes, Deacon let me choose whichever one I wanted."

She stands in front of the mirror, brushing her hair with a boar-bristle hairbrush. She doesn't realise it, but the brush belongs to Rhett and Deacon's mother, and this is the room she stays in when she comes to visit. The décor is floral and feminine, the walls papered in a delicate print that matches the thick quilted bedspread and pillows. There's even a matching en suite.

"It sucks about the caravan park," I say. "It was really lucky no one was hurt."

"I know," she agrees. "Really lucky. Now, do you think I should wear my hair up or down?"

"Down."

"It's just that it gets so big and frizzy if I leave it down."

"Look, there's something I've been meaning to ask you," I say, coming to stand next to her in front of the mirror.

"Yeah?"

"How *did* you get Deacon's barbecue to light?"

She stops mid brush stroke.

"What do you mean? I lit it with a match. You were there. You saw me."

"Yes, I was there," I say hesitantly. "But I saw you digging up flints."

She laughs. "I found a box of matches down there. How do you think I did it, silly?"

I look at her uncertainly, but she looks me right in the eye and her face shows no signs of insincerity. Could it be that I was mistaken?

Alicia sets the brush down on the table.

"That's better," she says, with a satisfied smile.

I follow her back down to the kitchen, where Kate is setting the table.

"Do you like pancakes?" Rhett asks Alicia

"Who doesn't?" Alicia smiles broadly.

What happened to all her shyness? It seems to have

vanished again. As has her wildness. Her hair looks smooth and styled today, not like a bedraggled orphan at all.

"I'll have some too, if you're making them," I invite myself. Rhett makes the best pancakes of anyone I know.

"Here, see if you can open this," Kate says, handing me a bottle of syrup. "It feels like the lid's been welded on."

There is a definite colour in her cheeks this morning, I notice and a certain bounce in her step that I haven't seen in ages. She has even ironed her shirt and put on some perfume, which is all very good, but at the same time a bit odd. I could have put last night's miraculous recovery down to alcohol, but she certainly isn't drunk now. It's almost as if Alicia has wiped all memory of Julio from her mind. I wonder what on earth she said to her?

I turn my attention to the bottle of syrup I'm supposed to be opening, clench it tight and yank as hard as I can, my face screwed up in concentration. Deacon strides in from the garden, and leans against the counter, watching my attempts with an amused look on his face.

"Here, give me that!"

He wrenches it from my grasp and twists off the lid as if it were no harder than opening a bottle of ketchup.

"I loosened it for you!" I say in my defence.

Deacon just laughs.

Rhett serves the pancakes and we all sit around the table, talking about the fire. It appears to have been a fierce one. Left a big, depressing cloud over the whole of Queensbeach. I doubt much of the caravan park survived.

Nonetheless, Alicia wants to know if any of her stuff survived, so we walk down there after breakfast to have a look. It's not good news. Not even the outer fence has been left intact. The place looks like a meteorite has hit it. It has literally been flattened – and blackened. Not a single, frazzled piece of grass remains, just the burned-out shells of the caravans and a whole lot of mess and mud.

"Hey, that's the owner," Deacon whispers to me, as a plump, balding man approaches. I recognise him as one of the men who were trying to put the fire out the night before.

"Looks bad, doesn't it?" he says, looking around at the charred remains.

"It happened so quickly," Deacon says. "There was really nothing you could do."

"No, I suppose not. Shame the fire brigade didn't get here quicker, but not their fault. Apparently, there was a bloody great van blocking the road."

"Do you know what caused the fire?" I chip in.

He shakes his head. "No, the police are investigating."

"They're not ruling out arson then?" I ask, with one eye on Alicia, who has gone to examine the place where her caravan used to be. I can't help it; I have to know.

"It seems unlikely. We've never had any of that kind of trouble round here before."

"It is a pretty quiet neighbourhood," Deacon agrees. "I hope you'll be covered by the insurance?"

"Should be, although you know what insurance companies are like. It'll be like pulling teeth." He looks guiltily in Alicia's direction. "We won't be covered for anything that was in the vans, I'm afraid. There wasn't supposed to be anyone living in them. We'd been renovating."

"So how come Alicia was staying here?" I ask curiously.

"I felt sorry for her," he says. "I found her sleeping rough on the beach, poor lass. I told her she could stay in one of my vans if she didn't mind the mess. I even gave her some of my daughter's old clothes. Of course they'll all have gone up in smoke now."

"Well, that settles it then," Deacon says, as we walk back over to the others. "Alicia will have to stay with us for the meanwhile. She clearly has nowhere else to go,"

"Are you sure?" I ask. "I mean, you barely know the girl."

He pats me on the shoulder. "She's your friend, isn't she? That's all I need to know."

"Well," I say faintly, "that's very…kind of you."

I bite my lip, wondering if I should tell him about my misgivings about Alicia. But what if I'm wrong? I wouldn't want her to end up homeless because of me, nor do I want to invite her to live with me. In fact, I'm more reluctant now than ever.

I owe her, I remind myself.

She still hasn't said a word to anyone about me nearly running her over. I don't think I'd ever hear the end of it if Deacon got wind.

"Hey, Isabel - what are you doing this afternoon?" Kate calls out.

"I don't know. I was thinking of going to the gym."

"I ought to go too – get my money's worth," she pulls a face, "but I really can't be arsed."

"It *is* rather pricey," I agree, "but luckily for me my free trial has been extended for another six months. Can you believe it? The manager called to tell me last week."

Kate's eyes bulge. "You're kidding! The first chunk came out of my bank account last month. No one offered me an extension. How did you get so lucky?"

"I've no idea!"

It's kind of strange, now that I think about it. Why am I getting a special deal, while Kate has to pay? After all, we joined at the same time.

"Anyway, I was going to suggest we take Alicia shopping this afternoon," she continues. "She's going to need some new clothes. I'm sure we can have a whip round to pay for it."

"Sounds good," I smile. After all, it can't hurt to get to know her a little better. Perhaps a shopping trip is just what we need to defuse some of the mystery.

Kate is right. Our friends and neighbours are very generous. Everyone wants to help out when they hear about the fire.

"I'd come with you," says Rhett, handing me a tenner for Alicia's clothing fund. "But I'm working this afternoon and it's double bubble. Let me know if you see any nice winter coats though."

"Like you need another coat!" I laugh. Rhett has the best wardrobe of anyone I know.

Red Rock Shopping Centre - 2 PM

So it's just the three of us who hit the shops that afternoon. It feels a little weird bringing a stranger along on a shopping trip, but Alicia fits in well – singing along to all the cheesy songs we listen to on the way and laughing in all the right places when Kate and I joke around. And although this shopping trip was supposed to be for Alicia, Kate and I stack up at least as many bags as she does. I even manage to persuade Kate to try on a couple of dresses. She doesn't buy any of them, but even trying them on is progress for someone who lives in jeans and combats.

We are on our way out of H&M when something catches her eye.

"How on earth did I miss those amazing jeans?" she exclaims, pointing to a pair of Levi's covered in rips and holes. I groan at her lack of taste, but she is totally oblivious as she pulls them off the rack and rushes towards the changing room. By this point even I've had enough shopping for one day. So, spotting some soft, comfy chairs, I sink down and ease the shoes off my aching feet. Alicia doesn't join me. Instead, she gazes in fascination at a pair of mannequins that have been stripped of their clothes and are looking rather sheepish in the corner. She reaches out and strokes their silky blonde hair, and as she does, a certain gleam comes into her eye. *I recognise that look*, I realise with a jolt. *It's the same one she had last night, when the caravan park was on fire.*

I look at the mannequins again, and the strangest thought

wafts through my mind. I picture their hard, plastic bodies melting into the fire. The mannequins look back at me with passive, unblinking eyes, but they no longer look embarrassed. Now they are afraid.

"I need something to drink," I announce abruptly, and whisk Alicia out of the shop. I take out my mobile and call Kate, telling her to meet us at the juice bar across the street. The heat of the mall is obviously getting to me.

We all sing along with the radio again on the way back to Queensbeach. The music is soothing, and helps me forget all about my stupid mannequin madness.

After I drop Kate and Alicia off, I curl up with Fluffy in front of the TV and order a takeaway from the pizza place in town. I've heard they have a hot new delivery man, so I go into the bathroom and touch up my make-up - you know, just in case. There is a knock at the door just as I come out.

"Wow, that was quick!"

I pull back the latch, but it isn't the delivery man who stands impatiently on the doorstep, a roguish grin on his face.

"Julio!"

"Well, aren't you going to invite me in?"

He taps his foot with mock impatience.

"What are you doing here?" I demand. "How come you didn't tell me you were coming?"

"I don't know. I just thought it would be better this way."

I usher him into the house and thrust a warm cup of tea into his hands. We've barely spoken since he walked out on Kate, but I can't deny I've missed him.

He is my brother, after all.

"So what have you been up to?" I ask. "Tell me all your news."

"Well, did you get your 'save the date' card?" he asks, his face taking on the puppy dog expression that drives the women crazy.

"Yes."

The card came this morning. I can't believe they've already sent them out.

"You seem to be in a bit of a hurry to get married. Is there anything I should know?"

"If you're asking if Holly is pregnant, then no. We just can't wait to get married. I just hope we get all the paperwork through in time – you know, for the divorce."

"Yeah, Kate told me."

"Is she OK?"

"Better than I would have expected."

"That's good."

"So what's she like, this Holly? Are you really sure you want to get married again so soon?"

"Absolutely, totally one hundred percent."

"Wow, you're really hooked, aren't you?"

"It's different with Holly," he says, setting his cup down on the table. "It just feels so right." A stupid smile flits across his face and I can see that he's smitten.

"Well, then I look forward to meeting her."

Julio beams. "Why don't you come for Christmas?"

"Christmas?"

"It was Holly's idea, actually. She really wants to meet you."

"That's really sweet of her," I say, stalling. It's not like I have any other plans for Christmas. Mum's going to be in Morocco, after all, but I'm not quite sure if I'd feel comfortable spending it with Julio and his new fiancée.

There's a reason why I'm a bit reluctant to meet Holly, and it's not purely out of loyalty to Kate, although that is a factor. The reason is this: I'm afraid that I'll like her. I know that sounds strange, but I can't help it. I find myself wondering if this love can really last, or if Holly will become another one of Julio's statistics. Because no matter how much in love with her he says he is now, there is no knowing how he will feel in six month's time. That's just the way he is.

Growing up, my brother always had a reputation as a heartbreaker. He's been like that since the age of twelve. Even then, he seemed to have a different girlfriend every week, and it was always me who ended up dealing with the hysterical women he left in his wake. But I never thought my best friend would be one of them. I don't know why I was so naive, but I just thought she was different to all his other women - stronger, more independent. I thought Julio had met his match with Kate. Turns out, I was wrong.

Ding-Dong!

"You expecting someone?"

"Yeah, that'll be my pizza."

"You ordered pizza?" he says, rubbing his hands with glee. "Fantastic! I could eat a horse!"

I pay for the pizza, and just for the record, the delivery man is definitely good-looking, though the goatee is a deal breaker.

I open the box of pizza and we dig in. With other men, I pretend to eat more daintily, but with Julio, I pig out. It's amazing how we can pick up just where we left off, even though we haven't spoken in months. It's always been like that between the two of us. He's so much a part of me that I can't just shut him out, no matter how hard I try.

"I'm really glad you came," I tell him, once all the pizza's been eaten and neither of us can manage another cup of tea.

He smiles his devilish grin. "Me too."

We both rise to our feet. I tower over him, even without shoes. He may have inherited his mother's Mediterranean good looks, but I got every inch of Dad's height.

My teeth chatter as I walk him out to his car. The warm weather has completely evaporated. We've gone from autumn to summer to winter in the space of a few days. The leaves are now crisp with frost and many of the birds have retreated back to their hideouts.

"So you'll let me know about Christmas?"

"OK."

"Oh, and one more thing, Izzy." He produces a brown cardboard box from the boot. "Can you give this to Kate? It's just some of her old stuff from the attic. I picked it up by mistake when I moved out. She'll probably want it back."

I nod, despite the knowledge that in order to give the box to Kate, I'll have to admit to her that I've seen him.

Well, there's no rush.

I'll wait till she's got over the shock of Julio asking for a divorce.

Mustafa's - Thursday Night

My shoulders feel a little tense as I walk through the door of Mustafa's. My friends are already there, and as always these days, the group includes Alicia.

"Isabel, we were beginning to wonder where you'd got to," Deacon says and he pulls up a chair for me. Alicia is sitting in my usual seat. I glance at her nervously. I'm still no closer to knowing what to make of her. At work she has already ingratiated herself with Sonya and she's even flirted with Stu, though I'm sure she wouldn't touch him with a barge pole. Everyone seems to like her, and yet there is something about her, something inexplicable that makes the hairs on the back of my neck stand up on end. I reach for the glass of wine Rhett's just poured me and take a large swig.

"Uh oh, what's going on?" Kate asks, watching the people at the next table being pulled from the comfort of their chairs. Tonight's entertainers, a 'traditional' Greek dance troupe from Portsmouth, are hauling everybody to their feet. They make us link hands, so that they can lead us in snake like formation around the chairs and tables. The dance gets faster and faster, and the heady speed is a little sickening, especially as I've just drunk half my wine.

Flushed and out of breath, we return to our table, where

we replenish ourselves with more wine. I look on as the dance troupe smashes plates on the floor and dances around in the resulting shards. I really hope these are props, as the whole thing looks rather dangerous.

"Oh, I got everyone key rings," I remember, pulling them from my bag and setting them down in the centre of the table.

"What are these?" Rhett asks, picking one up to examine it. "They're kind of…ugly."

"They're smoke detectors," I say, careful to avoid Alicia's eye. "I just thought, after the fire at the caravan park we should all be a bit more safety-conscious. It can't hurt, can it?"

My friends exchange bemused looks, much like the time Kate got us all suntan lotion for Christmas.

"That's really thoughtful of you," Alicia says sweetly. "I'll keep mine in my handbag at all times."

I am almost grateful to her as the others murmur in agreement, even though she is the reason I bought them in the first place.

"You know, I heard a rumour that they're reopening Millennium," Rhett says, sipping his Turkish coffee.

"Really?" Deacon looks at me in delight. "Maybe we can recreate our first meeting?"

"I don't think so!" I glare back.

"Why, what happened?" Alicia wants to know.

"Can you believe he threw me out of a nightclub?" I say, shaking my head in disbelief.

"I didn't throw you," Deacon objects. "I was very gentle."

❄

It was ten years ago and Kate and I were queuing to get into Millennium, the most popular - in fact, the only - nightclub in Queensbeach at the time. Kate had just turned eighteen, and although I was a few months younger, I rarely had a problem getting in as I was tall and sophisticated for my age, or so I liked to think. That night, however, there was a problem.

"You can go in," the bouncer told Kate. He was big and broad, with longish black hair and penetrating eyes. I made to follow her, when he put out his hand to stop me.

"Can I see some I.D, please?"

"What?" I was so taken aback by the question that I didn't even have the forethought to come up with a good story.

"But I'll be eighteen in a couple of months," I wailed, watching a group of my friends go inside.

"Come back then, and I'll let you in," he said firmly.

I was fuming, but there was nothing I could do. Angrily, I dragged Kate across the road to the Horse and Hare, which was much less fussy about its entrance policy. It wasn't nearly as much fun as Millennium though.

When we left a couple of hours later, I noticed that there was a different bouncer on the door at the club. Emboldened by the three or four WKD Blues I'd just downed, I decided to try again. This time, it was easy. The bouncer smiled at us, and with a polite "Evening ladies," we strode triumphantly inside.

For a while, I had a great time. We headed straight for the dance floor, where we swayed in time to Avril Lavigne or Pink or whoever it was that we were into then. But then I felt a heavy hand on my shoulder. Startled, I turned round and found myself looking up at that bloody annoying bouncer.

"I thought I told you you weren't coming in?" he said grimly.

"Well, I seem to have found my way in anyway," I replied boldly.

"You have until the count of ten to leave the premises."

But I had a stubborn streak. I folded my arms. "You can't make me."

That was probably the most stupid thing I've ever said. In one fluid motion, he swooped down and lifted me up over his shoulder. He carried me like that, fireman-style out of the club, with me banging my fists and kicking furiously as all my friends looked on and laughed. Once outside, he set me gently on my feet.

"*Did you have a coat?*" he asked. "*Give me the cloakroom ticket, and I'll go and fetch it for you.*"

But I wouldn't be placated. "*Don't bother,*" I said. "*I'll fetch it myself in the morning.*"

❋

"You were so angry with me!" Deacon laughs now, taking a contented sip of his wine.

"Can you blame me?" I demand. "You embarrassed me in front of all my friends!"

"Well, you never did learn to do what you're told, did you?" he teases.

"Shh!" Kate hushes us. "They're still doing their performance."

The Greek dancers have moved all the tables away from the centre of the room. A hush falls over the audience as some kind of fluid is poured in a big circle in the middle. A match is lit, and people gasp as a perfect ring of fire forms. Then the dancers begin clapping and singing, leaping in and out of the flames as if they were made of water.

A sudden cacophony of shrill, discordant bleeps pierces the night.

We all jump violently and it takes us a moment to realise where it's coming from.

"It's the key rings!" Deacon yells above the noise. "Quick, switch them off!"

We dive frantically into our bags and pockets, cheeks burning as our desperate fingers struggle to silence them. I feel the glares of the people around us, but the dancers continue with their performance as if nothing has happened.

The audience takes up their tune, clapping and whistling along, as the dancers whirl and twist inside the spectacular circle of fire. I feel Alicia's presence next to me as we both gaze intently into the flames. I sense that we are mirror images – her delight is my horror, my anxiety, her pleasure.

"Please," I whisper to her, but I'm not quite sure what I'm asking or if she even hears me. She doesn't reply, but then, as quickly as they were ignited, the flames are quenched, and the dancers step safely out of the circle to take their bow. The spell broken, I rush outside for some fresh air.

Kate follows me.

"Are you alright?" she asks.

"Yes, fine," I feel around in my pocket for my lighter. God knows what I've done with it. I borrow Kate's.

"Don't feel bad about the alarms going off," she says, as I light my cigarette. "I thought it was funny."

"Thanks."

"You sure you're OK?" she says, looking at me more closely. "You look tense."

"Just had a long day," I say, sinking down onto the window ledge.

How can I possibly explain to her about my concerns about Alicia? It all sounds so irrational.

"Look, I wanted to have a word with you anyway," she says, sitting down beside me.

"Sounds ominous."

"It's about Julio."

"Oh?"

"Alicia saw you with him, Isabel. Why didn't you tell me you were back in touch?"

I suck in my breath. "How would Alicia know? She's never even met Julio!"

"She happened to see you outside your house on Sunday night, talking to a guy in an orange Alfa Romeo. Who else would it be?"

"What was she doing there? Is she spying on me?"

Kate rolls her eyes. "Don't be ridiculous, Isabel! She went round to see you, but when she saw that you had company, she didn't want to interrupt. She thought Julio was some guy you were seeing."

"Hmm…" I bite my lip. Kate's explanation sounds plausible, but still, I don't like the idea of Alicia hanging around outside my house, watching me. I find it disconcerting.

"So it was Julio?" she prompts me.

"Yes, it was. Look, Kate it wasn't planned or anything, he just dropped in on me."

She takes my arm. "It's OK, Isabel. He's your brother. You have a right to see him, just don't keep things from me, OK? That's not the kind of friendship we have."

"I know. I'm sorry, I should have told you."

"So no more secrets?"

"No more secrets."

❄

I HAVE the dream again that night. The one where I nearly run Alicia over. I've had it several times since it happened. I play it over and over in my mind, just can't seem to get it out of my head. In this dream, it happens just as I remember, except for one thing – the expression on Alicia's face. It isn't fear that she looks at me with, as she slides to the ground.

It's pleasure.

I sit up, fully awake now. Was it just a dream, or is that how it really happened? What if the accident wasn't an accident at all? What if Alicia was hiding in the bushes, waiting to jump out?

What if she was crouched down in the darkness, waiting for me? She would have had to hide somewhere - behind the dustbins, maybe or else the iridescent glow of my headlights would surely have caught her? Was she down there, waiting until the very last moment to leap out, knowing that that I wouldn't be able to stop? Knowing that she would scare the living daylights out of me?

It was a very dangerous game if she was.

Robertson's Superstore - Monday Morning

"Morning," says Jon, the security man, as he holds open the door for me. The doors are supposed to open automatically, but they've been malfunctioning a bit recently.

"Morning. Did you have a nice weekend?"

"Not bad. Took the kids to Chessington."

"Sounds lovely."

Jon shrugs. "The little one chucked up in the minivan."

"Staff meeting in ten minutes," Sonya says, as I walk into the office. "Can you help me set up the projector?"

"No problem."

I pull it out of the desk drawer and follow her into the staff room, where we are greeted by rows of gooey glazed doughnuts.

My mouth waters. "Ooh, where did these come from?"

"Alicia brought them in. Apparently they were giving out free samples in the precinct. She persuaded the bloke to give her a dozen boxes."

I bet she did.

Sonya reaches over and takes one. "Hmm, delicious. But I really must start my diet tomorrow."

The staff reps surge in and devour the doughnuts like a plague of hungry locusts. The unexpected treat puts everyone in a good mood and we progress through the meeting with much less bickering than usual.

"Item 9," Sonya reads out, "I need more volunteers to cover Tuesday's night shift."

This announcement is greeted with a wall of silence. You could hear a pin drop, the room goes so quiet.

"Well, if anyone is interested, please let me know after the meeting."

The door creaks as Stu walks in.

He probably smelled the doughnuts.

"Anything you want to add, Stu?" Sonya asks politely.

"Yes, as a matter of fact, there is."

Sonya and I look at each other in surprise. Neither of us can remember the last time he actually contributed to a staff meeting. He comes to stand at the front.

"Great news!" he says with enthusiasm. "I've just been on the phone with head office and it looks like we will be replacing all our checkouts with self-service points. Isn't that great, everyone? No more boring checkout duty!"

I groan inwardly. How could he make such an important announcement without even discussing it with Sonya and me first? I bet he hasn't even spoken to any of the union reps. The usually quiet room erupts. Everyone starts speaking at once, all the checkout staff wanting to know what will happen to their jobs.

"Oh, I'm sure we'll work something out," Stu says blithely. "There's no need for anyone to worry."

Sonya dismisses the group, with a promise to update everyone as soon as possible.

"Isn't this great?" says Stu, as everyone files out of the room. I grip my hands tightly together. If I let them do what they wanted, they'd probably strangle him.

As a result of Stu's thoughtless announcement, I spend much of the morning fielding questions from irate checkout staff who refuse to believe that I don't know any more about the new tills than they do.

"There are going to be redundancies, aren't there?" demands a nervous father of five.

"I'm sure that won't be necessary," I try to reassure him. But I can't help but wonder what other work we could possibly find for some of the zombies who sit at the checkouts all day. I mean, obviously we'll need a few people to help the customers with the new self-service tills, but I doubt any of them will be up to that job. Their minds have become so automated, I really wonder if they are capable of being retrained.

"She must know something," says a rough looking woman, pointing at me with her jagged fingernail. "Come on, girly, out with it. How many are of us are going to be out of a job?"

Before I can think of anything to say, Sonya's voice fills the room:

"This is a colleague announcement. Can Isabel come to the Supervisor's office? That's Isabel to the Supervisor's office."

"Sorry," I say apologetically. "I have to run. We'll have to talk about this later."

I walk thankfully through the store. Sonya is waiting for me outside the office.

"We have got to get these people some answers," I tell her, "before we have a riot on our hands. Hey, what's wrong?"

I had assumed that she called me away to get me out of an awkward situation, but her expression is grim.

"The police are here, Isabel. They want to speak to you about the fire at the caravan park. I think you might be a suspect…"

5

The door slams ominously behind me.

Two plain clothes detectives sit side by side behind the desk; a tall, skinny man in a lilac shirt and a small, round woman with a wispy ponytail.

"Isabel Anderson?" says the man, beckoning me to sit down.

"Yes."

"I'm Detective Sergeant Penney, and this is Detective Constable Smith. We'd like to ask you a few questions about the fire at the caravan park last Saturday. You are aware that there was a fire?"

"Yes!" My voice comes out too loud and too fast. "Yes," I repeat, attempting to lower my voice. I seem to have lost control of my volume switch.

"We have reason to suspect that the fire was started deliberately," Penney continues. "Did you see anything suspicious?"

"No."

"But you were in the area at the time?"

"Yes. I was at a barbecue at Deacon Frost's house."

There is a pause as Penney glances down at his notebook.

"You were seen leaving the party just before the fire started. Can you tell us where you went?"

"I went for a walk," I falter, "on the beach. I can't have been gone for more than ten minutes."

There is a searching look in his eyes.

"Maybe twenty?" I guess. "I don't really remember."

The two police officers look at each other, eyebrows raised. Their telepathic communication unnerves me.

"Was it a good party?"

"It was OK."

"Why did you leave then?"

"I just wasn't in the mood. I felt like a walk."

"Did you meet anyone on this walk?"

"There wasn't anyone on the beach at that time – except Deacon, that is. He came to find me."

"And what time was this?"

"I don't know. I wasn't keeping track."

"And when did you first hear of the fire?"

"A little while later. One of the other guests discovered it as he was leaving the party."

They fall silent again, as if waiting to see if I have any more to add. I know they're expecting me to say something, but I really don't know what more I can tell them. Then, finally, Penney reaches into his pocket and pulls out what looks like a sandwich bag.

"What's that?"

He slides it across the table to me.

"Does this look familiar?"

I glance down at the metal object. It's my lighter, there's no denying it. Julio bought it for my birthday. My initials are embossed on it in fake diamond studs.

"Where did you get that?" I ask with trepidation.

"At the caravan park. It *is* yours then?"

I nod, because what's the point in denying it? It'll have my prints all over it.

I fold my arms, thoughtfully. "It's odd though. I could have sworn I lost it before the fire. We needed a lighter to light the barbecue and I didn't have it on me."

"So how did it come to be at the caravan park?"

"I really don't know, though I did go there with my friends when we heard about the fire. We wanted to see if there was anything we could do to help."

"The owner tells me you were there again the following morning, scrabbling around in the dirt."

"I wasn't scrabbling…" I break off, wondering how I got myself into this mess.

"My friend was staying there. We went back to see if any of her stuff had survived the fire. You can ask her if you like. Her name's Alicia McBride, she works here."

"Yes, we've already spoken to Miss McBride."

"You have?"

"Yes, she said she you left the party for a good thirty minutes."

"She did?"

"Yes."

Well, maybe I did, I don't remember.

There is another long pause. The detectives seem to have run out of questions.

You don't have anything on me, do you?

"I really don't think I can help you any further," I say, sounding a lot more brazen than I feel. "Can I go now?"

Penney nods grimly. "If you remember anything else, please give me a call."

He passes me a card with his number on it.

"Can I have my lighter back?"

"I think we'll hang onto in for now if you don't mind."

I decide not to push my luck.

I almost send Sonya flying as I walk out of the office. She must have been standing with her ear pressed right up against the door.

"Well?" she demands. "How did it go?"

"Well, they didn't arrest me."

"No?"

"No. Of course they didn't. I mean why would I burn down the caravan park? What possible motivation could I have?"

I march through the store, ignoring the prying eyes that follow me. I need to speak to Alicia, but she's on her break. Eventually, I go back to the office. The police have gone now and Stu is sitting at Sonya's desk, talking and laughing with a couple of his buddies from the warehouse.

"What do you call an Essex girl without a fake tan?" he chuckles.

"I don't know?" I say, walking into the room. "What do you call her?"

"Hey, Isabel! I hear you've been a bad girl," he smirks. "Let me know if you need me to bail you out." He makes an obscene gesture and the others laugh. I ought to report him to HR, but I couldn't bear the paperwork.

It is a long, long day of ridiculous jokes and innuendos. Not to mention the fact that half the checkout staff are still poised to go on strike. Finally, at a quarter to five, I grab my stuff and charge out the door. It's a little early, but I don't care. I've had enough.

I drive straight round to the Beach House. Alicia is already in the kitchen, setting the table for dinner. She blanches when she sees me. She knows she's done me wrong.

"What did you say to the police?" I ask, unable to hide my fury.

She ignores me and continues to set the table.

I grab the knives and forks from her hand and slam them down.

"What did you tell them?" I shout, my voice shaking.

"Who?"

"Who do you bloody think? The police! What did you tell them about me?"

"Just the truth," she whimpers, her eyes impossibly wide.

"You told them I left the party, didn't you? Why did you do that?"

"But why *did* you leave the party, Isabel?"

Suddenly, I explode.

"Are you're trying to set me up?" I grab her by the shoulders, ready to give her a good hard shake.

"Isabel! Get off her!" Deacon steps in between us. He looks from one to the other. "What the hell is going on here?"

"She told the police I left the barbecue!" I fume. "Now they think I'm the one who started the fire."

"Isabel, you're blowing this all out of all proportion," Deacon says, calmly.

"The police were here this morning and they talked to all of us. No one said anything that would have made them think you were the culprit."

"Well, thanks for giving me a heads up," I say bitterly. "Great friend you are!"

I stalk out to my car and sit there for a while, breathing heavily, too angry to drive. Now that I've yelled at Alicia, I ought to feel better, but I don't. She hasn't given me any of the answers I need, and now I'm feeling guilty all over again.

There is a soft knock on the window. It's Deacon. I wind it down.

"You were out of line, talking to Alicia like that."

"You wouldn't understand."

"Then explain it to me."

But I can't. He doesn't see Alicia the way I do. None of them do.

Robertson's - Tuesday Morning

I get to work early. Alicia is already on the shop floor.

I call out her name, but she pretends to be engrossed in what she's doing. She looks… scared when she sees me. I furrow my brow. Is it really plausible that she has nothing to do with all the strange events going on in my life? I just don't know anymore, it's all too confusing.

"Look Alicia," I say, walking over to her. "I'm sorry about last night, OK? I was just a bit upset. I shouldn't have taken it out on you."

Alicia pats my arm. Her touch is surprisingly warm, considering how cold the shop gets.

"Don't worry about the police," she says. "They're just trying to scare you."

Well, they're doing a pretty good job.

I join Sonya at the checkouts, where she is still taking grief about the automated tills. If Stu doesn't give us some solid answers soon, I think we should feed him to this lot, let them eat him alive like piranhas. A number of them have already told me they have unexpected dentist or doctor's appointments this week. I strongly suspect that they've been applying to Filbert's *en masse*.

"You're doing it again, Sonya," I say, pulling her hand down from her hair.

She has this horrible habit of pulling her hair out, strand by strand. It's a stress thing. She doesn't even know she's doing it. She'll have a bald spot the size of the Grand Canyon if she carries on like this.

"We've got to do something," she says in exasperation. "At this rate, Filbert's is going to take all our best people."

"I know," I agree. "If only we were allowed to run this place properly, without interference from that idiot."

I POP round to Kate's house for a cup of tea on the way home. I'm thinking about sharing my concerns about Alicia with her. Maybe she can tell me if I'm worrying over nothing.

"Come on in!" she says, as she answers the door. "Alicia's just made some tea."

"Alicia's here?"

I don't know why I'm even surprised anymore. She seems to pop up everywhere I go these days. I'm tempted to leave, but I make myself sit down at the table. I'm determined to play nice.

Alicia smiles at me.

"Would you like a cup, Isabel?"

For a moment, my suspicious mind works overtime, wondering if she's somehow poisoned the tea, or if she wants me to leave fingerprints on the cup so that she can plant more evidence at crime scenes. Given my misgivings, I should just say no, but instead I nod, numbly.

I watch as she pours the tea and swirls the leaves around in each cup, muttering something incomprehensible.

"What's she doing?" I whisper to Kate.

"She's going to read our tea leaves."

"Seriously?"

"It'll be fun!"

Reluctantly, I agree. I'm not sure I trust Alicia as far as I can throw her, but what harm can she do with a few tea leaves? And besides, it would be good to know what fate has in store for me, for a change.

We gulp our tea quickly, eager to get to the leaf reading. I'm not used to drinking tea made with loose leaves, and I splutter a bit as some of it goes down the wrong way. Kate pats me on the back.

"Do me first," she says eagerly, once I've stopped coughing.

Alicia leans forward and examines the little patterns in her teacup.

"What can you see, Kate?"

Kate scrunches up her face in concentration.

"Looks like a present?" she says, hopefully.

"Yes!" Alicia takes a closer look. "A parcel. That means a surprise."

"A good surprise or a bad one?" I ask.

Alicia shrugs. "It doesn't say. Maybe that depends on you."

Kate raises her eyebrows at me and I smile.

"So what about yours?" I ask.

Alicia gazes down at her own cup and a slow smile spreads across her face.

"I see a lover," she says, blushing.

"Ooh!" Kate claps her hands together. "Maybe it's that hot new pizza guy!"

Alicia giggles. "Let's do yours, Isabel."

I offer her my cup.

"What can you see?" she asks, as the three of us pore over the splattered tea leaves in the bottom of my cup. Mine looks a bit messier than the other two.

"Well, that blob looks a bit like Fluffy," I say eventually.

"Yes, a cat." Alicia confirms. "And next to it is a wolf."

"What's that, then?" asks Kate, pointing to the biggest shape of all.

"That's an hourglass."

"So what does it all mean?"

Alicia takes a deep breath. "Well, the cat is for deceit, or a false friend."

"Oh."

"And the wolf?"

"The wolf is for jealousy."

"And what about the hourglass?"

"Yes, the hourglass," Alicia looks me right in the eye. "That means that time is running out."

"Time for what?"

"Who knows? Maybe it means you need to make a change

in your life, or get something done. The signs can be very vague."

"You couldn't magic up a couple of lovers for us then?" I ask. "Not that I'm not grateful for my assortment of strange animals and warnings about punctuality."

Alicia laughs her squeaky little laugh. "Maybe next time. I can only work with the what the tea leaves give me."

"What do you think?" I ask Fluffy that night, as we watch Neighbours together.

"Can she really read tea leaves, or was she making it all up? 'The cat is for deceit, or a false friend,'" I say, mimicking her high-pitched voice. "She's obviously not a cat lover then."

Knock! Knock!

Who's that?

"I'm coming," I yell. I don't know why people don't just use the doorbell. There's nothing wrong with it.

I undo the latch and the door swings back.

It's the police. DS Penney and the other one.

"Who were you talking to?" Penney asks, looking around.

"Oh, just my cat," I say, gesturing towards the sofa, but Fluffy has already gone into hiding, the false friend that he is.

"So how can I help you?" I ask, glancing at my watch. It seems a bit late to be making house calls.

"We just have one question for you, Isabel. What happened to Rose Cottage?"

6

The summer I turned eighteen, Kate and I worked as play leaders at a children's holiday camp called Camp Windylake. While Kate's group charged up and down the football pitch, mine were more stylish and artistic. We had the best times in the arts and crafts tent, fashioning intricate hats and gloves from old scraps of material and decorating them with sequins, buttons and beads. We customised jeans and T-shirts with safety pins, ribbons and lace. Every one of my charges made something they could be proud of that summer, culminating in a big fashion show on the last day, where the kids strutted their stuff down a makeshift catwalk to Right Said Fred.

I started smoking that summer, actually. I know, most people start much younger than eighteen, but smoking had never interested me before. Yet somehow, sitting round the camp fire one night, I found myself accepting a cigarette. And despite many, many failed attempts, I've never managed to quit since. Not even after what happened to Rose Cottage.

The day camp finished, Julio picked us up in a cherry-red convertible he'd been working on, drawing numerous wolf-whistles from the girls, fellow camp leaders, and even one or two of the mums. This was way before he and Kate were ever an item, of course.

After dropping Kate off home, we returned to Rose Cottage, the holiday home Dad rented every summer since we were little. I dumped my bag in the hallway and ran upstairs to take a shower. Dad was out on a date that night (what can I say? Like father, like son) and Julio suggested we go out for a few drinks and catch up.

"How about here?" he said, as we walked down the High Street, in the direction of the Millennium nightclub.

"No," I said, glaring at the long-haired bouncer. He looked particularly smug that night, organising the crowd into an orderly queue and deciding who could go in and who couldn't. "I hear there's a new Turkish place that's just opened across the road. Let's go and have a look."

The raki poured freely that night, and it was gone midnight by the time we finally stumbled home along the beach.

Julio sniffed the air. "Hmm, smells like barbecue."

I blinked at the unfriendly lights ahead of us. "I don't think that's a barbecue. Something's on fire!"

We strained our eyes to see, and, perhaps because we'd had quite a bit to drink, we still failed to realise that the source of all the commotion was our very own Rose Cottage. Until we saw Dad, that is. He was walking across the sand towards us, his arms crossed, his expression as dark as the thunderous clouds of smoke above us.

"OK, which of you did it?" he demanded. "I've just been speaking to the fire crew and they think it was probably started by a cigarette."

Julio and I looked at each other in horror. We had each had one before heading out that night. But I'd stubbed mine out, I was certain of it. Poor Dad, he had no idea either of us smoked.

"It wasn't me!" Julio said indignantly, his body language mimicking his father's.

"Well, it wasn't me, either!" I defended myself. "I wouldn't be that careless!"

And so it went. I blamed Julio, and he blamed me. We never did get to the bottom of it. That was the end of our holidays at Rose Cottage though. The place was damaged beyond repair.

❉

"So you admit that you started the fire at Rose Cottage?" Penney asks. The man has ants in his pants. He keeps pacing up and down, seems unable to sit for longer than ten seconds. His partner, meanwhile, lounges back on my sofa, taking in the stack of fashion magazines on the coffee table and the orderly row of shoes, lined against the wall. These are not all my shoes, by the way, just the ones that don't fit in the shoe cupboard.

"We never found out for sure," I say cagily. "It could have been me, but it could equally have been my brother. It was a long time ago and an accident at that. I really can't see what it has to do with the fire at the caravan park."

"Except that it's another unexplained coincidence," Penney points out.

"Look Isabel, we don't want to do this, but if we find any more of these little 'coincidences', I'm going to have to turn you over to my boss, and she's not into these cosy little home visits, if you get my drift. She'll want to question you properly."

"Down the station," adds his partner, as if I'm an imbecile.

"Look, I know this looks bad," I say, in exasperation, "but there's really nothing more to tell."

"So this is going to be the last time we'll need to speak to you then?"

"Yes. Absolutely the last."

Next morning, I am awoken by the sound of the phone ringing.

Groggily, I reach for it.

"Hello?"

"Isabel? It's Sonya. Are you OK?"

"Yes, fine. Why?" I ask, rubbing my eyes.

"It's gone half past nine. Are you still in bed?"

"Oh, bollocks!" I glance at my bedside clock. "I must have

overslept. Sorry, Sonya – I had trouble getting to sleep last night."

"You OK?"

"Yes, fine, just had the police sniffing round again last night."

I don't know why I told her that, Sonya isn't exactly the soul of discretion.

"About the fire?"

"Yeah."

"That's crazy! They should stop wasting your time and catch some real criminals."

"Tell me about it."

"Well, I'm glad you're all right, anyway. I'll see you at work then."

"Yeah. I'll be as quick as I can. Sorry about oversleeping."

"Not to worry, it's kind of dead today, anyway."

I thought she was just trying to make me feel better, but I get a bit of a shock when I walk through the door of Robertson's an hour later.

"Hey, where is everyone?"

Stu walks out of his office.

"Something's not right," he says, pointing out the obvious. "Maybe you should go over to Filbert's, Isabel and see if it's quiet there too."

"I really don't see how checking out the opposition is going to help," I object. "Wouldn't my time be better spent helping with the inventory?" I glance at Sonya for support.

"No, I think they're up to something," Stu insists. "Just go and have a look."

"I suppose it can't hurt," Sonya agrees.

I didn't want Stu to be right, but when I reach Filbert's, the car park is so packed that I have to drive round in circles for ten minutes before I can get a space. What's more, their trolley bays are all empty. Meaning either they've had a major trolley theft, or every single one of them is in use.

What's going on here?

That's when I see the sign: 'Half price Friday! Everything half price!'

How did I miss this? How did we all miss this?

Why are they doing this? They must be making a massive loss!

But look how many people there are! They've taken most of our customers and then some! I fight my way into the store and look around. Shelf stackers work furiously to replenish the stock, but they're no match for the bargain hungry shoppers, some of whom have taken more than one trolley. I'm tempted to do a little shopping myself.

I follow the crowd towards the checkout. No zombies here. They have fully automated tills, with helpful assistants on hand to advise people on how to use them. All the staff seem ultra smiley and efficient. They must invest a lot more in staff training than we do.

Hey - I wonder if they pay more than Robertson's?

Boldly, I walk over to the customer service desk.

"Hi, do you have any vacancies?" I ask.

"Yes," says the smiling assistant. "We're currently looking for customer service personnel and shelf stackers."

"What's the pay like?"

"Very competitive," says a voice behind me. I turn round and find myself looking at Bernie Greengrass, the store manager. He needs no introduction - his picture is in the local paper just about every week.

"But I'd have thought junior manager would be more suitable for you, Isabel?"

"You know my name?"

"I make it my business to know," he says with a smile. "If you're really interested in a position here, just let me know. Our pay and conditions are very generous."

He hands me his business card.

"Thanks, I'll think about it."

"You do that. We have an excellent fast-track programme, and just think - you wouldn't have to work for that idiot, Stu, any more!"

He flashes a cheeky grin, then he's gone, his attention diverted as a local TV news crew walks through the door.

❆

I race back to Robertson's to tell Stu and Sonya all I've discovered - well not quite all - I don't mention Bernie Greengrass' job offer. Sonya looks riled enough.

"It's just a stunt," I reassure her. "They can't keep that up for long, unless they're looking to bankrupt themselves."

"But what else have they got up their sleeves?" she wonders, grasping at her hair with her hands. "Don't you remember, when Filbert's first opened, a lot of people said Queensbeach was only big enough for one supermarket. What if they were right?"

"I can't believe we missed this," I say, shaking my head. "They must have advertised on the radio and in the papers."

"Not in the papers I read," Stu says.

"No, well they probably didn't advertise in the Beano," Sonya mutters, flicking through the newspaper stand. "Here it is, front cover of the Queensbeach Echo. No wonder this place is deserted."

The store is so quiet that Sonya lets me leave early, despite my late start. It makes a pleasant change to get out while it's still light. I head for the High Street, intending to make a start on my Christmas shopping, but a shimmering green dress immediately catches my eye. It's in the window of a little boutique I've never been in before. Curiously, I push open the door and walk inside.

The predatory eyes of the shop assistant watch as I finger the cool, silky fabric.

"That's a lovely dress," she says approvingly. "Would you like to try it on?"

I glance at the price tag. I know I shouldn't, but I find myself nodding and following her to the fitting room, where it takes less than a minute to shimmy out of my black tailored suit and into the dress.

I admire myself in the communal mirror. The material hugs my figure in all the right places, neither too tight nor too loose.

"Oh, my!" The shop assistant gasps. "It looks like it was made for you!"

I know that they'll say anything to make a sale, but I can't help feeling she's right on this occasion. The colour complements my complexion perfectly, as does the shape.

"Would you like to take it?" she asks.

My conscience tugs at the hem of the dress. It is both expensive and elaborate, so there won't be many occasions when I could wear it. But Kate and Deacon get complimentary tickets to a posh ball run by the hospital every year. It would be perfect for that.

"What shoes do you have?" I ask.

As it turns out, not only do they have great shoes, but also stoles and handbags. I leave the shop with parcels tucked under each arm, my face flushed with guilty pleasure.

"Hi Isabel, can you get me a beer?" Deacon asks, when I arrive at the Beach House for dinner.

"Nice to see you too," I mutter, opening the fridge. "Anyone else?"

"Yes, please," Kate says.

As I shut the fridge, I notice a familiar cream coloured invitation card pinned to the door.

"You're going to the Christmas ball then?" I say, casually placing the beers down on the table.

"Yeah," says Kate, twisting hers open. "I'm taking Rhett as my plus one."

I look expectantly at Deacon.

"How about you?"

"Actually," he says, "I thought I'd ask Alicia this year. You don't mind, do you?"

7

"Hi everyone!" Alicia calls, as she skips through the door. "Oh, hi Isabel!" She slides into the empty seat next to Deacon and it takes every ounce of my strength not to kick it out from under her. My stomach churns as he casually rests his arm on the back of her chair. The jealous wolf inside me has reared its ugly head.

"You're really OK about Deacon taking Alicia to the ball?" Kate asks when I give her a lift home.

"Course, it's no big deal," I lie. "I've got another party that night anyway."

"Great - you should come round to my house so we can get ready together."

"Maybe."

"Oh, come on! We can open a bottle of wine and put on some music to get us in the party mood. Besides, I might need fashion advice."

She's got me there. One year, she tried to wear legwarmers under her cocktail dress, claiming her legs were cold. I definitely need to quality check her outfit before she sets foot outside the door.

"Well, OK." I reluctantly agree. "I'll get ready at yours."

Robertson's - Three Weeks before Christmas

"If I hear Jive Bunny one more time, I'm going to ram a Christmas tree down someone's throat!" Jon the security man tries to shield his ears, but it's impossible to block out the sound.

That's one of the many joys of working at Robertson's at this time of year, they bombard us with diabolical Christmas music all day long. I've tried talking to Sonya about it, but apparently it's a head office directive. We have to play Christmas music to get the customers in the spending mood. And so we do - all day long. I've heard the American government used the same technique on prisoners in Guantanamo Bay. I bet it was effective.

The Christmas shopping season has begun in earnest, but not as ferociously here as at Filbert's, where the kiddies are queuing round the corner to see Santa.

Sonya rushes up to me, her face flushed.

"Isabel! I need a favour."

"What is it?"

"I've just caught the elves conducting themselves in..er…"

"Un-elfly behaviour?" I supply.

She nods. "I've had to send them both back to the agency, so I was wondering if you could take over, just till they send someone else? Santa can't cope on his own."

"Surely there's someone else who could do it?"

Sonya tugs at the hair at the back of her head. "Isabel, I'm asking you. I don't want any more screw ups, I just want to know that it's under control."

"Well, OK." I reluctantly agree, "But I don't really have to wear a costume do I?"

"It's in the office."

It is a long, long afternoon. Stu comes over to leer at me in my ridiculously short belted tunic and curly toed shoes.

"There's a pot of gold at the end of the rainbow," he croons, in a terrible faux Irish accent.

"That's leprechauns, you ignorant bastard," I hiss. "Oh, sorry!" My hand flies to my mouth as I remember too late that I'm surrounded by small children. Their mothers look at each other and shake their heads in consternation.

The promised replacement elves never materialise, so I have to prop up Santa all afternoon. Finally, at five o'clock, I stalk off to the toilets to change, feeling hot, sweaty and irritable. The cheap, tacky green tights leave an inky stain as I peel them from my legs, and my feet hurt from being squished into those stupid shoes. I wriggle thankfully into my normal clothes, bundling the hated costume into a ball and contemplate flushing it down the loo.

Sonya couldn't be more apologetic, but her apologies don't make up for my humiliation. Bernie Greengrass' business card feels like a brick in my handbag as I stomp out of the store. Just one phone call and I could be out of here and onto something better. The idea of telling Stu where to go appeals more and more by the minute, but I don't feel good about deserting Sonya. I'm not sure how she'd cope without me. I picture her tearing what remains of her hair out. But one way or the other, I've got to make up my mind and soon. Bernie doesn't strike me as a patient man, and I have a feeling his offer comes with an expiry date.

The Night of The Christmas Ball

My gorgeous green dress watches with melancholy, as I pack my bag to go to Kate's on Saturday night. But no one is going to be wearing fancy dresses where I'm going. Jeans and a jumper are my best bet, jazzed up with a pair of kitten heels. I wasn't lying when I said I had a party to go to. Stu's having a

Christmas get-together at his house for all the staff. I hadn't in a million years intended to go but now I feel like I have to, to prove to my friends that I'm fine about Deacon taking Alicia to the ball.

Kate answers the door in a navy blue trouser suit.

"How do I look?" she asks.

"Like you're going to a job interview. Why don't you wear the purple dress you got for your birthday?"

"But none of my shoes match."

"Don't worry, I've got some options in my bag."

If I'm missing the ball, then I'm damn well not letting her go dressed like an estate agent. I follow her upstairs to her room, then take a sharp intake of breath.

Alicia is standing in front of the dresser, styling her hair.

"Hello, Isabel!" she calls, gleefully.

I glare at Kate.

"You didn't say she was going to be here," I hiss.

"I didn't think you'd mind."

"I don't…"

"Well, then."

While Kate slips into her purple dress, I tip the shoes out onto the bed and arrange them in neat pairs.

"I think the red ones," she says, uncertainly.

"No, the pink." Alicia chips in.

Kate looks at me. I want to disagree, but Alicia is right.

"Definitely the pink."

"Aren't you getting dressed up?" Kate asks me as she applies her make up. Alicia leans over and wipes off the clown-like blusher, just like I normally would. In fact, she's doing everything I normally do, pouring the wine, turning up the radio and singing along - badly. I feel like I've been superseded.

"No, it's not that kind of party," I say, pulling my hair into a simple ponytail. I can't be bothered to do anything else with it. I'm just not in the mood.

The doorbell rings.

"Can you get that?" she pleads, "I'm not quite ready."

"Course."

I trudge down the stairs and open the door. It's Rhett and Deacon, all dressed up in tuxedos. They remind me a little of Batman and Robin, before their transformation.

"You look nice," Deacon greets me.

"You too. You should wear a tux more often."

He smiles, but his attention has been diverted. Alicia is descending the stairs, dressed in a ruffled pink cocktail dress. Her long black curls are piled high on top of her head, a few ringlets cascading over her smooth white shoulders.

He smiles appreciatively and walks towards her.

"You look breathtaking!" I hear him whisper, as he kisses her on the cheek.

I lean back against the wall. I feel sick.

The taxi journey into town is long and uncomfortable. Deacon and Alicia sit close together, laughing at some private joke that makes sense only to them. Rhett and Kate don't seem to notice. They're too busy perusing the evening's programme and discussing who's going to be there. Last year, the newly divorced Mayor turned up with a contestant from a popular reality TV show on his arm. This year, rumour has it, he'll be bringing a page three girl.

The taxi drops off my friends first. I watch as they all shuffle up the steps of Queensbeach Civic Hall. The door is opened by a doorman, and I get a tantalising glimpse of the ballroom, with its five piece orchestra and elegant tables laid for lobster and champagne.

Then the taxi runs me half a mile up the road, coming to a halt outside Stu's seedy bachelor pad. I am tempted to ask the driver to take me home again, but Stu's spotted me from the window. He comes running out of the house.

"Isabel! I knew you wouldn't be able to resist a party!"

The smell of cheap aftershave almost knocks me off my

feet as he steps forward to hug me, pressing his sweaty body against me for slightly longer than is strictly necessary. He is wearing tight leather trousers with a revolting electric-blue shirt, unbuttoned practically to the waist to display his hairy tangerine chest to full effect.

Against my better judgement, I follow him inside. There are a few curly sandwiches laid out but I'm not particularly hungry. I feel as though a ship has dropped anchor in my stomach. I accept a glass of eggnog despite the fact I've always hated the stuff, and swig it back in one determined gulp.

Sonya is in the kitchen, wearing a snowman jumper, paired with a voluminous skirt, which does nothing for her figure. I make a note to myself to take her shopping for some decent clothes in the January sales.

"Stu's a real pig, isn't he?" she says, by way of greeting.

"I never doubted it."

I rifle though the cupboards.

"What are you looking for?"

"Drink."

"Try the fridge."

I open it, but there is nothing but row upon row of jellies.

I find a spoon and taste one.

"What's in it?"

"Vodka."

We fight our way back into the living room, armed with jelly shots. The only people I recognise are the blokes from the warehouse. They sit in a dark damp corner, surrounded by beer cans, making the same lude jokes they do at work.

Sonya is telling me how Stu screwed up her computer, but I'm not really listening. My treacherous mind drifts back to the ball and I picture Deacon dancing with Alicia, her delicate arms wrapped around his neck. Why can't he see through her? He's a doctor for goodness' sake – he's supposed to be clever.

When I can't take it any longer, I pull out my mobile and dial Kate's number.

The phone goes straight through to voicemail.

Oh well, it's probably for the best. I don't want her to think I'm checking up on them.

"Wanna dance?" Stu looms over me, trying to look sexy.

"Um, no thanks."

"Oh come on, it's Phil Collins."

With the most impeccable timing, my phone starts to ring.

"Sorry, I have to get this."

I turn my back on him. "Kate? Call you? Er, no – I must have been butt dialling."

I'm a terrible liar – I don't know why I even try.

"So are you having a good time?" I ask, trying to keep my tone casual.

"Yeah - you won't believe this but Lenny Lopez is sitting at our table!"

"What? Didn't he used to be on Neighbours?"

"Yup – apparently his sister works at the hospital. Anyway, I got him to autograph my napkin for you."

"Thanks."

But really, what good is a signed napkin? This is just so unfair. If it weren't for Alicia, I would be meeting Lenny for myself.

"So how's your party?"

"Great," I lie. "You wouldn't believe the cocktails." I glance down at the tray of quivering jelly shots and shudder. "So, er..What about Deacon and Alicia? Are they having fun?"

"Oh, they've been on the dance floor for ages! You know how Alicia loves to dance."

I didn't, but I suppose I don't really know much about her at all.

"So how's it going between them?" I hate myself for asking.

"Great. I mean, they seem to be getting on well. You don't mind do you?"

"Mind? Why would I mind?"

"Well, you know, you and Deacon have always been close."

"Oh, don't be silly! I was just curious, that's all."

"OK."

"Really. Now I'm going to get back to my party. You have a great night!"

"Yeah, you too."

I turn the phone off and slip it into my bag.

I feel like Cinderella, stuck at home while my ugly sisters go off to the ball. Except my fairy godmother has failed to show up, and I'm stuck at a stupid party with a bunch of pumpkins.

"I've had enough of this for one night," I say, turning to Sonya. "You want to get out of here and go to Mustafa's?"

"Sounds good – just one thing before we leave."

"What?"

"Follow me."

She leads me upstairs to the bathroom.

"What are we looking for?"

"This!"

She flings open the cabinet to reveal box upon box of tanning spray.

"Look at it all!"

We both giggle.

"Shall we hide them?" Sonya suggests, with a wicked grin.

"Sonya!"

I laugh even harder as she starts pulling the boxes out of the cupboard.

"There are so many! Where can we possibly hide them?"

"We'll put them in the airing cupboard, under all the towels. He'll never think of looking there."

She walks down the hall, her arms full.

"Grab the hair dye, Isabel. We'll hide that too. Tomorrow, he's going all natural!"

I watch as she crams all the boxes into the cupboard. It's really silly, but somehow, it's just what I need.

"Come on, let's get back downstairs before anyone sees us."

"One last thing."

She pauses in front of the master bedroom.

"What are you doing?"

"Just taking a peek."

She pushes open the door and switches on the light.

"Silk sheets," I whistle. "Fancy!"

Sonya smiles. "I think Stu could do with an early morning wake up, don't you?"

She walks over to the alarm clock, sitting on the bedside table and starts fiddling with the settings.

"What shall we change the station to? Do you think he likes German industrial music?"

I smile, but I feel a bit bad as we walk back downstairs. After all, Stu did invite us into his home.

Still, I suppose he had it coming.

"I'll grab our coats," Sonya says, heading back to the kitchen.

"Thanks for the party Stu," I say, so as not to be totally rude.

"What? You're leaving already?" He looks a little bewildered. "But you've only just arrived!"

"Yeah well we've got another party to get to. Busy night."

"Do you really have to go?" he asks in a whiny voice.

He looks quite forlorn - until he notices something:

"Hey, we're standing under the mistletoe!"

"What?" I glance upwards. He's right, this part of the ceiling's totally covered with it. Before I know what's happening, he's pressing his lips against mine. His breath smells of cheese and onion crisps. I pull back, repulsed, just as Sonya returns.

She raises her eyebrows. "You ready to go?"

"Very."

"Oh, you know you loved it," Stu calls after my departing back. "All the ladies do. Once you've had Stu, no one else will do!"

❆

I MAKE the call just before work on Monday morning. I reason that a successful businessman like Bernie Greengrass isn't one to loll about in bed, so I'm sure he won't mind me calling him a little early.

"About time!" he chuckles, when he hears my voice. "How about you pop in to see me, and we can discuss the details."

"Sounds great. When?"

"Let's see - I've just had a lunch cancellation, actually. Can you do twelve o'clock?"

Wow, this is all happening so fast!

"OK, I'll see you then."

"Morning Isabel," Alicia bounds up to me in the car park when I get to work. She has the energy of a Labrador puppy.

"Hi," I reply cautiously. "How was the ball?" I was dreading this conversation, but somehow, with the lunch-time meeting in my pocket, it's not quite so bad.

"It was incredible! Deacon's such a great dancer!"

She giggles. – I don't know what at.

"Did you have fun at your party?" She leans a little closer. "I heard you and Stu kissed!"

"Yeah, well don't believe everything you hear."

I brush past her into the store.

"Have you seen Stu?" Sonya asks with glee. "His skin is definitely a few shades lighter today!"

I smile, but to be honest I can't tell the difference. "Um, Sonya, is it OK if I take a long lunch break today? I need to go to the post office and you know what the queues are like this close to Christmas."

"Course, just make sure you're back by two."

So at half past eleven, I head off for my interview.

"Good luck," Alicia whispers, as I walk by. I look at her sharply. How the hell does she know? But Alicia just smiles sweetly, in that annoying way she has.

Must be a lucky guess, I tell myself. I bet half the staff here are job hunting at the moment.

I arrive at Filbert's a little early, so I sit in the car and smoke a cigarette while I think about what I want to get out of this meeting. Obviously, I want a pay rise, but I also need to know what my career prospects would be, though they couldn't be any worse than they are at Robertson's.

I'm just stubbing out my cigarette, when a loud beeping sound makes me jump. I reach into my bag and pull out my keys. It's my bloody smoke detector. It doesn't usually go off when I smoke. So why's it become so sensitive all of a sudden? Slowly, I look up.

Crap! There's a car on fire!

I can see flames coming out of the boot.

I know I should call 999, but I can't from here. I can't be around fire. Not when I'm already under so much suspicion. With shaking hands, I stick the keys back in the ignition and speed towards the exit. As I wait for the woman in front of me to pull out, I glance back at the car that's on fire. It's a beautiful, shiny new Jaguar, with customised registration plates that read 'Bernie1'.

I speed back to Robertson's, violating about twelve different traffic laws along the way.

"That was quick," says Sonya, as I walk back into the office. "I thought you'd be at least an hour."

"Yeah, well the queue looked a bit too crazy. I'll go another day. Have you seen Alicia by any chance?"

I have to know if she's behind this.

"She's on her lunch break."

"Down in the canteen?"

"No, she said something about going into town."

Which means it could have been her who started that fire!

I don't know what that girl's up to, but I don't trust her. Not one bit.

8

I tip my sodden clothes into the dryer. The machine whirls and then judders as it picks up speed. I watch for a moment, as my clothes whiz round and round and the thoughts tumble around in my head in a similar manner.

Until now, I forced myself to give Alicia the benefit of the doubt, because the alternative was way too sinister for me to even comprehend. I thought I was being crazy, paranoid. But not anymore. Now, there has been one fire too many and like DS Penney, I don't believe in coincidences. I don't know why Alicia is out to get me or how she's setting all these fires but it's about time I found out.

To start with, how did the police know to connect me to the fire at Rose Cottage? It happened all those years ago, and it's not like I have a criminal record. And how is it that Alicia has ingratiated herself with my friends? Somehow, she's made them all trust her instantly. My friends have become her friends. Anything she wants to know about me, she can get from them, the people who know me better than anyone. And yet I know nothing about her.

That has to change.

I think back through all the time we've spent together, but

she leaves very few clues. She has a skill of turning the conversation around to other people and since people love to talk about themselves, I don't think anyone ever notices.

I sit down in front of my laptop and type her name into Google. It takes some time to trawl through all the Alicia McBrides, but none look or sound like her. She has no Facebook profile, no obvious Twitter account. I draw a big fat blank.

A car honks outside. I go to the window and peer out.

Damn, I'd forgotten Kate was picking me up. Quickly, I run a brush though my hair and grab my handbag. Normally, I spend ages getting ready for a night out but I was too engrossed in what I was doing.

"So, what are you doing for Christmas?" I ask, as I fasten my seat belt.

"Staying here in Queensbeach," she says, reversing out of the driveway. "I'm on call at the hospital, so the family are coming to me."

"I was thinking of going away for a few days," I tell her. "Do you think you could feed Fluffy?"

She glances at me out of the corner of her eye.

"You're going to see Julio?"

"Yes."

"And his new fiancée?"

"Yes."

She bites her lip and an awkward silence descends.

"So you've got all the family coming to stay?" I ask, in an attempt to resuscitate the conversation.

"And Alicia."

This time, it's my turn to bite my lip.

"Doesn't she have a family of her own?"

"No. Not that she talks about, anyway."

Poor little orphan Alicia. I know I should probably feel sorry for her but instead I just feel annoyed. How dare she intrude on Kate's family Christmas? How dare she take advantage of her generous nature?

The knot in my stomach tightens as Deacon and Alicia walk into Mustafa's, hand in hand. I can barely look at them, either of them. I pick up my glass of wine and drink it straight down.

"So when are we having our Christmas dinner?" Kate asks, oblivious to my pain.

The four of us always get together for a Christmas meal before everyone leaves town for the holidays.

"How about next Sunday?" Rhett suggests. The others nod in agreement.

"Hey, how about I host it this year?" I suggest brightly.

They all look at me blankly.

"Oh, I assumed we'd be having it at Rhett and Deacon's," Kate says awkwardly.

"I just thought it would be fun to have it at my house for a change. It's been ages since I've had you all round."

"You're, erm, going to cook?" Deacon asks dubiously.

"Yeah, why not?"

He rubs his chin. "Can you… cook?"

"Of course I can!" I say with indignation. "I just don't do it very often."

"That sounds lovely," says Rhett, ever the diplomat. "How about I bring the pudding?"

"That would be great."

❄

NEXT MORNING, I try once more to get Bernie Greengrass on the phone to apologise for missing my interview, but his assistant refuses to put me through.

"I'm sorry, but Mr Greengrass is a very busy man. He doesn't have time to reschedule your appointment."

"I understand. Please let me know if an appointment becomes available."

I put down the phone.

Damn Alicia, she's ruined everything.

I see Stu coming my way and hurriedly disappear into the shoe aisle, the memory of his repulsive Christmas kiss still fresh in my mind. I wait until the coast is clear, then hot-foot it back to the office, where I pull up the personnel files on the computer.

McBride, Alicia. *No middle name.*

I flick through her details. Her age, date of birth and national insurance number all look completely normal. I scroll down the page. No work history and the only person listed as a reference is me. I'm also her next of kin. Not much to go on. I press print anyway.

"Hi Isabel."

I jump as Alicia herself appears in the doorway, her eyes impossibly wide and childlike.

"Alicia! What are you doing here?"

"Sonya asked me to put the kettle on. Do you want a cup of tea?"

"No thanks, I'm fine."

"You sure?" She seems to look right through me. "I could read your tea leaves for you?"

"No, that's fine," I say sharply. Some of her last predictions were a little close to the mark.

The room is filled with a droning sound as the ancient printer bashes out her file, line by agonising line. Sonya's been on at Stu for a new printer for ages but he insists we can make this one last a little longer. It screeches in protest.

"I think it's stuck," Alicia says, walking over to investigate. She peers down at the printer.

"I can handle it, thanks," I tell her. I rip the page from the printer and stuff it into my pocket.

Alicia smiles knowingly.

"Just trying to help."

Sunday - 7 AM

I get up early to go shopping. I shop not just for food and drink but also for extra pots and pans and an apron. Good thing Robertson's is open 24 hours a day or I'd be in trouble. My friends didn't look particularly impressed when I offered to cook Christmas dinner, but I'm going to prove them all wrong. Even if this is the first time I've used all four rings on my cooker. I fill a glass with sherry and pore over the cookbook, frowning with concentration.

Wow, turkey takes bloody ages, I'd better put it on first.

Rhett and Kate both ring at various intervals to ask if I need any help but I insist I can handle it on my own. They don't have to know that I had to ring mum four separate times, one of which was to find out what I'm supposed to do with the turkey baster.

By the time my friends arrive - a polite fifteen minutes late - there is cranberry sauce in my hair and my top is covered in flour. My apron, I am proud to say, remains spotless.

"I'll just pop this in the kitchen," says Rhett, staggering in with what looks like a very heavy plum pudding. He puts it down on the side and opens the oven to check the turkey.

"Beautiful!" he says, approvingly. Then he lifts the lid off the saucepan. "These carrots look done. I'll take them off the heat, shall I?"

Rhett is my saviour. He puts on a Christmas CD and hands out glasses of sherry and mince pies while I dash upstairs to change into my glamorous green dress. Well, where else am I going to wear it?

"You look fabulous, darling!" he says, as I re-emerge. "Where do you want us to sit?"

I shoot him a grateful smile. He has even laid the table for me and folded the napkins into little swans. But even his efforts don't make up for the fact that my dining table is meant for four. Five is a bit too much of a squeeze.

Why did Alicia have to come?

Thanks to her, I have to go next door to Mr Krinkle's to borrow an extra chair and he keeps me talking for ages before he finally condescends to lend me one. Luckily, Rhett has the sense to turn down the oven so the turkey doesn't burn.

"Well, Isabel, this all looks surprisingly good," Deacon says when we're finally seated at the table. I suppose that's as close as I'm going to get to a compliment.

"Shall I carve?"

I smile smugly as he doles out wafer-thin slices of turkey and try to ignore the fact that he and Alicia are probably playing footsie under the table. My cooking may not be in Rhett's league, but this is definitely edible.

After we've eaten our fill of turkey, I warm up the pudding in the microwave and pour warm brandy over it, ready to light.

"Wait!"

Rhett gets up and turns out the lights.

"OK, go ahead."

I feel in my pocket for a lighter.

"Here, let me do it," Alicia offers, picking one up from the table. Her eyes gleam dangerously.

"No!" I cry. I try to grab the lighter from her hand, but with a flick of her thumb, the flame ignites and I can only stare in horror as it dances up my sleeve.

For a second, I can't move.

"Isabel, you're on fire!" Alicia shrieks in delight.

"Ahh!"

She leans over and makes a big show of swatting the flames with a tea towel, which only makes it worse.

"Get off me!" I yell.

"Let me help you!"

"You? Help me?"

I push her away, and dash into the kitchen, where I plunge my arm into the washing up water, quenching the flames.

Deacon rushes after me.

"Are you OK?"

"I'm fine." I withdraw my arm from the murky water and examine the scorched fabric of my sleeve.

"Have you hurt yourself? Let me see."

He takes my arm and holds it under the cold tap.

"My arm's fine. It's my dress that's ruined."

"What on earth was all that about?" he asks, as I towel myself off.

"Why did you grab the lighter from Alicia's hand like that?"

"She could have set the house on fire," I mumble. But even as I'm saying this, I can hear how stupid it sounds.

"What do you have against Alicia?" he asks with frustration. "You've been funny about her from the start."

"That's not true!"

"Yes, it is, Isabel. I've seen the way you look at her. I thought she was supposed to be your friend?"

Over my shoulder, I can sense the presence of someone else. Someone whose eyes bore into me so deeply, I feel their heat on my shoulders.

"It's nothing. Now if you don't mind, I'm going upstairs to get changed. Start on the pudding without me, before it gets cold."

Deacon shakes his head, but allows me to slip upstairs to my room.

I sit down on the bed. My eyes feel hot and heavy with tears. I don't know if it's the shock of what just happened, or the fear or what's to come, but I can't let Alicia see me like this. With determination, I discard my ruined dress and pull on jeans and a jumper. I am just coming back downstairs when the doorbell rings.

That'll probably be Mr Krinkle wanting to know if he can have his chair back.

The bell rings again.

"Wow, he's impatient."

Kate, who's nearest, jumps up and answers it.

"Isabel!"

"Yeah, I'm coming."

But it isn't Mr Krinkle. It's DS Penney and his partner. They both look very serious.

Penney steps forward. "Isabel Anderson, we'd like to speak to you about a fire at Filbert's Supercentre. Where were you at twelve noon on Monday 14th December?"

I open my mouth to answer, but Alicia's voice floats out from behind me.

"She was with me."

9

I swing round to face Alicia.
What is she doing? But there are no clues in her wide, innocent eyes.

She has the perfect poker face.

"That was the day we went Christmas shopping," she continues, unprompted. "Don't you remember, Isabel?"

Penney regards her coolly.

"I suppose you have receipts?"

I shift uncomfortably from one foot to the other.

"I'll have to check," I say. "I might have thrown them away."

"I've got receipts," Alicia says, without missing a beat. "Back at the Beach House. I can show you, if you like."

I watch incredulously as she slips on her coat and leads them out the door.

Against my better judgement, I follow.

I sit in nervous silence in the back of the police car. Beside me, Alicia yaps on about Christmas shopping and the shops we supposedly visited while I was sitting in Filbert's car park, watching Bernie's car go up in smoke. Just what, exactly, is she up to? And why the hell am I going along with it? I think of the till receipts we use at Robertson's. They have the time and date printed on them. If Alicia set the fires, how could she possibly produce receipts? And if it wasn't her, then why is she covering for me?

We draw up in front of the Beach House and get out of the car. The little voice inside my head tells me to run but I hold my nerve. Without a hint of urgency, Alicia unlocks the door and we follow her up the stairs to her bedroom.

And there we wait. We wait for a horrendously long time as Alicia performs an elaborate search of the room. Oh god, why did I go along with this? Did I really think she was going to be able to produce those mythical till receipts, like a rabbit from a hat?

The police are getting restless. Penney's partner keeps sighing and glancing at her watch.

"Would you like a cup of tea?" I offer for the second time.

"No thanks, just the receipts," she responds curtly.

"I'm sure they're somewhere around here," Alicia mutters, digging through her desk drawer. A search of her cupboard, dressing table, and wardrobe has failed to turn up anything besides a hair slide she thought she'd lost. The police glance at each other with exasperation and I wonder, with a sinking feeling if she's doing all this to taunt me.

I clench and unclench my fists as she pulls an old shoe box out from under her bed and begins rifling through it, with the same lack of urgency as she's conducted the rest of the search.

"Ah, here they are."

I look up in surprise. Triumphantly, she pulls something out of the box.

Penney and his partner take a closer look.

"The times and dates look right," he confirms.

She nods.

"So do I still need to come down the station?"

They look at each other.

"I think we'll leave it, for the time being."

I sink back against the bed as their footsteps retreat. I don't want to stay here in Alicia's room but neither do I have the strength to get up. I can barely even string a sentence together.

"Don't worry, it's going to be OK now," Alicia tells me, putting the box back in its place.

"But why did you do that?"

She smiles sweetly. "Anything for a friend."

"But why did you?"

"I didn't want you to get into trouble."

"But why did you think I'd get into trouble?"

She flicks some fluff from her jumper.

"I knew you were at Filbert's that day."

"How?"

"Oh, come on – you were acting shifty all morning. Where else would you be going? It's not like anyone else is recruiting - not at this time of year."

She's right.

"Well, thanks, I guess."

I feel more confused than ever.

※

I DON'T SLEEP VERY WELL that night. I wake up at two, and then again at three and four, and end up pacing around the living room with the shopping channel on in the background.

What the hell is going on? Nothing makes sense anymore.

I'm supposed to be driving over to Julio's in the morning but I'm nervous about leaving Alicia alone with my friends. If only I knew for sure whether I can trust her. Still, there's no backing out now. Julio's really looking forward to introducing me to his fiancée. And besides, I have to admit I'm kind of curious. I try to picture Holly, but it's useless. My brother doesn't have a type, unless it's female. Sometimes I wonder what all these women see in him.

Since I'm unable to get back to sleep, I set off early, before the traffic has a chance to build up and I pull up outside Julio's new house just before lunch-time. It isn't hard to figure out which house is his. The dismembered body of an old Morris Minor litters the driveway. The poor thing is leaking buckets of oil, and spare parts are splayed out like guts all over the grass. A familiar pair of boots sticks out from under the car.

I'm just considering how to rouse him, when the garage door opens and someone, presumably Holly, teeters out on high heels, carrying a tea tray. She is tall and blonde, with endlessly long legs and rather well-dressed for my dishevelled brother.

"Oh, hello! You must be Isabel!"

"And you must be Holly!"

"I am!" Her smile reveals a slight overbite, which only adds to her appeal. "Julio! Your sister's here!"

My brother slides out from under the car and makes a futile attempt to dust the dirt off his overalls. He tries to hug me, but I bat him off.

"Not in those clothes!"

"Go and take a shower," Holly tells him. She's what my mum would call 'well spoken'."

"Come on in, Isabel. I've just made some tea."

The two of us sit in the living room drinking tea and eating Jaffa Cakes. The coffee table is stacked high with bridal magazines and honeymoon brochures. Holly talks enthusiastically about the wedding, which is due to take place in the spring. She seems keen to include me in their plans, which is very sweet, but kind of awkward since it wasn't so long ago that I was helping Julio plan his wedding to Kate. This would all be so much easier if I could dislike Holly, but so far, I see nothing to dislike.

"It all sounds like a fairytale," I say, admiring the lavish dress designs she shows me. She nods. "We're getting married barefoot, down on the beach. I was thinking it might be fun to arrive on horses, but Julio doesn't have a clue how to ride. Still, I'm sure he can learn in time. And after the ceremony, we'll have the wedding breakfast in the grounds of Seymour Castle."

"Sounds lovely."

"And instead of a disco, we're going to finish with a candlelit dance. Doesn't that sound romantic?"

"It does."

It really does.

I don't think Kate was that bothered about the details when she married Julio. Theirs was a very simple wedding. She didn't even wear the traditional white meringue. It just wasn't her. I'm not sure a big fancy wedding is really Julio either but then, my brother is a chameleon. He twists and changes with every woman he's with. Sometimes, I'm not sure I know the real Julio at all.

His capriciousness weighs heavily on my conscience. Holly is so excited about this, she's making so many plans, spending so much money. What if he ditches her just like he ditched Kate and all the others?

I have to say something. I can't just let her do this, not knowing what my brother's really like.

I take a deep breath, and the words all come rushing out at once.

"Don't get me wrong, Holly – you seem fantastic, but are you really sure you want to marry my brother?"

Holly laughs. Yes, actually laughs.

"Don't worry about me, Isabel. I know his reputation. I know what I'm getting myself into."

I feel a little taken aback. This isn't the reaction I was expecting.

"Well, just as long as you know. I would hate for you to get hurt."

"Don't worry," she says, with a dismissive wave of her hand. "Julio's met his match with me, I can promise you that."

Well, she seems sure enough!

I wrap my cardy a little more tightly round me as a cool draft blows through the room.

"Are you cold?"

"No, I'm fine."

Despite my protests, Holly strikes a match and lets it flutter onto the coals. I hadn't realised it was a real fireplace. I'd just assumed it was gas, like mine.

For the first time in weeks, I enjoy the hiss and spit of a fire, without worrying about whether the house is going to burn down. Holly puts on some soft, soothing music and we warm ourselves in companionable silence. My eyes begin to droop as the blue and orange flames crackle and snap in front of me.

"Izzy?" I hear Julio coming downstairs.

"Shh! She's asleep."

I am in that no-man's land between the waking world and the sleeping one. I am aware of Holly and Julio tiptoeing around me, but my closed eyes are still faintly focused on the fire. I can almost make out a ghostly face amidst the black plumes of smoke. I see a girl with pale skin and wild curls. She throws back her head and laughs. I struggle to shake off the image, but I am no longer in control. I give in to the lull of sleep.

"Hi, sleepy head," Julio says, when I finally emerge from my nap.

"Sorry - I didn't sleep very well last night," I apologise, rubbing the sleep from my eyes.

"We were thinking of going to the pub over the road if you fancy it?" Holly suggests.

"Sounds good. I just need to freshen up."

"Of course, come on – I'll show you your room."

She leads me upstairs to a neat little guest room. I smile politely while she points out the bathroom and explains the trick for getting the hot water going in the morning. I wait until I hear her feet pad back down the stairs before I ring Kate.

Kate sounds a little frosty when she answers.

"You're at Julio's then?"

"Yes."

"So what's she like, his new fiancée?"

"She's…" I pause. Kate wants to hear that Holly's a screaming lunatic with a hunch-back and a heroin habit but after all Holly's lovely hospitality, the words stick in my throat.

"You like her, don't you?" I can hear the hurt in her voice.

"She's…" I search desperately for something negative to say.

"She's not you," I finish truthfully.

❄

Holly wakes me on Christmas Day with yet another cup of tea and a piece of homemade gingerbread. It's the first Christmas in years that I've been allowed to sleep in late. Mum seems to start the festivities earlier and earlier every year. Not so much out of enthusiasm, but an eagerness to get it all out of the way. Last year, we were both tucked up in bed by half past nine in the evening. I try not to hold it against her though. After all, I like to be up bright and early to hit the Boxing Day sales.

I put on my dressing gown and walk downstairs, eager to begin opening my presents.

"Here - I saw this and thought of you," Julio says, holding out a large, rectangular parcel.

"Thanks!"

I rip open the paper. It's a framed picture of a little girl gazing out of her bedroom window at a purple moon.

"I can't believe you remembered this!"

"Of course I did!"

When I was a little girl, I would often dream of a purple

moon – it became a bit of an obsession. Every night, when I was supposed to be asleep, I would wrap my duvet around me and tiptoe over to the wide bay window. There, I would sit and watch, waiting to see if the moon changed colour. I often fell asleep like that, my face pressed up against the glass, my warm breath leaving a strange smudge on the window that mystified my poor Mum in the morning.

"This is really lovely, thank you." I smile guiltily, remembering what I said to Holly about him yesterday.

Oh god, I hope she's not going to tell him.

But I get the feeling Holly is someone who can be trusted. Somehow, I don't think she's going to repeat my warning to Julio.

"So how are Deacon and the others?" my brother asks later, over Christmas lunch.

I adjust my paper hat. "I don't know. Everything's a bit weird at the moment."

"How do you mean?"

I fill them in on the situation with Alicia.

Holly takes a deep breath. "You should be careful," she says, stabbing a pea with her fork. "There are some very weird people out there. I should know - I meet enough of them in my line of work."

"Why? What do you do?"

She flicks back her long, shiny hair.

"I'm a private detective."

"Wow! That sounds exciting."

"Hardly. I spend most of my time sitting in the car waiting to take pictures of cheating wives and husbands."

My eyes flicker to Julio.

Ha! Ha! You aren't going to get anything past this one, Julio.

"So what would you do, if you were me?" I ask.

"Well, first of all, I wouldn't have let her give me an alibi!" she says sternly. "It's not like they've got any real evidence against you, anyway. The CCTV images would have put you in the clear – if they had any."

"That's it!" I exclaim, snapping my fingers. "There must be cameras outside Filbert's – why don't they look at those to find out what happened?"

Holly shakes her head. "They don't always help. Some cameras only record the last 24 hours and others only show live feed, so there would have to be someone monitoring them at the time."

"What? Can't they go back and look at the footage?"

"Only if they were recording. And now you've lied and said you weren't there, it's probably for the best if they don't have anything on camera."

"I suppose so."

"So what do we know about this Alicia girl?"

"Very little. She gives nothing away."

"Have you managed to find out anything at all?"

"Well," I say hesitantly. "I did manage to get a copy of her personnel file."

"Oh, you bad girl!" Julio clicks his tongue in mock disapproval.

"It didn't tell me much, though."

I reach into my handbag and pull out the crumpled piece of paper.

"Leave that with me," says Holly. "I'll do some digging around."

"Oh, would you? That would be great!"

"I can't promise that I'm going to find anything," she warns. "But I'll definitely take a look."

I nod, appreciatively. It's so great to finally have someone I can talk to about this stuff. Holly doesn't seem to think I'm mad, and with her help, I may finally have the upper hand.

"And in the meantime, it would be best if you keep your distance from this girl."

"That's easier said than done. She's got in pretty deep with my friends."

"Well, you be careful. And whatever you do, don't let her know we're investigating her. It sounds like she could be dangerous."

Her words send a chill down my spine... *I'm not imagining it, then.*

Three Hours Later

"Are you sure you can't stay another night?" Holly asks, as I collect up all my stuff. "We'd love to have you."

"I wish I could, but I've got work in the morning."

I peer through the window. It's already getting dark outside.

"Well, take care, then." Holly says. "It was lovely to meet you."

"You too. You'd better hang on to this one," I whisper to Julio, as I hug him goodbye.

The roads are eerily empty on the way home. There is nothing but a series of cat's eyes that stretch out in front of me in the darkness. I turn on the radio for company but I can't help feeling that something isn't quite right. There are hardly any cars on the road, yet the one behind me has been tailgating for a while now. I glance in my mirror, but I can't make out the driver's face. Are they watching me or the road?

Five minutes pass and then ten. The car is still right behind me, uncomfortably close. This isn't right. I'm starting to get really freaked out.

I just have to make it to the next services. Then I'll be safe.

It seems like forever before the knife and fork sign looms out of the darkness. I wait until the last possible moment to indicate, and then spin off to the left. For one, heart-stopping moment it seems like the white car is going to follow, and then the driver seems to change their mind. They swerve back onto the main road, and I heave a huge sigh of relief.

Feeling rather wobbly, I pump some petrol into my car and get a latte from the shop. But as I sit, sipping my drink at the counter, my uneasiness returns. It's so dead out here that the few people who are around seem very sinister. I take a final gulp of my drink and toss the paper cup into the bin.

As the roads are so empty, I take a liberal interpretation of the speed limits for the rest of the drive home. At last, the lights of Queensbeach twinkle tantalizingly on the horizon. I wind down my window and gulp down big breaths of sea air.

I pull up outside my house and hurry up the path, not even bothering to get my overnight bag. I ram the key in the lock and throw open the door. I am about to switch on the lights on when I hear a creaking sound coming from upstairs.

"Fluffy?"

There is a loud thud. *That's no cat,* I realise, my heart in my mouth. *There's someone in my house!*

10

I freeze.

What should I do?

I stand stock-still and listen. Whoever it is has gone silent.

With shaking hands, I reach for my mobile, but something stops me before I hit the third 9. The police have not exactly been my friends lately. I'd better handle this on my own.

I let out the breath I've been holding. I shouldn't go up there, I know I shouldn't. And yet I have to. I creep into the kitchen and grab the largest knife I can find. I grip the handle tightly as I steal up the stairs, wincing at every creak.

I pause at the top of the stairs. A shaft of light spills out from under my bedroom door.

Someone's in there.

I edge my way along the cold, dimly lit hallway, my breath coming in short, sharp gasps. Then I burst into the room, hoping to catch whoever it is by surprise. As I do so, the knife slips from my grasp and clatters loudly to the floor. I grab it quickly, scanning the room urgently with my eyes. The bed is made, the curtains drawn and the nightstand just as I left it. I throw open the wardrobe door and rifle frantically through the clothes. There is no one there.

I spin round, my eyes fixed on the bed. The duvet seems strangely lumpy. I whip back the covers. But it's just my old teddy bear, Gerald.

This is ridiculous. What am I doing?

There is nowhere to hide under the bed or behind it. I must simply have left the light on. The wind rattles against the window and I notice my watering can lying on the floor. It must have fallen down off the shelf. That must have been the sound I heard. I stoop down to pick it up. And yet…as I stand there, berating myself for my own stupidity, I distinctly hear someone - or something - breathing.

My eyes dart from left to right.

There! There it is! That bulge behind the curtains. I can't believe I didn't spot it before.

My heart is in my mouth as I step forward and wrench them open.

An ear-splitting scream fills the room.

"ALICIA!"

"Isabel! You scared the life out of me!" She steps out of the shadows, looking the very picture of wide-eyed innocence.

"What are you doing in my house?" I demand, my shoulders trembling with fury.

"Kate asked me to feed Fluffy," she says, as though it's the most obvious thing in the world. "She got stuck working an extra shift at the hospital."

"So what are you doing up here?"

"She said your plants might need watering."

She indicates the drooping plants on the window sill.

"So why were you hiding?"

"Me?" Alicia's eyes grow wide. "Why were you creeping around like that? I thought you were a burglar!"

"Me too."

She catches sight of my knife.

"Oh my god! What were you going to do, stab me?"

"I…I…"

But then she laughs her irritating Minnie Mouse laugh and I can see she's not serious.

I smile weakly and accept surrender. She's got me. Again. My brain aches.

We traipse downstairs and I watch as she pulls on her boots. I hadn't even noticed them, lined up by the front door.

"Well, Merry Christmas," she smiles.

"You too," I echo lamely. It's really dark outside and I should probably offer her a lift but I just want her out of my house. Besides, there's no way I'm getting in a car with her again. She lingers on the doorstep, as if expecting me to offer, but I just say good night and shut the door. I watch from the window as she skips off down the path. I wait until I'm sure she has gone, then I bolt the door behind her. Exhausted, I collapse into my favourite armchair. My poor, jangled nerves.

The phone shrills, making me jump. I ignore it. Let the answering machine pick it up.

"Isabel, it's Holly. Just checking you got back all right?"

I make a grab for it. "Hi Holly, I just got in."

"Everything OK? You sound a bit shaky."

"Alicia was in my house!" I blurt out. "Kate gave her the key."

"You'd better change your locks then. Tonight if possible."

"Tonight?"

"Yeah, you shouldn't take any chances."

I touch my throat. Oh god, she's right. Alicia has a key to my house.

Why, oh why didn't I ask for it back?

I think back to the expression on Alicia's face when I caught her in my bedroom. It wasn't fear, was it? It was pleasure. Just like the day she jumped out in front of my car. She's getting a kick out of scaring me, the sick little freak.

And just in case you ever think of ringing a locksmith at

eight PM on Christmas Day, don't bother. Forty-five minutes later, the saucer I've been using as an ashtray is completely full and I'm no closer to getting the locks changed. What to do, what to do? I drift around the house, checking that every window is shut tight, then drag the coffee table over to the front door and wedge it up against the handle.

Ding-Dong!

At last!

I peer through the peephole. But it isn't the locksmith.

"Deacon?"

"Who were you expecting? The Dalai Lama?"

"Yes, he always pops round for tea about this time. Just wait there a minute and I'll let you in."

I scramble about, pulling the coffee table back to its original position, and then I unbolt the door.

"What was all that about?" he asks as he strides inside. "Sounded like you were rearranging the furniture."

"Er, yes - I was, but I decided it looks better the way it was."

He raises an eyebrow and perches himself on the sofa.

"I came to give you your Christmas present."

"You already gave me a Christmas present," I remind him, pulling a face. He left me a book called 'Managing your finances' when he came for dinner.

"Your real Christmas present, silly. I wanted to see your face when you opened it."

"Oh!"

He reaches into his coat pocket and pulls out an envelope.

"What's this?"

"Why don't you open it?"

I slit it open.

"Depeche Mode tickets? Oh my god, this is amazing! You're the best!" I hug him violently. "I have wanted to see them forever."

"I know. I couldn't believe it when I heard that they're

finally coming to the Arena. The tickets are for Saturday night. I know it's a bit short notice but I really wanted to surprise you."

Wow!

I start mentally thumbing through my wardrobe, deciding what I should wear.

But wait...A big grey cloud drifts into my thoughts.

"There are only two tickets. What about Alicia?"

"Oh, she won't mind. I mean, it's Depeche Mode. They're a bit before her time, aren't they?"

I smile, but inside, my stomach is churning.

This is Alicia we're talking about. I can't accept Deacon's invitation.

"You *do* want to go?" he asks, studying my face carefully. "You've gone awfully quiet."

"Of course I do!" I hug him again. "Best gift ever!"

I'll just have to come up with an excuse in the morning.

But I can't face telling Deacon the next day or the next. Finally, on Thursday night I force myself to drive over to the Beach House after work.

"Isabel!" Rhett greets me. "Wait till you see what I got in the sales!"

He pulls me into the kitchen, where Deacon is sitting at the table, reading the newspaper and eating a roast beef sandwich.

Rhett bounds up to his room and returns, wielding a Frankie Morello shoe box.

"Wow," I say eyeing his expensive new trainers. "They're pink!"

"I know!"

"How much?"

"40% off!"

"Nice."

He places the shoes back in their box, tenderly wrapping them back up in their tissue paper. He keeps all his shoes like that, never even wears half of them. Still, whatever makes him happy.

"So what did you get in the sales?" he asks me.

"The sales?" I repeat. "Oh, I haven't been."

Deacon looks up from his newspaper.

"*You* haven't been to the sales?" he repeats in disbelief. "Why not?"

"I just didn't feel like it this year."

He leans over and puts his hand to my forehead. "You don't seem to have a temperature."

I smile weakly. The truth is, shopping hasn't been terribly high on my agenda lately.

"But Isabel," Rhett gasps, "shopping is your life. I thought we were kindred spirits!"

"It's really not such a big deal," I say lightly. "I've just been busy, that's all."

"Hmm…" Rhett is still looking at me like I'm from another planet.

"So about Saturday night," says Deacon. "Do you want me to pick you up, or shall we meet at the Arena?"

"Deacon, about that…"

"What?"

"Look, I'm really sorry but I don't think I'm going to be able to go."

"Why not?" he folds his arms. "I thought you were looking forward to it."

"I was, but I just found out I have to work that night," I lie feebly.

"On a Saturday night?" Deacon frowns. "Look Isabel, if this is about Alicia…"

"It's not about Alicia."

"Cos I already talked to her and she's fine with it."

I bet.

Alicia!

I sense her watching from the banisters. Her eyes are lasers, scorching the back of my head.

"I really have to work that night," I say more emphatically. "I'm sorry you went to so much trouble."

Alicia chooses this moment to make her entrance.

"Hi Isabel, what's up?"

"Isabel has to work on Saturday night," Rhett fills her in.

"Oh no, isn't the concert on Saturday?"

I nod.

"Oh, that's a shame." Her large eyes are wide with pity. "And you were so looking forward to it."

"Well, it can't be helped."

"Hey, how about I talk to Sonya?" she says, snapping her fingers. "Maybe I can cover some of your work?"

"No really, it's fine."

"It's worth a try though, isn't it?" Deacon says. "If you do still want to go?"

"Of course I do."

"Well, then."

❄

"There's rubbish on your lawn," Mr Krinkle points out as I arrive home. This is the probably the highlight of his day, poor man.

Gingerly, I stuff the discarded chip papers into the bin, and hurry down the path towards the house. I'm not in the mood for small talk.

"There's another bit on your doorstep," he calls after me.

I glance down and find a sliver of brown film. I bend down to pick it up. It appears to be a strip of negatives. I didn't think anybody used those anymore.

Inside, I hold it up to the light. It's hard to make out, but they appear to be the negatives of Kate's Camp Windylake pictures. They must have fallen out of the box Julio brought round. I pull out the box from under my bed, where I'd shoved it. I didn't even attempt to give it to Kate when she came for Christmas dinner. I didn't want to spoil the mood by bringing up my brother. It is still taped up, but there are a couple of hand holes for carrying it. The film could have slipped out of one of those. I open the box and riffle through it for the corresponding photographs but I can't find them. Which is a shame because I never took any photos at Camp Windylake. I kind of wish I had.

Alicia bounces up to me as I walk into work the next day.

"It's all set," she announces, her eyes sparkling.

"What is?"

"Saturday night, of course. I just had a word with Sonya. She wasn't even aware you were meant to be working on Saturday. Must have been a mix up with the schedule. Anyway, she said she'd be happy to swap you to another shift."

"Thanks." I am more confused than ever. Does she actually want me to go the concert? Or is she playing games with me, pawing at me like a cat with a ball of yarn? It's impossible to tell.

I am so busy puzzling over this, I almost forget to pick up the photographs. I dropped off the negatives at the 24-hour pharmacy on the way to work. I flip through the prints as I walk out of the shop, first quickly, then more slowly. Kate's going to laugh her head off when she sees these.

What was I wearing? How could I have ever have thought ponchos were a good look?

I drive home, where a confused Fluffy circles around me as I go from room to room, checking for intruders. Although the locks have now been changed, I still can't rest until I'm absolutely certain Alicia isn't in the house.

Once I'm satisfied I'm alone, I make myself a cup of tea and take out the photos again. I just can't seem to put them down. There's something that bugs me about them, but I can't quite put my finger on it.

What's this?

I'm looking at a picture of Kate, aged eighteen, surrounded by children from the camp. And there, sitting on her knee is a young girl of about ten years old. A young girl with wild black curls and big doe eyes.

I suck in my breath.

Is it really possible? Alicia is a good few years younger than us. She would have been around that age when the photo was taken. I study the photo carefully. There's no mistaking it.

It's her! It's Alicia.

And I'm betting she's come back into our lives for a reason.

11

I am on her trail.
 Alicia has never mentioned Camp Windylake. She doesn't want us to know she was ever at that camp. She doesn't want us to know we've met before.
 Excitedly, I pick up the phone.
 "Kate, can you meet me at the Beach House in twenty minutes?" I ask. "I have something to tell you all."
 "What? Why can't you tell me over the phone?"
 "Just meet me at the Beach House," I insist. "I'll explain all."
 I set the phone down, and lean back with satisfaction. It's time to expose Alicia for what she really is.
 I hum to myself on the short drive over there. For some reason, I am not the least bit scared of confronting Alicia. In fact, I'm looking forward to it.
 "This is all very mysterious!" Rhett says, as he lets me in.
 "Don't tell me. Gucci's having a sale," Deacon guesses, without looking up from his paper.
 "No, it's something much more important than that," I say, pulling off my boots.
 "Well, come on, out with it."

"No. We have to wait until Kate gets here. We all have to be here."

A nervous buzz of energy pulses through me as Kate arrives. I wait until everyone has sat down. Then, feeling a bit Miss Marple, I slap the incriminating photo down on the kitchen table.

Explain that, Alicia.

For the teeniest fraction of a second, a hint of colour rises in her cheeks, but it's gone in an instant, and she's all dimples and smiles again.

No one says anything. I don't think the rest of them have got it yet.

"Look closely." I urge.

They all look.

"Wow, doesn't that little girl look like me?" Alicia bursts out. "Where did you say this was again? Camp Windmill Lake?"

"Camp Windylake," I correct her, though I'm sure she knows damn well.

"Wow, wouldn't it be an amazing coincidence if this really is Alicia?" Kate whistles.

"A bit too much of a coincidence, don't you think?"

But they don't seem to be getting it.

"They do say that everyone you meet is just seven connections away," Rhett says.

"I once read about these twins who were separated at birth but found each other years later. And get this – they lived less than a mile apart."

"Well, I got talking to this girl in the pub the one time, and it turned out we lived next door to each other when we were 5." Kate jumps in.

"This is different!" I interject.

But it's no use. Nobody is listening to me anymore. They're all trying to outdo each other with ridiculous tales of coincidence. I glance in Alicia's direction and she flashes me a triumphant smile. With a sinking feeling, I realise I should have kept this to myself. It was a mistake to reveal my hand so soon. A big, colossal, gigantic mistake.

The Night of the Concert

I try on practically every item in my wardrobe on Saturday night, before finally deciding on skinny jeans, a long-sleeved T-shirt and Ugg boots. I refuse to let this latest business with Alicia ruin my night out with Deacon. I have decided I'm going to go to the concert, and what's more, I'm going to damn well enjoy it.

Also, it's occurred to me that my friends might be right. I mean, Alicia was just a kid at Camp Windylake. I suppose it's plausible that she really doesn't remember me, or even the camp. After all, I don't remember her. I don't know, this whole thing is so confusing. I would give anything to have it all go away. No better still, to have her go away. Crawl back to wherever it was she came from.

I outline my eyes in grey and smudge a little shadow into the sockets. Now, what shall I do with my hair? I try plaits, but they make me look too babyish, so I take them out again. Maybe a French braid? This is silly. Why am I spending so much time on this? It's not like I'm going on a date! I run my brush through my hair till it gleams and set it down on the nightstand. There. Done.

All this messing around means Deacon's been waiting a while when I finally arrive at our meeting place.

"Sorry I'm late."

"I was beginning to think you weren't coming."

But he's relaxed and smiling, as if he half expected me to be late.

He's shaved, I notice, and he smells of soap. His breath is warm on my face as he leans in and kisses me on the cheek.

And when he pulls away, I have to fight the urge to pull him back again.

"You look great," he tells me. I wait for the punchline, but instead he glances at his phone to check the time. "We'd better get going."

The atmosphere in the Arena is electric. The warm-up band is just finishing and people chatter excitedly as they wait for Depeche Mode.

"Where are we sitting?"

"Let me see…"

As he stops to examine our tickets, I feel a pair of eyes on me. I glimpse a face in the periphery of my vision. Pale, with curly black hair. I turn my head to look, but she's already melted away, into the crowd.

"I hope this is OK," he says, leading me to a row near the back. "I couldn't get anything closer to the front."

"This is great," I assure him, scanning the stands. I can't see her, but I know she's here somewhere, watching. I just wish I knew her plan.

The lights go down and everyone cheers as the first notes sound. My spine tingles with excitement as they start to play one of my favourite songs.

I won't let Alicia ruin this for me.

Then someone in front of me flicks on their lighter and waves it about in time to the music. One by one, lighters light up around the arena. They look fantastic in the darkness. Smiling, I reach for my own lighter and give it a flick.

The flame bursts into the air, three times higher than normal, narrowly missing my fringe, and the back of the girl in front of me.

"Whoa!" I snap it shut quickly and stuff it back into my bag. Alicia must have tampered with it.

I glance at Deacon, but he's so caught up in the music that he hasn't even noticed.

I need something to steady my nerves.

"Do you want a drink?" I whisper in his ear.

"Yeah, I'll have a beer, thanks."

I head for the loos first, amazed to find there's no queue. I walk into a cubicle and set my bag down on the ground, then I hover gingerly over the seat. I try to pee, but I can't go. I squeeze my eyes shut. Sometimes that helps.

What was that?

My eyes snap open. For just a second, it felt like there was someone in the cubicle with me. I glance around.

Nope, no one here.

Hold on.

There! There it is!

A hand.

Reaching under the wall that separates this cubicle from the next. Small, pale fingers close themselves around the straps of my favourite green Prada handbag and begin to tug it from view.

"Hey!"

I grab hold of the handle and try to pull it back. For a moment, we both tug, and then my beloved bag disappears from sight.

"No!"

I yank up my jeans and struggle with the zip.

To my surprise, the bag slides back into view. I grab it back. The hand slips away.

I am up and out of the cubicle as quickly as possible but the thief has already made a run for it, leaving the door to slam in my face. I run out and look up and down the corridor.

"Did you see who just came out of the toilets?" I ask a group of girls standing outside.

"Was it someone famous?"

"No, I just…"

"Was it Madonna? I heard she's here tonight."

"No, it wasn't Madonna."

"Lily Allen?"

"No, I…oh, forget it!"

I stalk off and join the queue at the bar. While I'm waiting, I look through my bag to see if anything's missing. To my relief, my wallet, cards, keys and phone are all still in there.

So what on earth was she after?

If only I could know for certain if it's Alicia doing these things.

I take out my phone.

"Hi, Rhett. It's Isabel."

"Oh, hi Isabel."

"Is Alicia there?"

"She's in her room."

"Could you get her for me?"

"I think she's sleeping. She said she was going to have an early night."

"Please? I really need to speak to her."

"Well…OK."

"What can I get you?" asks the man behind the bar.

"One beer and one red wine please," I say, holding the phone to my ear.

"We don't do wine, just beer and cider," he says, pointing to the sign.

"Just the beer then."

"Isabel?" says a voice on the other end of the phone.

"Alicia?"

"What's wrong?" she asks. "Rhett said it was important."

"Oh, er…" For a moment I'm completely flummoxed.

"Hello?"

"Um, I couldn't find Deacon, but it's OK, I've found him now. Sorry to get you up for nothing."

"That's OK, Isabel. What are friends for?"

I stuff my phone back in my bag and pay for Deacon's drink. This doesn't make any sense. How can I have seen Alicia if she isn't even here? And who just tried to take my bag? And more to the point, why did they give it back?

I make it through the rest of the concert without any further incidents, though I can't really enjoy it. While Deacon watches the band, I watch the crowd, unable to relax until the very last note has sounded.

"Right, let's go and get some fish and chips," Deacon says as we squeeze out of the Arena.

"OK but no mushy peas," I say, pulling a face. I've always had a slight horror of the lurid green things.

Deacon laughs. "Don't worry, they're not compulsory."

We cross the road to the chip shop opposite.

"Oh no, it's closed!"

"Damn, I'm starving."

I glance at my watch. "Nothing else will be open at this time of night."

"Never mind, we'll go back to my house," Deacon invites me. "I'll make some toasties. No mushy peas, I promise."

For a moment, I hesitate. But it's been ages since I had Deacon all to myself, and Alicia is in bed already.

Isn't it worth the risk?

We find the Beach House in darkness.

Deacon switches on the light in the spotlessly clean kitchen and goes to the fridge.

"What do you want? Cheese and ham?"

"Sounds great."

I fill the kettle, then rummage around for a couple of mugs while Deacon assembles the sandwiches. Soon, the room is filled with the sound and smell of sizzling cheese.

"So what's going on with you lately?" he asks me as we sit down at the table to eat.

"What do you mean?"

"Well, first this business with the police, and then setting yourself on fire the other night. You always seem to be in the wars lately."

"I have been having a bit of a funny time," I admit. I

really want to tell him what's been happening, but I'm afraid he'll think I'm losing my mind.

"I had a good time tonight," he says, when I don't elaborate.

"Me too," I grin, and for a moment, I'm able to forget all the weird, freaky stuff.

He takes my wrist and turns it towards him to look at my watch.

"You won't get a taxi at this hour. You'd better stay the night."

"OK."

He looks at me for a little longer than is strictly necessary. I swallow.

"So, you and Alicia," I say nervously. "Is it... serious between you?"

"Does it matter to you if it is?"

I meet his gaze.

"Hmm, that smells delicious," says a voice from the doorway.

Alicia.

I almost drop my cup.

"I'm sorry, did we wake you?" Deacon asks, calmly.

"I couldn't sleep anyway," she says, slinking up to him and giving him a kiss.

I can't help noticing her expensive Chinese silk pyjamas. I wonder if he bought those for her? Her small, pert breasts are clearly visible through the fabric.

"Can I have a bite of your sandwich?" she asks me.

"Here, finish it," I say, instantly losing my appetite. "I think I'm about ready for bed."

"Would you like to borrow some pyjamas?"

"No, that's OK."

We both know full well that they wouldn't fit me anyway.

❄

It's cold in the guest room at the end of the hall. I should have picked one at the other end of the house, but I wanted to be as far away from Alicia as possible. I close the window and sink down under the covers but still, I find it very hard to sleep. How can I, knowing Alicia could be lurking just outside the door? That the room could fill with soot and smoke at any moment?

I snooze fitfully, waking at every sound. I don't think I've ever been so relieved to see daylight streaming in. I grab my things and sneak downstairs, intending to slip out before everyone wakes.

I am not expecting to find Rhett in the kitchen, mixing batter for pancakes.

"Morning," he says pleasantly.

"You're up early."

"Yeah, I've still got some shopping to do. Wanna come?"

"Not today."

He shakes his head. "I'm starting to worry about you. Don't tell me you're on a budget?"

"Nothing like that," I laugh. "I just have stuff to do."

"Well, at least stay for breakfast. We've got fresh blueberries."

I pause. On the one hand, it would probably be safer to leave. But on the other, Rhett's pancakes are amazing and I've woken up with one hell of an appetite.

"Oh, OK," I agree. "Is there anything I can do to help?"

"No, I've got it all under control. But you could go and wake Alicia. She needs to be up for work."

"How about I fry the pancakes while you wake Alicia?"

Rhett pulls a face. "No offence, but you might burn them."

I rack my brains for a good excuse, but it doesn't come to me.

Instead, I find myself marching up the wooden stairway to the enemy's lair.

The door is slightly ajar.

Impulsively, I push it open, without knocking. I don't know exactly what I expect to see – maybe I'll catch Alicia doing voodoo, or concealing a small nuclear arsenal under her bed. Instead, I find her dressing for work, pulling a hideous lime-green Robertson's shirt over her head. She's fast, but I still see it; the word 'FRY' branded into the small of her back.

I stumble backwards and knock my elbow against the wall. "Ow!"

Alicia whirls round. Her eyes flash dangerously.

I don't know what this means, but I think I've just found her weak spot, her Achilles heel. And boy, does she know it.

12

Rhett looks up as I rush back into the kitchen.
"Something came up. I've got to go."
"What about breakfast?"
"Sorry, another time."
"Well, what about Alicia? Did you wake her?"
"She's awake."
I glance nervously behind me. I hear footsteps on the stairs.
"Gotta go – tell Deacon thanks for last night."
"Isabel?"
"I really have to go."
I do not stop to explain any further, just grab my bag and shoot out the door.
I stride quickly, cutting across the car park and take the road that leads into town. There is no one behind me, and yet I still feel like I'm being followed. I quicken my pace, walk for some minutes, but still can't quite seem to shake that feeling.
Eventually, I flop down on a bench and pull out my phone. I see a missed call from Holly and ring her back, eager to hear if she has an update.
"Well, I checked Alicia's references for you," she tells me.

I sit up straight. "They're no good, are they?"

"They're fine, Isabel. Her national insurance number is real, date of birth too. I even got a friend on the force to check her police record. It's clean. Either she's innocent of what we suspect her of, or she's devious enough to have never been caught."

Dammit!

"Well, thanks for trying, Holly."

"No problem. Just let me know if there's anything else I can do to help."

"Actually…" I chew my lip. "There *is* one more thing. If you have time, that is?"

"Yes?"

"Could you look into Camp Windylake for me? I have a feeling that's where this whole thing started."

The phone rings again the minute I hang up. This time, it's Kate.

"Just wanted to check what time you wanted to meet tonight?" she asks.

"Tonight?" I repeat, blankly.

"You do know what day it is?" She sounds a bit exasperated.

"Yes, of course." I quickly consult the calendar on my phone.

"It's New Year's Eve!"

"So what time do you want to meet?"

"Eight. Let's meet at eight," I say decisively.

"Great. See you at Mustafa's."

Why didn't I know that? I wonder, staring at my phone. I'm so out of things lately, it's not funny. I'll be forgetting what year it is next!

Mustafa's - Four Hours to Midnight

Mustafa's is packed when we arrive that evening, and the celebrations are already in full swing.

"It's a good thing I booked," says Kate, looking around. "There are even more people here than last year."

This is the fifth New Year my friends and I have celebrated here. This owes less to the quality of their food and entertainment and more to the price of the drinks and their laid-back approach to closing time.

As if to prove how much time (and money) we spend here, Mustafa himself comes over to our table with a tray of complimentary cocktails.

"Drink! Enjoy!" he implores us, in his strong Turkish accent.

We all smile politely and thank him for his generosity, but in truth, the drinks are the colour of toilet cleaner and don't taste much better. We all wait until his back is turned before feeding them to the pot plant in the corner.

"Hey, where's Alicia?" I ask, washing away the terrible taste with a sip of wine.

"Running late," says Deacon.

Hallelujah!

It's so lovely to kick back, just the four of us. It's just like old times, Rhett giving a running commentary on what everyone's wearing and scoring people out of ten for their prowess on the dance floor.

"What's she wearing?" he asks, nodding towards a girl dressed in a sheet.

"I think she's supposed to be the ghost of Christmas past."

"Well, someone should tell her Christmas has passed!"

He chuckles at his own joke. He always does that – he'd be useless at stand-up. Kate thinks it's endearing.

Deacon looks on in dismay as baskets of fish and chips are placed in front of us.

"Who ordered these? They're tiny."

"They're supposed to be miniatures," I tell him. "They're cute."

I laugh as he tries to pick up one of the dainty delicacies with his big, clumsy fingers.

"What?"

"You look so funny!"

"Thanks."

"Don't worry, that's just the starter. There's lamb for the main."

"Thank god for that!"

Kate looks up from her phone and regards the food with suspicion.

"Has dinner shrunk or have I grown?"

I sit back in my seat and rest my head against the comfortable old cushions.

This is so nice, so normal. I wish it could stay like this forever.

But all too soon the serenity is shattered. The double doors swing open and Alicia makes her entrance. She is dressed head to toe in white, with silver tinsel woven into her hair. Not many people could pull off that look but she, who has the devil inside her, looks just like an angel.

The temperature in the room rises as people turn to look, men with adoration, women with envy. Alicia is a force of nature, impossible to ignore, no matter how demure she pretends to be.

"Who needs a drink?" she asks. "I'm going to the bar."

"I'll get them," Deacon tells her, placing a hand on her shoulder. "You take a seat."

"Thanks, that's so kind of you."

She slides into the empty seat beside me, sits very close, her bony elbow sticking into my ribs. Nervously, I glance around. Rhett and Kate are heading onto the dance floor. Panic rises inside of me.

"I'll go and give Deacon a hand."

"No." She reaches for my arm. "Sit and talk to me."

I try to send Kate an urgent message with my eyes, but she just smiles and turns her back on me.

Come back! Don't leave me alone with her!

Hesitantly, I meet Alicia's gaze. Her eyes are deep pools of tranquillity, but I fear the psychosis that lurks beneath.

"Look, about what you saw earlier," she says. "I would appreciate it if you'd keep it to yourself."

She smiles pleasantly but grips my hand so tight, it hurts.

"Of course."

"Good." She treats me to one of her saintly smiles. "And you know you can count on me to keep your little secret."

"What secret?"

"Oh, you know," she says with a wink.

"I did not start those fires! You know I didn't!"

"Of course not," she says hastily, as if trying to placate me. "Though you do seem to be under a lot of pressure these days?"

"I'm fine!"

"Are you sure? You have such dark circles under your eyes. I'm really quite worried about you."

"I'm just a little tired, that's all."

Why am I even trying to explain myself to her?

"Oh dear! Not sleeping well? Maybe you should see a therapist? I'm sure Deacon could recommend someone."

"What's that?" Deacon asks, as he sets the drinks down on the table.

"Nothing!"

I reach for my drink and consider pouring it all over her, but that would only add fuel to the fire. Besides, I've never been one to waste wine. Alicia glances at me out of the corner of her eye, as if to see if I'm ready to break yet. Well, I'm not about to give her the satisfaction. Bored by my silence, she turns her attention to Deacon, rubbing his neck and shoulders and making him smile.

"Get your hands off him!" I want to yell. But he seems to like it.

I've had enough. I throw back the rest of my drink and head to the bar. Unfortunately, there is a quite a queue.

"Do you want to put that on your tab?" The barman asks, once I finally get served.

"Yes, please."

"Where are you sitting?"

I point to my table, where my friends are sitting around, talking and laughing. As if sensing my presence, Alicia turns to face me, her eyes glinting dangerously as she tilts back her head and laughs. As she does, a small blue flame bursts from her mouth. I rub my eyes, unable to believe what I'm seeing. She is literally breathing fire.

"Fire!" I scream, pointing at her. "Fire! Fire!"

But as I look back at Alicia, I realise she isn't breathing fire anymore. She's just sitting there, sipping her drink and looking as perplexed as the rest of them. I don't know exactly what happens next. I just feel a little strange. I grab the bar to steady myself and knock into the girl standing next to me.

"Hey!"

People are turning to stare at me.

"Where? Where's the fire?"

"Er…false alarm! Sorry!"

I lean heavily on the bar, feeling both sick and embarrassed. I wish I could just press the 'undo' button, and stop them all from staring at me.

A big burly doorman looms over me.

"I think you've had a bit too much to drink, Miss."

"She's fine," Deacon says, appearing at my side. "I'll take her outside for a bit of fresh air."

The doorman nods. "All right, but any more hysterics and she's out."

Deacon takes me by the arm and pulls me towards the exit. Alicia makes a move to follow us, but to my relief, Rhett chooses that moment to drag her onto the dance floor.

"What happened?" Deacon asks, as we sit on the stone steps outside.

"Didn't you see her?" I ask.

"Who?"

"Alicia! She was breathing fire!"

"We were drinking flaming sambucas, Isabel. Believe me, nobody was breathing fire. It was just a bit of fun."

"But her mouth! It was on fire! I saw her. She was breathing flames!"

I didn't imagine it, I know I didn't.

"Perhaps hers was still alight as she drank it," he says frowning.

I scratch my head. "Is that…possible?"

"Of course. How else would you explain it?"

"Well, I thought…I thought…"

But what exactly, can I tell him? That for that moment, she didn't look quite human. That it was like staring into the unblinking eyes of a demon. That she'd become something I've never even believed in, and never wanted to acknowledge could be real.

Oh, what's the use? How can I possibly expect him to understand?

The door opens, and I jump slightly as Alicia herself strides out, Rhett unable to hold her off any longer.

"Is she OK?" she asks Deacon, as if I'm an invalid. Her voice drips with sympathy.

Deacon nods, seems to sense that I don't want a fuss. "She's fine now. Aren't you, Isabel?"

Alicia peers at me sweetly. "Oh, but you're so pale! Would you like me to call you a taxi?"

"No!" I sit up abruptly. "No, I'm fine. My eyes were just playing tricks on me, that's all." I force a smile onto my face.

"So you want to go back inside?"

"Yes," I say, though it's the last thing I feel like doing. "I'm not going to bloody well miss the New Year."

Not because of her.

As I follow them back into the restaurant, I feel a gentle tap on my shoulder. It's the owner, Mustafa.

"Isabel, isn't it?"

"Yes, that's right."

"Did you enjoy the cocktail?"

"Er…yes, thanks."

"Maybe you'd like another? On the house of course."

I shudder. "That's alright…I'm on the wine now, thanks."

"Wine it is then," he says, signalling to the barman to pour me a glass.

"Well, thanks. That's very kind of you. Cheers!"

What does he want?

I take a tentative sip and turn to walk away.

"I hear you were worried about fire safety?"

"Just a misunderstanding," I say, embarrassed.

Mustafa rubs his bushy moustache. "Maybe, but you can't be too careful with fires."

"There have been a lot of them round here lately," I agree.

"Still, I think most of the businesses have done OK out of the insurance money." He sticks his hands in his pockets. "As long as the police can't prove it was arson."

How cynical!

"In fact, I could do with a bit of that insurance money myself!" he laughs. "I bet we all could."

I smile politely, thinking he's finished, but he goes on,

"As long as the family was away, say, on holiday, for example. Then there would be no chance of anyone getting hurt. We're off to Turkey at the end of next month, as it happens."

I gape.

What is he saying?

He lets out an unconvincing laugh.

"Ha! Ha! Something to think about, anyway!"

I stare after him as he disappears into the kitchen.

What on earth just happened? Did he proposition me…to burn down the restaurant?

I shake the craziness out of my head.

What a night!

I return to my table and my friends, but the night has lost its magic.

As the clock strikes twelve, I feel strangely removed from everything. My friends kiss and hug, but I feel hollow inside. Someone hands me a glass of champagne and I down it before anyone even has a chance to clink my glass.

"Are you sure you're OK?" Deacon asks, as he sees me into a taxi. "You'd be welcome to stay at ours again."

"No, I'm fine," I insist, pulling my pashmina tightly around my shoulders. Alicia materialises next to him and wraps her serpent like arms around his neck, staking her claim. I climb into the taxi and a lump forms in my throat as it pulls away. I don't want to think about what goes on between them, but I really can't help it. I imagine them laughing and tumbling into bed together and I feel queasy at the thought.

"I'll drop you on the corner, love, if that's all right?" the driver says, as he turns into my street. I nod. One of my neighbours is having a party and the street is chock-a-block with cars. I pay my fare and start to cross the street when another car catches my eye, a dirty white escort. I can just make out the registration plate in the moonlight: F-R-Y. FRY. I stop abruptly and try to get a look at the driver, but the car begins to pull away.

"No, wait!" I yell. I run after it, chase it all the way down the street until it picks up speed and roars away. And still, I run after it, but my stiletto-clad feet are no match for a car and finally, I have to admit defeat.

SMASH!

What was that?

For the first time, it occurs to me that this is not such a great neighbourhood to walk through in the middle of the night. I clutch my bag and walk faster, my heels click-clacking noisily on the pavement. I hear footsteps behind me and walk faster. The footsteps quicken too. I glance round in fear, but it's just a young boy mimicking me. His friends laugh.

"What's the rush, darling? Left something in the oven?"

I smile nervously, feeling a little foolish, but I keep moving. My heart pumps loudly in my chest until I'm back in my house, with the door safely locked behind me.

Upstairs, I find Fluffy stretched out contentedly at the foot of the bed. I climb in and close my eyes, listening to the soft, rhythmic hum of his snores. But every time I start to drift off, Alicia's demonic face flashes before me.

"Haven't you figured it out yet?" she cackles, her whole mouth aflame. "Don't you understand the significance of FRY?"

❆

I RISE at the first light of dawn and head for the only place I know that's open at such an ungodly hour – the gym. I have so much pent up energy that a workout might be just what I need.

I do a token warm up, then jump on the treadmill and set it for a run. The machine squeaks in protest as I adjust the pace, faster and faster. Faster than I've ever run before. Sweat streams off my body, and still it's not enough. I can't get that terrible image out of my mind.

My face is as red as a beetroot as I make my way to the showers. I shed my clothes and step under the jet, enjoying the soothing sensation as the cool water washes over me. I close my eyes and massage shampoo deep into my scalp. Oh, that's so relaxing.

"BEEP! BEEP! BEEP! BEEP!"

Is that… the fire alarm?

I jolt to life, leaping out of the cubicle and skidding on the tiled floor. I lunge for my towel, pausing only to wrap it round me and rush towards the door. As my hand closes around the handle, I glance back at the other women in the room.

"Why isn't anybody leaving?" I ask nervously.

"I'm not going outside in a towel!" one girl laughs.

"Don't worry. It'll just be a false alarm," her friend says. "It happens all the time."

"But what if this is the real thing?"

"Hey, aren't you the one who was yelling 'Fire!' at Mustafa's last night?"

"I…"

"I thought so! Look, when we smell smoke, we'll leave."

I stand anxiously in the doorway, unsure what to do.

"Someone's been deliberately starting fires," I warn them. "This could be the real thing. We've got to get out of here!"

But nobody is listening to me.

13

I scuttle out into the gym, my towel wrapped tightly around me.

Out here, people seem to be taking the alarm much more seriously. I follow the throng out through the fire exit, into the biting cold January morning.

My teeth chatter noisily as I shift from one foot to the other. It's bitterly cold. My hair is wet and my towel damp from the shower.

"Brr…" I hint loudly, but nobody's kind enough to offer me their jacket.

"Hey, love, you're dropping your towel!" someone says, helpfully.

Cheeks burning, I wrap it more tightly around me, the remainder of my self-respect forming a puddle on the floor. Why did I have to pick this morning to walk here? If only I had driven, I would now be snuggled up in my nice, warm car.

A few more people trickle out of the building. The place isn't nearly as busy as normal, being that it's New Year's Day. But the real fitness fanatics are all here. I watch as the girls from the changing room swan out, now fully dressed. They giggle as they walk down the street, apparently unconcerned by the whole thing. Before I met Alicia, I probably would have been one of them, but things are different now. I have to treat every fire drill as if it were the real thing.

"Hey, is that smoke?" someone says, sniffing the air.

"Fire!" someone else exclaims in excitement. "There really is a fire!"

The gym manager gesticulates wildly, urging everyone to move away as a turret of grey smoke billows out from an open window.

Nee-Naw-Nee-Naw-Nee-Naw

The crowd whistles and cheers as a fire engine whirls into sight. I watch with admiration as firefighters leap out and start tackling the blaze. Then another sound fills the air. More sirens. The police are coming. Heat rises in my cheeks. I can't let them catch me at the scene of another fire.

I have to get out of here!

My arms and legs have turned to jelly, but I will them into action. Frantically, I elbow my way through the mob and dart round to the back of the car park. I gaze down the dark, damp alleyway. Then at my naked feet. Dare I?

I dare. I start to run, slowly at first, then faster, faster. Soon I am running as fast as I did on the treadmill. I try not to care how much the gravel stings my feet, how narrowly I miss stepping on a broken bottle. I don't have time to worry about any of that. I have to get away from the fire.

You can do this! You can do this!

Sheds and back gardens fly by. My house isn't that far away, or at least, it never seemed so before.

My heart fills with relief as I charge down the street to my house. The chipped red paint and unwashed windows have never looked so charming. I collapse in a delighted heap on the doorstep, a huge stitch in my side and I reach down for my keys. And that's when I realise. My keys are in my handbag. Which is in my locker. Which is at the gym.

How could I be so stupid? In my blind panic, it never occurred to me that I had no way of getting into the house. I hold my head in my hands. I am at a total loss for what to do. It's bitterly, bitterly cold. My hands and feet are starting to turn numb and yet I can't go back to the gym, not when it took so much effort to get here. And not while the place is swarming with police.

I have to think quickly. Do I wait it out here, or should I try to get to a friend's house? Kate's is probably the nearest, but even her place is a ten minute walk.

Or… I could go next door. Mr Krinkle would probably let me use his phone to call Kate and ask her to pick me up. I sigh. The thought of having to explain myself to Mr Krinkle is horrendous, but I don't have any better ideas.

I stagger next door, my feet cut and bleeding. I ring the doorbell and wait. When there is no response, I ring again. Still nothing. I peer in through the window, but it looks dark inside. I can't believe it. Mr Krinkle never goes out!

Dammit!

I walk back to my house and try the door, in the vain hope that I forgot to lock it when I left the house this morning. I didn't. My eyes flit over the house. There must be some way to get in.

The front window is slightly ajar.

It's very small and rather high up, but maybe, if I could find something to stand on, it might be possible to haul myself in? I wander round the front garden and return with a large flowerpot. I set it down and pray that it will take my weight.

Gingerly, I step up onto the flowerpot and reach for the window ledge. I push the latch and the little window opens further. It looks like there is just enough room for me to crawl through. There's nothing much to break my fall on the other side, so it looks like I'm going to have to do a nosedive down onto the living room carpet. This could hurt, but I don't care.

I start to heave myself through, inching forward on my

stomach, squeezing myself through the very small space until I am ready to make my descent. I am just about to take the plunge, when…

"Arrgh!"

Someone is grabbing my ankle.

"Help!"

"Come down from there!" a voice commands.

I kick out as hard as I can, but I'm no match for the strong arms that bring me crashing back down into the garden.

I struggle to my feet, attempt to run, but I am shoved against the wall.

His eyes meet mine. They are cold and unfriendly.

Oh god, it's the police.

Not Penney and his mate, but a couple of others, one male, one female.

"Do you live here?" he asks, his arm firmly on my shoulder.

"Of course I do!"

"Do you have any identification?"

"No, I'm locked out and I don't have any pockets." I gesture down at my towel which, by some small miracle, is still wrapped around, or rather welded to, my body.

"Is there anyone who could verify your identity?"

"Mr Krinkle next door…except he's not in at the moment."

"What about your other neighbours?"

"I don't know them. They're new."

I shiver uncontrollably. I was so close, I could cry.

The female officer looks at me with concern. "You must be freezing. Why don't you come down to the station with us while we sort this out? We can get you some nice, warm clothes to wear. "

No!

"Please, this really is my house! If you'll just give me a leg up, I can get back inside and then I can show you some ID."

The nice officer looks at her partner, but he shakes his head.

"Come on," she says, "I bet you could use a hot drink."

"Am I under arrest?" I ask nervously, as they shoo me into the police car.

"Oh no," Nice Police Lady assures me. "We're just going to get you some warm clothes and check that you are who you say you are."

Well, that doesn't sound so bad…

I keep my head ducked down low as we drive through the streets of Queensbeach. Luckily for me, it's still early in the morning and on New Year's Day to boot, or I'd be the gossip of the town.

Nice Police Lady ushers me quickly into the police station. She provides me with a dry towel, an old tracksuit and a pair of plimsolls. I pull the clothes on gladly, not caring how I look.

"That's better. Now if you'll follow me, I'll get you a nice, hot drink."

She leads me through a maze of corridors, ending in a dark, dingy room.

I freeze in the doorway.

"Isn't this an interrogation room?"

She laughs. "It's an interview room, yes. There isn't much space I'm afraid. We have to use whatever room is available. "

Cautiously, I step inside.

"Do sit down. Hot chocolate do you?"

"Um, yes, thanks."

She leaves, closing the door behind her. I shudder. The room is cold and forbidding. There are no pictures and no windows. The clock on the wall is stuck on twelve, yet it keeps on ticking. I sit down, but then jump up again. If I listen carefully, I'm sure I can hear the echoes of all the people who were here before me; the guilty and the innocent, each protesting their case with equal vigour, an endless stream of questions and accusations, ricocheting off the walls.

What's taking so long?

I glance down at my wrist but my watch is still at the gym along with everything else. Where is Nice Police Lady? It seems like she's been gone ages, though it might only have been a matter of minutes. I edge towards the door, am about to turn the handle, when it comes swinging open and almost knocks me flying.

"Sorry about that." Nice Police Lady hands me a steaming hot cup – it's one of those plastic ones you get from a vending machine. "Got a bit caught up. Do take a seat."

She sits down at the table. Reluctantly, I sit down opposite.

"OK, so we've verified who you are, but I have to admit, I'm still rather curious as to how you came to be in this predicament?"

I bite my lip. "Like I said, I got locked out of my house."

I pick up my drink and take a tentative sip.

"Oh, so you have one of those doors that locks when you close it?"

"Not exactly."

"Then how did you get locked out?"

I scour my brain for a feasible explanation, but nothing comes to mind. I take a deep breath.

"There was a fire at my gym," I reluctantly explain. "I'd been waiting out in the cold for a long time and I thought it would be quicker to just go home. I only live around the corner."

Her eyes widen. "You walked home in just a towel? And without your keys?"

"Yeah, well I probably wasn't thinking straight," I admit. "It was really cold."

There is a knock at the door and another police officer walks in.

He looks at me with a smug, satisfied smile.

It's my old friend, DS Penney.

"Isabel Anderson," he says grimly. "Well, isn't this a surprise?"

I glance back at Nice Police Lady.

"What's going on?"

"My colleague here just wanted to have a word with you. I understand you've met DS Penney?"

I nod, slowly.

"What's this about?"

"Just a little chat."

"No," I shake my head. "I'm not talking to you anymore without a lawyer."

I had hoped mentioning a lawyer would put him off, but he nods his approval.

"I'll see if the duty solicitor is available."

Now what?

He returns a few minutes later accompanied by a stern-looking woman who reminds me of my old headmistress, in her brown suit with a gold scarf tied around her neck.

She introduces herself, but I am too nervous to catch her name. Penney and Nice Police Lady leave us alone to confer.

"I didn't do anything!" I tell her, as soon as he's gone. "Someone's trying to set me up."

She nods doubtfully, as if she's heard it all a thousand times before, which she probably has. I tell her the whole story, from the beginning and she nods thoughtfully, but I'm not sure she really buys it.

"When they ask you a question, just say 'No comment'," she tells me.

"Shouldn't I just answer the questions? I've nothing to hide."

She shakes her head, adamantly. "No. Just say 'No comment'."

Penney and his colleague come back in. Penney switches on the tape and reads me the caution.

"Isabel, you've already admitted that the lighter found at scene of the caravan park fire was yours. Is that correct?"

"Well, I..." I glance at my lawyer. "No comment," I mutter.

"You already admitted it was yours when Constable Smith and I spoke to you at Robertson's Supercentre."

I look down at my thumbs.

"No comment."

Penney presses his lips together to hide his annoyance.

"At 9.30 this morning you were present at the scene of another fire, at the Waterfront Gym, weren't you Isabel? And this time, you've admitted to sneaking away."

I shift uncomfortably. "I know how it looks, but I had nothing to do with that fire – or any of them."

This time it's my lawyer who looks at me in annoyance.

"I..I mean no comment."

There is a knock at the door and Penney is called away. He returns, stony faced a few minutes later.

"You can go," he mumbles.

"Really?"

"Why, what's changed?" My lawyer demands.

"The preliminary investigation suggests that the fire at the gym was caused by the deep fat fryer in the cafe kitchen," he reports, with reluctance. "They don't think it was arson."

"It wasn't?" I say in surprise.

Is it possible?

Nice Police Lady escorts me back out to the front desk. There is no pleasant small talk this time. I'm not sure I trust her anymore.

"Would you like to ring someone to come and pick you up?" she asks.

"Yes, please."

I consider my options. I really don't feel like answering twenty questions from Kate or Deacon, so I ring Rhett. He comes straight round to collect me.

"Thanks for getting here so quickly," I say, as we walk out into the daylight.

"No problem."

I look up and down the street for his zippy little sports car, but can't see it.

"Where did you park?"

"Over there," he says, reluctantly. I look again.

Deacon's dark red BMW.

Deacon winds down the window.

"Hello, Isabel."

I glare at Rhett for giving me away, but he just shrugs and hops in the back.

Deacon opens the passenger door for me and I climb in, but he doesn't start the car.

"So, are you going to tell me what's going on?"

I blunder my way through the story of how I got locked out of the house. I'm getting really sick of telling it by now. I can tell he's miffed that I called Rhett instead of him. Not that it's really any of his business.

He drives me back to the gym to get my stuff, but we find it closed. I don't know what I expected. It was on fire, for Pete's sake.

"How about we go to Kate's and get the spare key?" Deacon suggests.

"Kate doesn't have a spare anymore," I say, looking down at my hands.

"She lost it?"

"No, I changed the locks."

He blinks. "Why?"

"It's complicated."

"So you want to stay at ours tonight?"

"No," I say, a little too sharply. "I mean, it's OK, I can crash at Kate's."

"We've got more room," he says, logically.

"No really – I'll be fine at Kate's."

"As you wish."

❄

To MY RELIEF, the gym is open is for business again the following morning, so I am able to collect my keys.

"Fluffy?" I call, walking into the living room. I listen out for the jingling of his bell, but the house remains silent.

"Fluffy?"

I walk into the kitchen and am about to unlock the back door when I notice his food bowl. He hasn't touched any of the food I left out for him yesterday morning, before I went to the gym. I feel a lurch in my stomach.

"FLUFFY!" I bawl.

There is no reply.

14

I pound on the door of the Beach House.

"I'm coming! I'm coming!"

A bleary-eyed Deacon opens the door. He is still in his dressing gown, hair tousled, face unshaven.

I look past him into the hallway.

"Where's Alicia?"

"Just left for work."

"Good."

I barge my way in and stomp up the stairs, flinging open the door to her bedroom.

"Fluffy?" I holler.

I yank open her wardrobe, but there is nothing there but a few neatly ironed clothes and a couple of pairs of shoes. Nothing under the bed, either.

Deacon folds his arms. "Are you going to tell me what all this is about?"

"Fluffy's gone," I say impatiently, marching into the en suite.

"What's that got to do with Alicia?"

"I think she's taken him."

"Why?" He looks perplexed.

"Because she's evil."

He laughs. He thinks I'm joking. But when I don't laugh too, his face grows serious.

"Come on, you don't really mean that, do you? You're just upset."

"I mean it."

I prise the lid off Alicia's laundry basket and peer inside, examining its contents.

"Look, this is silly." Deacon says, folding his arms. "Why on earth would Alicia take your cat? And if she did, she would hardly hide him in the laundry basket, would she?"

"Where, then?"

He shakes his head. "We'll find Fluffy, don't you worry. He's probably just sulking because you weren't home last night."

"I really hope you're right."

But what if he's not?

"I can come back to yours and help you look, if you like? I'm not seeing any patients till this afternoon."

"Would you?"

"Of course. Just give me ten minutes to have a shower. There's seed cake in the kitchen if you want."

"Seed cake?" I murmur, pretending to consider this. But I'm not really interested. As soon as he's gone, I resume my search, going through every drawer, bag and box in Alicia's room. There must be a clue in here somewhere.

She has so few possessions that under different circumstances, I would feel sorry for her, but as it is, it makes my job a bit easier. I'm just in the middle of rifling through her underwear drawer when my phone rings. It's a number I don't recognise.

"Hello?"

"Why aren't you at work?" a squeaky voice demands.

Alicia!

I nearly drop the phone. She's never phoned me before. I didn't even know she had my number.

My heart begins to pound.

Does she know I'm here? In her bedroom, this very minute, going through her things?

No, she can't know. That's impossible. She's at work. Isn't she?

"Isabel?" she prompts, "I do hope you're not ill?"

"No." I clear my throat. "I'm looking for Fluffy."

"Your cat?" she asks innocently "Oh, is he missing?"

You know damn well he is!

"Any idea where I should look?" I ask, through gritted teeth.

"No idea. You know what cats are like. They turn up in the most unexpected places."

Is that supposed to be some sort of clue?

"Like where?"

"I don't know. Have you checked all the outhouses in your street? Or maybe one of your neighbours has seen him?"

"Do you think he'll be OK?" I ask, my voice breaking a little.

"Well, that's down to you."

"What does that mean?"

She just clicks her tongue, signalling that the subject's closed.

"You should really get to work now, Isabel. It's getting busy. Sonya looks like she's going to blow a gasket."

"But what about Fluffy?"

The line goes dead. For a moment I just stare at it, dumbfounded.

Then I look down at my hands. This is ridiculous - I'm actually shaking!

Snap out of it. You have to find Fluffy.

I survey the room. What was I even thinking, coming over here? All that searching and not so much as a cat hair. But of course she wouldn't be stupid enough to bring him back here. If he's even still….

"Isabel?"

Damn, Deacon's coming. I quickly close the drawer and check the room, careful to leave everything just as I found it.

"Come on, let's go."

We scour my neighbourhood, but nobody's seen or heard anything, not even Mr Krinkle, who can usually tell you the comings and goings of every single person, vehicle and animal in the street.

"What we need are some posters," Deacon suggests, "with a picture of Fluffy and a contact number. Somebody must have seen him."

"Good idea."

We plod back to my house.

❄

THE PHONE IS RINGING as we walk through the door.

It's Sonya. "Isabel! Where are you? I've been trying to reach you all morning."

"Sorry. I've been stuck in bed with a migraine."

How smoothly the lie comes.

"You've got a migraine? Alicia said something about your cat going missing?"

Damn.

"Yeah, that too. I'm having a really bad day."

"I'm not having such a great day either, Isabel. Stu screwed up the canned goods order and the computer's playing up again. I could really use your help."

"Sorry."

I try to feel guilty, but I can't. I've got too much else to worry about right now.

"Well, OK," she relents. "Take the rest of the day off if you have to, but I need you in first thing in the morning."

"Of course," I promise. "I'll see you tomorrow. Thanks, Sonya."

I switch on my laptop and do a quick mock-up of a poster while Deacon investigates the contents of my fridge.

"Half a bottle of wine and a manky old avocado? Is that all you've got?"

"I haven't had time to shop."

"But you work in one, don't you? You'd think it would be easy enough to pick up a few groceries."

"So you would think." I manage a tiny smile.

"Come on, let's go and get some breakfast. We can put up some posters on the way."

We walk down to the greasy spoon on the corner - not my first choice, but Deacon is hungry and I'm not in the mood to argue. We hand out posters as we go, stick them to every bus stop, telephone box and lamppost we pass. I even stick one on the noticeboard at the cafe, while we're waiting to be seated.

"Table for two?"

We are taken to a booth by the window and Deacon orders a full English.

"I'll just have a coffee," I say halfheartedly.

"Bring her a muffin as well," Deacon tells the waitress.

He looks across the table at me. "I know you're upset, but you've got to eat."

"OK," I reluctantly agree.

He rests his hand on mine. "Try not to worry. I'm sure Fluffy's just hiding out somewhere. He'll turn up safe and sound."

"I hope so."

But the phone call from Alicia has not filled me with confidence. Horrible images keep flashing through my mind; Fluffy locked in a cold, dark cellar, Fluffy lost and injured, Fluffy tied to the railway tracks…

"Isabel?"

"Huh?"

"I have to ask," he says, handing me a napkin.

"What made you think Alicia would have taken him?"

I want to tell him, I really do. But I'm scared he won't be able to see past her big Bambi eyes.

So I just shake my head. "You won't tell her, will you? I don't want her to think…"

"That you don't trust her?"

I look at him uncertainly.

Then the waitress brings over our order and breaks the mood with some idle speculation about the weather, which seems to get wetter and wetter with every day that passes.

While Deacon ploughs through his bacon and eggs, I drink my coffee and nibble half-heartedly on my muffin. The waitress comes over and refills my coffee and I drink a second cup and then a third.

"Should you really be drinking that much caffeine?" Deacon asks, wiping his mouth.

"Probably not."

But without it, I'm not sure I could function.

I put down a fiver for the bill, and excuse myself to go to the Ladies.

As I walk into the loos, I get a chill, remembering the bag thief. Why do they have to make public toilets so creepy? Although it's daylight outside, the room is poorly lit and badly ventilated. Plus, there's a constant drip, drip, drip from a faulty tap.

Clutching my bag tightly, I walk into one of the little cubicles. There's a slight chemical smell, like someone's been applying nail polish. I sit down and try to be as quick as I can. Why did I have to drink so much bloody coffee?

Typical - no loo roll.

I look round to see if there's a spare roll on the tank. And that's when I see it; written in a shiny blood-red scrawl, the word 'FRY,' dripping from the wall.

What the…?

FRY

I practically jump out of my skin. And yet I can't quite tear my eyes away from it. How did she know I would be here, at this time, in this very cubicle? My first instinct is to flee, but instead I push open the door to the next cubicle and peer inside. There it is again - FRY. The glistening letters shimmer on the wall. I reach up and touch it. The varnish is still wet.

Why is she doing this to me?

It's just too much. My legs give way and I sink, quivering, to the floor.

Time probably passes. I don't know how little or how much. But I'm aware of someone banging on the door.

"Are you OK in there?"

The waitress walks in. Her jaw drops when she sees me.

"What's wrong with you?" She sounds more annoyed than concerned.

Then she looks up, her eyes drawn to the blood-red graffiti. Her hand flies to her mouth.

"What have you done to the walls? Do you know how hard this is to clean?"

"It...it wasn't me."

"Then why have you got wet paint on your hands?"

I jerk my head up to look at her and the world seems to spin a bit faster.

"It wasn't me!"

"Leave this to me OK?"

Deacon swims into view. He takes my hand in his.

"Come on, Isabel. Let's get you home."

❄

NEITHER OF US says anything as he leads me back to my place. Once there, he sits me down at the kitchen table.

"I know how strong and independent you are, Isabel, and I know you don't like to ask for help. But it's obvious something's not right and I want to help. If you'll just let me."

"Yes," I agree, wearily. "That would be nice."

He takes a deep breath, as though he hadn't thought it would be this simple.

"Good," he says. "So why don't you tell me what's going on?"

Once I start, the words just come tumbling out. Not just about what happened at the cafe. All of it, from the moment I first met Alicia. It's just such a relief to get it all out. I haven't even told Holly in this much detail. I was afraid she might think I was bonkers.

Deacon sits in perfect silence, no interruptions, no questions, just listens.

"So can you help?" I ask, when I've finally finished.

He looks at me gravely. "Yes, Isabel. I think I can."

"Thank god!" I fling my arms around him.

"Look, I've really got to get to work now, but can you meet me after?"

"Of course. Where?"

"Why don't you come to my office?"

"Good idea."

Not much chance of running into Alicia there.

I feel as if some of the weight I've been carrying these past few weeks has been lifted off my shoulders.

"Well, I'd better go and put up some more posters," I say, but as I get up from the table, I find that I'm still a little wobbly.

"Why don't you do it later?" he says. "You should go and lie down for a bit. You're deathly pale."

"Well, maybe just a short nap."

I snuggle up on the sofa and to my surprise, I sleep for most of the afternoon.

Queensbeach Medical Practice - 5.30 PM

"You're going to have to get some better reading material for the waiting room," I tell Deacon, when he comes out of his office. "I just found a copy of Vogue that was two years out of date. Oh, sorry…."

I hadn't realised there was somebody with him.

Deacon smiles. "Isabel, this is my colleague, Jim."

I smile politely. Jim is tall and skinny with limp hair that sticks to the sides of his head. He looks at me expectantly. I glance back at Deacon.

"What's going on?"

"Deacon was saying you've been having some problems lately?" Jim says, softly. "He thought perhaps I could help?"

"What?"

I stare at Deacon.

"Haven't you been listening to a word I've said? Alicia's the crazy one, not me!"

"Calm down! I just thought it might be helpful for you to speak to a therapist."

"I am calm!" I bellow. I know this isn't the best time to display my anger, but this is really all too much. "I thought you wanted to help me!"

"I do!"

"Not by setting me up with a therapist," I explode, eyeing Jim in dismay.

"I just needed you to believe me."

15

I storm out of the office and back to my car. I drive aimlessly for a while, too het up to think about where I'm going. A flock of seagulls circles overhead as I turn south and take the coast road. Almost without realising it, I find myself nearing the familiar turn-off for the Beach House.

What am I doing here?

I don't park directly in front of the house, but close enough that I still have quite a good view. The light is on in the kitchen - probably Rhett, cooking dinner. My phone rings. It's Deacon. My heart aches, but I can't speak to him. Not yet. I'm still too angry.

It's not long before he rolls up outside the house. I note the hassled expression on his face as he shuffles up the steps. But he doesn't go inside. Instead, he glances back at the road. As if he's waiting for something. *Or someone.* A few minutes later, a second car pulls up.

Kate! Kate's here.

Deacon goes to greet her and they disappear into the house.

Oh, this is stupid!

I get out of the car and walk up to the house. I stand at

the door, my hand poised to knock, when their voices float out to me through the open kitchen window.

Oh god, they're talking about me, aren't they?

I can hear their conversation quite clearly,

"What if," Kate murmurs. "What if there is something in what Isabel says? What if Alicia really is trying to set her up? She seems so convinced."

Yes! Yes!

I silently punch the air. Kate is on my side. Maybe she can talk some sense into him.

"It isn't Alicia who's acting strangely though, is it?" Deacon reasons. "I've heard of cases like this before, where the patient grows gradually more deluded, creating increasingly elaborate stories."

"But what about her cat going missing?" Kate persists. "Seems a bit of a coincidence, don't you think?"

Deacon sighs. "The sad thing is, Fluffy's disappearance is probably her own doing."

What?

His words hit me with a force.

How could he even suggest I would hurt Fluffy?

I will never forgive him, never!

"But she loves that cat!"

"I know, I know. But she isn't herself right now. If we really want to help her find Fluffy, we need to persuade her to get help."

How could he? I seethe with unadulterated rage.

I thought he knew me.

I turn and run. Once back in the car, I sit and stare blankly at the controls, as if I've just boarded an alien spacecraft. I've lost him. Alicia has won. Reluctantly, I start the engine. I let my anger take the wheel – I speed up at every bump in the road, aim straight for every muddy puddle. I take a masochistic delight in every thud that bumps the car, a sick pleasure at every muddy shower.

Maybe I'm the one who's crazy after all? Who knows?

I stare up at the ceiling for hours that night, my body rigid at every crack or creak. If only there was someone I could talk to. Someone who'd be on my side, for a change. Someone like Holly.

I haven't heard from my brother's fiancée since she checked Alicia's records, but I know she'll take me seriously, even if no one else will, and if anyone can help me, surely it's a private detective? I just have to get her to dig a little deeper.

It's ironic, I think, as I dial her number. Holly was a stranger to me just a couple of weeks ago. Now she and Julio are my only allies.

I wait anxiously as the phone rings and rings.

Oh, why doesn't she pick up?

Finally, there is a click on the other end.

"Holly!" My heart floods with relief.

"This is Julio," a sleepy voice answers. "Do you know what time it is?"

"Oh - sorry," I gulp. "I just really need to speak to Holly. Things are getting so crazy here."

My brother sounds extremely irritable.

"I'll get her to ring you in the morning, Isabel. Now get some sleep. Before you start losing your grip."

"But…"

It's no use arguing with him. He's already gone.

❄

I SLEEP FITFULLY, but the house seems cold and empty without Fluffy. A couple of times, I jolt awake, convinced I can hear his cries. But there is nothing there but the darkness.

It is some time later that the sound of birds twittering seeps through my consciousness. I raise a hand to shield my eyes from the light.

What time is it?

FRY

I reach for my phone, which is lying on the pillow beside me. It's gone nine. Why didn't the alarm wake me?

Probably because I didn't set it.

I get up and pull on my dressing gown. I'm halfway to the shower when something stops me. I can't go in. I can't face her.

I ring Sonya.

"You're not coming in, are you?"

"I'm sorry. My migraine's still really bad. I haven't had a wink of sleep."

Well, that part's true, at least.

Sonya sighs. "You will be in tomorrow, won't you? We're really struggling without you."

"Yeah, I'll be in tomorrow." I assure her. "Of course I will. I just need a bit more rest."

How easily the words trickle from my lips.

I throw on some clothes and head out into the street, armed with a wad of posters and a reel of sticky tape. Someone must have seen Fluffy. Someone must know where he is.

That's strange, I think, as I pass a lamppost close to my house, I thought I put a poster there yesterday.

I grab another one from my bundle and tape it up where people will see it. But as I pass the bus shelter, I notice that poster's gone too. And the one on the newsagent's notice-board. I feel a tightness in my chest.

Someone's been taking down my posters!

For the rest of the day, I stomp around, plastering posters to every conceivable surface and pressing them into the hands of bemused passersby. I work with an energy I didn't know I possessed. People look at me strangely, fearfully, even. But I don't care. I'll do whatever it takes to find Fluffy

Time starts to lose all significance. Day blends into night and night blends into day. Drained by lack of sleep, the word 'FRY' reverberates around in my head like a marble. It is the last thing I see before I close my eyes at night and the first thing I see when I open them in the morning.

I ring Holly incessantly. Probably make quite a pest of myself, begging her for updates. I offer to pay her anything she wants. She refuses to take a fee and patiently warns me – yet again that the business of a private detective can be slow and that it might be a while before she finds anything.

People look at me strangely in the street. Some with sympathy, others with suspicion. I don't know if it's just my tired appearance, or if word has got round that I'm losing it, but I'm definitely not imagining it. The man who owns the garage where Julio did his apprenticeship gives me a wink as I pass him in the street. I keep getting free coffees from Mustafa's and the manager of the beauty salon comes out of her shop to offer me a free haircut, even though she's known for being a tightwad.

I have probably been off work for a week or more, when I find myself curled up on the sofa one night, the remote in one hand, and a glass of cheap red wine in the other. I flick from one music channel to another, but each song in turn annoys me. I switch over to the style channel instead and start to watch a programme about military-inspired hats.

This is really boring. Maybe I should just go up to bed?

I switch off the TV and sit in silence for a moment, unable to will myself off the sofa. There is a slow, creaking sound as my letterbox starts to open.

I freeze.

What's happening?

A pair of eyes peer through.

Alicia?

My heart in my mouth, I dive behind the sofa, and hunch there, quaking.

What does she want from me? Why doesn't she leave me alone?

It seems like an eternity before her voice floats out to me.

"Coo-ey! Isabel? Are you there?"

It's just Kate!

Wiping the sweat from my forehead, I get up and go to the door.

"What are you doing here at this time of night?" I ask as I start to unbolt the door. But I leave it on the latch while I peer behind her to check that Alicia's not lurking in the shadows.

"Night? It's half past seven in the morning, Isabel! I'm on my way to work and so should you be."

"Did Deacon ask you to come round?"

"He's worried about you and can you blame him? You have to admit you've been acting rather strangely lately."

"If I'm acting strangely," I snarl, "It's because fires start wherever I go! My cat's been kidnapped, and Alicia's out to get me, only none of you bloody well believe me!"

"Calm down!" she says. "I've never seen you like this."

"Well, nothing like this has ever happened to me before. She's destroying my life."

Kate shakes her head.

"Look, are you going to let me or what? It's freaking freezing out here."

"Yes, of course, come in."

I take the chain off the latch and pull her inside, taking care to lock and bolt the door after her.

"Now, first things first," she says, taking her coat off and hanging it up in an orderly fashion. "Let's get some light in here."

She goes to the window and pulls back the curtains, letting in a stream of daylight. Then goes into the kitchen and puts on the kettle.

"I'll make us both a nice cup of tea."

"Are you sure you have time? I don't want to make you late for work."

Kate smiles. "What are friends for?"

I give an involuntary shudder. I'm sure she means it nicely, but that sounds exactly like something Alicia would say.

While Kate is in the kitchen, I clear a space on the coffee table, which has become cluttered with the wine glasses, coffee cups and cigarette packets that have become the mainstay of my diet. She returns a minute later with two strong cups of coffee and a plate of chocolate biscuits, which she must have brought with her, because there were none in the cupboards.

"You're out of milk so I made coffee instead."

"Thanks."

I eye the biscuits.

"Go on, help yourself."

I devour one after another.

"Hungry?" she says, sounding concerned. "No offence, Isabel – but if you can't remember to feed yourself, isn't it possible you forgot to feed Fluffy, too? Maybe he's wandered off somewhere to find food."

"I never forget to feed Fluffy." I say, through a mouthful of biscuit. "Just go and look in his food bowl, if you don't believe me. It's full to the brim."

"But that's what Deacon thinks too, isn't it?" I say, after I've wiped the crumbs from my mouth. "That I neglected Fluffy, and that's why he disappeared."

"He's just worried about you. We all are."

"Well, it's him and Rhett you should be worried about. They're the ones living under the same roof as that psycho."

Kate frowns, as though she can't quite comprehend this argument. "You know - maybe you should go and see that psychiatrist," she says, softly. "If only to put everyone's minds at rest."

"You think I'm crazy!"

"I didn't say that, I just want to make sure you're alright."

I am about to argue when a strange thought pops into my head:

Maybe this psychiatrist guy could help me. Maybe if I go

and see him, he can help me convince them all that I'm not crazy. Then they'll have to believe me.

"Perhaps you're right," I say slowly. "Maybe I will go and see him, after all."

"Good!" Kate hugs me in relief. "Good for you!"

Queensbeach Medical Practice - 1 PM

This whole thing is totally cringe worthy, I think to myself as I sit in the waiting room later that day. I half expect Deacon to come out and check I'm really here, but he doesn't. I suppose he must be tied up with his own patients.

"Isabel Anderson?" The receptionist calls my name in such a soft voice that I almost miss it.

Setting aside my magazine, I walk up to Jim's office and knock tentatively.

"Hi," I say sheepishly, remembering the way I acted the last time we met.

To my relief, he acts as though nothing happened.

"Come in, Isabel. Take a seat."

"Where?" I ask, looking around at the mismatched assortment of chairs.

"Wherever you like."

I plump myself down in a big comfy armchair. The chair is very relaxing, and as he rattles off his preliminary spiel, I feel my eyes start to droop.

"Isabel?"

"Yes!" I sit up sharply and force myself to pay attention.

"How are you sleeping, Isabel?"

"Not very well," I admit.

How can I, with all this hanging over my head?

He nods. "You know, sleep deprivation can play terrible tricks on the mind."

"That isn't the problem."

"Why don't you tell me about it, then?"

So I spill the whole story. His frown grows deeper and deeper, the longer I talk. I suppose I can understand that. It sounds crazier every time I tell it. When I've finished, I lean over and peer at his notes. He looks a little taken aback, but does not attempt to hide them. My nostrils flare with indignation as I see what he's written: *"Has a morbid fascination with fire"*.

"I do not have a morbid fascination with fire!"

"What's that in your hand, Isabel?"

I glance down. "My lighter."

I hadn't even realised I was holding it. It must be a subconscious thing.

"Look," I tell him. "If I'm obsessed with fire, it's because she's made me that way."

He does not argue.

"So you believe me?"

"I can see that you believe that that's what's going on."

"That's not what I asked!" I say angrily. "I want to know what you think."

But he won't give me an answer.

I let myself out, seventy pounds out of pocket, and no closer to the answer.

As I stand outside the office, smoking a cigarette, I sense him watching me from the window. When I turn to look, he has his head buried in his notebook. I can just imagine what he's writing: *"Exhibits smoking behaviour"*.

This was clearly a very bad idea.

I return home to find Mum's left me a voicemail on my landline. She doesn't like calling me on my mobile, in case I'm driving or something. I think she's getting worried though, because I haven't been in touch. She even left me a private message on Facebook last week. I'd better send her a quick reply, just to stop her worrying. I'll tell her that I'm swamped with work or something.

I open up my laptop and log in. After replying to mum, I

notice someone has invited me to join the Robertson's Facebook group. I didn't even know Robertson's had a Facebook group.

Hang on, if Robertson's is on here…

Almost before my brain has a chance to register, my fingers have typed in the words 'Camp Windylake'. There's a hit. I scroll through the page. How do I know this is my Camp Windylake and not one in Canada or somewhere? No, this is definitely mine. I recognise a couple of the members. I skim through a potted history of the camp. According to the site, it closed down nine years ago, just after I was there.

Oh look, group photos!

I flick excitedly through the album till I come to summer 2003. There are a few of me and Kate and a couple of other people I recognise, dancing like idiots at the disco on the last night of camp. And who's that? As I click to enlarge the picture, a chill runs through me.

But it can't be…

Standing next to us, a tight scowl on her lovely face, is Alicia. Not the sweet little ten-year-old Alicia from Kate's photos, but a mature, grown-up Alicia. And she looks about the same age as Kate and I.

16

OK, think rationally, Isabel. This cannot be Alicia. And yet...I click to enlarge the picture. Just look at that curly black hair, the dark piercing eyes. It looks so much like her. I don't know how long I sit there, staring at that picture, completely unable to grasp what's going on. It seems quite some time before the penny finally drops:

There are two of them. That's how she does it!

The realisation jars my body. Alicia has a double, a doppelganger. Probably an older sister or cousin. It seems like a bit of a crazy conclusion to come to, but I feel in my gut that it's right. I can't understand why one person would have such a grudge against me, let alone two but it all seems to fit. Whoever it is, they are working together to spy on me and make my life a misery.

My mind flicks back to the day I was with Deacon at the concert. I saw Alicia in the crowd. At least, I thought I did. And yet she was there on the end of the phone when I rang the Beach House. If there are two of them, then it is entirely possible that Alicia's double started the fire at the caravan park while Alicia herself was still at the party. And that could have been her I saw in the rear mirror, following me home from Julio's on Christmas Day. She could have even followed me into the cafe and written on the toilet walls that day, making me think I was going mad.

I bet she's out there right now, watching, waiting.

Perturbed, I go to the window and look out, but there is no way of knowing if anyone is out there in the darkness. I shudder. We're not just talking about Alicia skulking about in the shadows anymore. It's much, much more sinister if there are really two of them. And if I'm right, her double, whoever she is, has a car.

Why are they doing this to me?

In the picture, she is standing right next to me. I might have known her once, must at least have met her. I try desperately to remember, but the memories don't come. Judging from the age of this girl, she's much too old to have been a camper. Most likely, she was a fellow play leader. I wish I could ask Kate – she was there too, after all. But I don't dare in case it gets back to Alicia.

I need something to calm my nerves.

I go into the kitchen and twist the top off a bottle of wine. I'm about to pour a glass when I think better of it. *No, I mustn't drink. Not now. Not when I need to keep a clear head.* My mind is whirling. *Who sets the fires? Alicia or her double? And why, just to frame me?* It seems such a reckless crime. People could get hurt. People could die.

Are they equal partners in all this, the two of them, or is one of them in charge? I think of the word 'FRY', branded into Alicia's back. I can't imagine anyone choosing to have such a thing done. Could it be that Alicia's not the one in the driving seat? Even though she seems so very, very creepy. Has she been tutored, coerced? It's impossible to say.

More than ever, I yearn to know the true meaning of FRY. What is it? And what does it have to do with me? I sit back down at the computer and go through the rest of the Camp Windylake album, examining each picture in turn, but none of the others show anything out of the ordinary.

What to do? What to do?

If only I could ask the other members of this group. Someone must remember something. Maybe they can help me? But how do I broach the subject, without raising suspicion or looking like a complete weirdo? I click my fingers. What if…What if I pretend to be organising a staff reunion for Camp Windylake? I could ask the other members of the group to send me names and contact details of all the play leaders who worked there. Someone's bound to remember this girl, surely?

Seized with inspiration, I start typing. I am deliberately vague about exactly when and where the reunion will be. The only person I don't invite is Kate. Luckily, she doesn't really use her Facebook account, so she won't have seen this group, and I want to keep it that way. I can't risk this getting back to Alicia. I just hope I get some responses. And fast. Because who knows what she and her evil double have in store for me next.

My message sent, I wait anxiously for a reply. After a few minutes, I hit refresh, but there are no responses. Full of impatience, I drum my fingers on the table top and refresh again.

It's like watching a kettle boil.

In an effort to distract myself, I google FRY, and get an array of confounding hits, from the Former Yugoslav Republic of Macedonia, to a group offering tax and financial aid, none of which bring me any closer to the truth. I flit back to Facebook, but there are still no responses. I drum my fingers on the table top.

Now what?

I'm quite hungry, actually, pipes up a little voice inside my head.

I glance at the table, where I had some fruit, but the peaches and plums have turned sour in the bowl. Maybe I should nip down the chippy and get myself some dinner? Someone might have responded by the time I get back.

The chip shop is only a fifteen minute walk from my house, but I'm too creeped out to walk, so I take the car and drive into the centre of Queensbeach. I hadn't expected there to be so many people out, talking and laughing in loud, booming voices, enjoying themselves as if nothing has happened. I see girls dressed up in…well, not very much, considering it's winter, shivering in the queue for the night-club. But it's just another ordinary night for them, I suppose.

"One portion of fish and chips please," I tell the man at the fish bar. "No mushy peas."

I hand over my money and sit down to wait, my tummy growling at the smell of the hot chips frying. Idly, I pick up a copy of the local gazette someone's left lying around. Thumbing through it, I notice an article on the recent spate of fires in the area, including the one at the caravan park. There have been blazes at several businesses around the town over the last few weeks. Apparently, the police are following up a number of leads, whatever that means. I bet they have no idea.

I am so engrossed in the article that I barely register the presence of another customer walking up to the counter.

"Four portions of fish and chips, please."

It's Deacon.

I watch out of the corner of my eye as he takes out his wallet and pays with crisp, new notes. He hasn't clocked me yet, and I'm not sure I want him to. We haven't spoken since the night he introduced me to Jim. The night I overheard him saying those awful things about me. So I keep my head ducked down low, try not to listen as he discusses football with the owner.

"Fish and chips, no mushy peas," the server calls out when my order is ready.

Deacon whirls round.

"Isabel? How long have you been sitting there?"

"A little while."

"Great minds think alike, hey? Why don't you come back to the Beach House and eat with us?"

His face is kind and earnest, but I can't forgive him. Can't ever forget those terrible things he said.

"No thanks."

I reach over him for my parcel of chips, try not to notice the hurt and confusion in his eyes. See, the thing is, I'm not sure we can be friends anymore. I'm not sure we can be anything.

❄

I CHECK the computer as soon as I get in, but still no responses. I'm going to have to be patient. Maybe someone will post something in the morning. I pick at my chips while I try to figure out my next move. Absent-mindedly, I break off a piece of fish and hold it out for Fluffy, but of course, he's not there to take it.

What am I going to do, Fluffy?

I could confront Alicia about her doppelganger. But, damning as it seems, I have a feeling she'd be able to talk her way out of it like she has everything else. And I can't afford not to be believed. Not again. No, I need to keep this quiet. Do some digging.

What I need is help, professional help and not the kind Deacon's friend Jim was offering. Like it or not, I'm going to have to ask Holly – again. The trouble is, how can I get her to take my call? I've been hassling her so much lately that the only conversation I'm likely to have with her now is with her answering machine – or Julio. But I really need her, more than ever. There must be some way.

❄

Mr Krinkle is outside, watering his plants as I set off the next morning.

"Hello, Isabel," he says, eyeing my overnight bag, nosily. "Going away for the weekend?"

"Just visiting my brother."

"That's nice. Do you want me to water your plants while you're away?"

"Oh no, I won't be gone that long. But thanks for the offer."

He looks disappointed. I bet he would just love to have a snoop around my house, tell Mrs Norris at number nineteen about all the washing-up left in the sink.

"There is something you could do for me though."

"Yes?"

"Well…" I hesitate – is this really a good idea? "I did read something in the paper about there being a rise in burglaries in this area."

"Really?" A look of concern etches itself onto his face.

I'm a terrible person, worrying an old man like this.

"Yeah, and I was just wondering if you wouldn't mind keeping a bit of an eye on my house while I'm away? I wouldn't want to come back to find an intruder."

"Yes, of course," he says, nodding solemnly. "I'll mention it to Mrs Norris opposite. I'm sure we can keep a look out between the two of us."

"That's really good of you, thanks."

I start to back towards my car before he can ask me any more about the burglaries. I don't feel good lying to him, but what is the world coming to if you can't harness the power of nosy parkers for your own good?

I really hope they're in, I think nervously as I approach Julio and Holly's road a few hours later. A sensible person probably would have rung ahead to check, but I'm just going to have to take my chances. If I had told them I was coming, I'm fairly certain they would have tried to put me off. As it is, I'm just hoping they won't have the heart to turn me away. Not when I've driven all this way.

To my relief, there's a dismembered old Beetle blocking their driveway. And where there's a beaten up old car, you can usually find Julio. There he is, sure enough, delving around in the engine.

"Julio?"

"Izzy!" he looks up sharply, nearly banging his head on the bonnet.

"I'm really sorry to bother you, but I've found out something important and I need to talk to Holly."

Julio frowns. "Well, it will have to wait until she gets home from work."

He produces a cloth from his pocket and wipes his greasy hands.

"Oh," I say, unable to hide my disappointment. "Well, I suppose I could wait in the car."

He takes in the state of me - the lack of make-up, the unkempt hair, the dark rings around my eyes and seems to relent.

"Don't be silly. Come on inside. I'm due for a tea break, anyway."

"I don't even remember her," I babble, as I finish telling him about the girl in the picture. "So why in the world has she got it in for me?"

"Are you sure it's not just Alicia winding you up again?"

"What do you mean?"

"I mean, how do you know the picture's genuine? It could have been photoshopped."

"It looks real enough."

"Show me."

I pull up the picture on my phone. "Here."

He stares at it for a moment, a strange expression forming on his face.

"What? Is it real or do you think it's been messed with?"

"Yeah it's real," he says, his face a little pale now. "And, I think…no, I'm sure… I used to go out with that girl."

17

"But you didn't even go to Camp Windylake!"

"No, but I came to visit you often enough, didn't I?"

"So this is all about you?"

I don't know why I'm so surprised. Julio has gone out with most of the women I know at one time or another. Why should this girl be any different?

"Oh, what was her name? Josie. No, Jody!"

"Jody," I repeat. "You're sure?"

"I think so."

"Do you recall a last name?"

"Erm…"

"Could it be McBride?"

It's a stab in the dark. I mean, I don't even know if that's really Alicia's last name, but a flicker of recognition appears on Julio's face.

"Could be. Definitely Mc something or rather."

"Honey, I'm home!" Holly calls out, as she walks through the door. Then she sees me.

"Oh, hello Isabel." She shoots Julio a worried look. I can't really blame her, after all those endless phone calls.

Quickly, we fill her in on what we've just discovered.

"Did you break up with her?" Holly asks him.

"Of course he did," I snort. As far as I know, Julio's never been dumped in his life, more's the pity. And even those girls who know of his reputation don't seem to be put off by it. Kate was adamant that she was going to be the one to change him, just as Holly is now.

"But do you remember why?" I press. "Was there another girl?"

Julio frowns. "It was a long time ago. I really can't remember."

"Do you remember anything about her at all?" I ask. "I mean, what was she like?"

"I don't know. Kind of…quiet. And serious."

"What I can't understand is why she's going after Isabel," Holly says. "Why not you? And why now?"

"Search me."

"We are in the phonebook, after all. You wouldn't be too hard to find."

"She *is* crazy," I point out. "At least, if she's anything like Alicia, she is."

But Holly isn't satisfied.

"Wait a minute - Julio did you…two-time this girl?"

"What?"

"Oh, don't look so shocked. "I know what you were like."

She turns to me. "The question is, if he did two-time her, did you know about it?"

Julio and I look at each other helplessly.

"I honestly can't remember."

"Me neither."

She rolls her eyes. "You've both got memories like sieves! Well, let's say that's what happened. Julio cheated on her and Isabel knew about it. That will have to be our working assumption for the time being, unless anyone can come up with a better one."

"It still doesn't make sense," Julio says. "Why would she even care about some bloke who dumped her ten years ago?"

Holly says nothing. She doesn't have to. I know what effect Julio has on women. I've seen it too many times before.

"What if she never got over it? What if she hasn't had another boyfriend since?"

"Oh come on," Julio laughs. "Give me a break!"

But I'm not so sure and by the looks of it, nor is Holly.

"Do you think we should go to the police?"

"And tell them what exactly? They'd think we were nuts."

"Yeah, I've been getting that a lot lately." I sigh. "So what should I do in the meantime?"

"Act as if everything's normal," Holly says, decisively. "Surround yourself with people. And don't take the same route to and from work every day. You need to vary your routine. Swap things around a bit. Make some last minute changes. Make it hard for them to figure out where you're going to be and what you're going to do next."

I nod. I don't tell them that I've been off work for the last couple of weeks. I'm too embarrassed to admit how much Alicia and Jody have got to me.

"Meanwhile, I'll see what I can find out about this Jody person."

She eyes my bulging bag, sitting by the door.

"Are you staying the night, Isabel? I can make up the spare room."

"No thanks," I say, getting to my feet.

"I've got work in the morning."

Now I've got them on side again, I don't feel quite so hopeless. It's time to take control of my life and it's definitely time I went back to my job. If I still have one, that is. I mean — Sonya's been understanding and all, but there's only so far you can push it. Especially as I haven't even bothered to return her phone calls for the last few days.

I drive home, ready and alert for Jody's white Escort to

appear in the rear mirror, but to my relief, it doesn't. Once home, I set my alarm for 6.00AM and get an early night.

※

Butterflies flutter in my stomach as I march into Robertson's the next day, ignoring the nosey looks of the checkout girls. Everybody knows about my meltdown. Alicia's taken care of that.

Sonya is in the office, swearing at the computer.

I knock gently. "Can I come in?"

"Oh, thank heaven! See if you can fix this. I don't know what the hell I've pressed, but it's coming out sideways!"

"Let me see," I lean over her shoulder and correct the error with a few strokes of the keys.

"Thanks – ruddy thing's out to get me."

"Bastard. Yeah, it's got a mind of its own."

"So you're back?" she asks, seriously.

"Yes." I meet her gaze.

"You're sure? Because I can't really afford to be left in the lurch again. In fact, Human Resources have just sent over a pile of CVs from people who would love to interview for your job." She drops her gaze. "But you know I'd much rather have you."

I bite my lip. "I really am sorry, Sonya. I won't let it happen again."

"Well, OK then, just as long as I can rely on you from now on."

"You can. I promise."

We spend the rest of the morning working through the backlog in the office, which suits me fine, as it means I don't have to face the gossips on the shop floor. And more importantly, I don't have to face Alicia.

"Are you coming down to the canteen?" I ask Sonya, as twelve o'clock rolls around.

"Um, not today," she says, a flush of colour creeping into her cheeks.

I look at her closely. "Why? What's going on?"

"I've, er...I've met someone. His name's Michael and he's taking me out for lunch."

"Wow," I say, a little blown away. Sonya's been single for as long as I can remember, longer than me, in fact. "How did you meet?"

"I ordered him over the phone," she says, with a giggle.

"You what?"

"Actually, it was just a pizza I ordered, but I got a bit more than I bargained for. The delivery man was gorgeous!"

"Well, I'm really pleased for you," I say, as sincerely as I can manage. If I had the energy to worry about such things, I would probably feel just a teensy bit envious. I mean, I want her to be happy – of course I do. It's just…seeing her radiant, smiling face reminds me of my own non-existent love life.

Holly rings me later.

"I just wanted to give you an update on Jody."

"What have you found out?"

"Well, she doesn't have a police record, but she did spend time on a psychiatric ward when she was younger."

"Really?" My heart jolts. "What for? Pyromania?"

"Haven't been able to get that info, but she definitely had a drug and alcohol problem in the past."

"Anything else?"

"I'm still trying to get her current address but she was last seen in Sandford Dunes."

"Sandford Dunes? That's not far from me."

"Which makes it all the more plausible that she's involved in all this."

When I log into Facebook, there are developments there too. Someone has replied to my suggestion for a reunion. Soon the wall is buzzing with replies, some from people I vaguely remember, others, I haven't a clue about, but still no mention of Jody. I only thought of a reunion as a way of getting people to send me information about her, but the idea seems to have sprouted legs. Almost without me having to do anything, a venue is agreed and a date set. I just hope somebody will be able to tell me something about Jody.

In the meantime, I do as Holly advises. I accept invitations, I go out and while I'm about it, I manage to have a little fun. I make sure I'm home as little as possible, staying at Kate's a few times, even at Sonya's once, after a few too many glasses of wine. My friends all heave a collective sigh of relief, assuming I've recovered from my little meltdown. But I don't go over to the Beach House anymore, and I tinker with the roster at Robertson's so that Alicia and I are scheduled to work together as little as possible. Avoiding her is the only way I can keep sane.

But if I thought for one minute that Alicia would just give up and leave me alone, I was very much mistaken. One evening, as I am sitting in front of the TV, I hear something scratching at the door.

"Fluffy!" I cry, rushing to the door. "Fluffy, is that you?"

I throw back the bolts and open the door.

"Fluffy?"

But there's no one there. I grab my phone from my pocket and use it to shine a light around the garden.

"Fluffy!" I call, a little louder now. "Are you there?"

If I listen intently, I can hear definitely hear something.

There it is again! What is that?

It's the sound of a bell jingling. A miniature cow bell – just like the one I bought Fluffy for Christmas.

"Fluffy!"

I wait for the sound of padded footsteps, running up the path towards me.

But the only sound that greets me is laughter. Hard, callous laughter. It's Alicia.

I recoil in horror, jump back inside, slamming and bolting

the door as quickly as my shaking hands can manage. I should have known it was her – just as I thought she'd finally left me alone. Just as I thought I'd found Fluffy.

I stand stock still, hope in vain that she'll go away, but my silence just makes her crazier. She knocks furiously, pummels the door with her delicate fists. I am amazed at how strong she is, amazed to see the whole door shudder and shake.

"Is-abel" she calls out in her singsong voice.

"Is-abel! I know you're in there!"

I back into the kitchen, where she can't see me.

But I can still hear her at the front door, calling out my name.

So what's that scratching at the back door?

"Fluffy? Fluffy?" I hiss, peering out through the kitchen window.

But it is not a cat, but a ghostly figure that greets me.

"Is-abel. Is-abel!"

"Shit!"

How did she get there so quickly? Or…wait a minute. I stare back in horror. Could this be Jody? It's hard to tell in the darkness, but she seems a little taller, her voice a little huskier.

So I was right - they're are two of them!

Both of them scratch at the door and call out my name.

"Is-abel! Is-abel."

They're just trying to freak me out, I tell myself, as I squat down behind the kitchen cabinets. I cover my ears with my hands, desperate to block out the sound, but all the time I have one eye on the smoke alarm and the other on the phone.

Eventually, they fall silent. I assume they've gone away, but you never can tell. I curl up on the sofa and fall asleep with my pocket smoke detector snuggled against my chest.

❄

I'M dog-tired when my alarm goes off in the morning, but I

force myself to get up and dressed. I have to get to work. I have to show Alicia that she hasn't got to me.

Sonya waves me into the office the minute I arrive.

"I need you to do me a big favour."

"Yes, of course," I agree, suppressing a massive yawn. "What is it?"

"I need you to cover the night shift tonight. I was going to do it myself, but now I've got plans."

I force a smile. "Are you seeing your new man again?"

"He's taking me to see Cats."

Oh, Fluffy!

"That's great!" I try to swallow my sadness. "What are you going to wear?"

But as she debates between her leopard print halterneck and her little black dress, my mind wanders. I can't help noticing the calendar sitting on her desk. Today is the 26th February. Isn't there something significant about this date? I think hard, but my tired mind is as fuzzy as a snow globe. Then I remember.

The reunion! It's tonight!

"Oh no, Sonya – I've just realised. I've got something else on tonight."

"Come on Isabel, I've cut you a lot of slack recently. Surely you can do this one thing for me?"

I swallow. She has a point. I do owe her. But what am I going to do about the reunion?

"Don't worry – I…I'll work something out."

"Thank you."

She walks over to the table, where Alicia has once again laid out doughnuts.

"I don't know how many times I've asked Alicia to stop bringing these in – they're ruining my diet."

The temptress!

But she takes one regardless and swallows it in three large bites.

I pull out my mobile.

"Holly, I've got a problem."

"Maybe," Holly says, when I've finished explaining. "Maybe, I could go in your place?"

"But you didn't even go to Camp Windylake!"

"They don't have to know that," she laughs. "It's been such a long time, I doubt anyone will notice."

"Do you really think it could work?"

"I don't see why not. I do this kind of thing all time for work."

"Well, I suppose," I say.

But I still feel uneasy.

Sonya sends me home for the afternoon, so I can get some sleep before I come back for the night shift. I arrive back at Robertson's just as the afternoon shift is streaming out and hide in my car until they are all out the door. According to the roster, Alicia was scheduled to work this afternoon, and I really don't feel like running into her.

Once I'm sure the coast is clear, I walk inside.

"Oh, there you are!" says Sonya. "I was a bit worried you'd overslept."

"No, I'm here," I reassure her. "Let me just go and grab my cardy."

I head to the staff room and punch in the combination for my locker. The door swings open with a loud creak.

"What on earth?"

I rub my eyes in disbelief, because there, right in front of me, taking up my entire locker, is a huge can of petrol.

18

Someone's coming!

I slam the door shut and lean against it just as Sonya walks in. I feel a bead of sweat trickle down my brow as she turns and looks at me.

"Thanks for doing this, Isabel. I really appreciate it."

She pauses in front of the mirror to check her make-up.

"That's fine."

My mind is transfixed with horror. I can feel the huge can of petrol wedged against the closed locker door. If I move so much as an inch from this position, I feel certain it will tumble out and spill its guilty contents all over the staff room floor.

"Isabel?" Sonya has noticed I'm not paying the least bit of attention to her. "Are you OK?"

"Of course I am." My voice comes out in an unnaturally high pitch.

What the hell am I going to do?

Oh god, I wish she would just leave. I'm amazed she doesn't smell the petrol fumes.

"Hey, can I borrow some perfume?" she asks.

"Sorry, I haven't got any."

"Are you sure?" She eyes me with suspicion. "I thought you kept a bottle in your locker?"

"Er…yeah, I ran out."

She looks put out. "Couldn't you just check? I don't want to go out smelling like old boot."

I press my back against my locker. There's no way I'm letting her see inside.

"Sorry, I just had a clear-out. Why don't you use one of the testers from the cosmetics aisle?"

"I suppose I'll have to," she says, a little huffily. She must think I'm holding out on her, but I can't worry about that now.

As soon as the door shuts behind her, I shove the petrol can further into the locker and lock it again quickly, before anyone else walks in.

How did Alicia know I'd be here tonight? My covering this shift was unscheduled. It wouldn't have been on the roster.

I walk out onto the shop floor. Whatever I'm going to do about the petrol can, it'll have to wait until Sonya's gone. Not that she seems in any particular hurry to leave.

"Can you make sure the rosters are printed out for the morning?" she asks. "I was going to do it earlier, but the printer was getting overheated."

"Yes, of course."

"Oh, and another thing, don't forget to get the baked bean aisle re-stacked. We should be getting a shipment in later tonight."

"Don't worry," I say, in the calmest voice I can muster. "I've got it all under control. You go and enjoy your evening."

"Yes," she smiles, the perfume incident temporarily forgotten. "I suppose I am worrying for nothing. I know Robertson's is in safe hands with you."

Once I'm sure she's gone, I go back to the staffroom and carefully reopen my locker. A crazy little part of me is hoping that it's all been a figment of my imagination, that there isn't really a massive can of petrol in there after all. But as the door swings back, there is no denying its existence. It has a strong, pungent odour. The cap is loose, the seal broken. I screw it back on, tightly.

What in god's name am I going to do with it? Pour it down the sink? But I'm not so sure that's a good idea. This is a lot of petrol. I don't know what effect it might have. It would reek the place out if nothing else, and I'd still have to get rid of the empty can, somehow.

I long to shove the thing in Alicia's locker. But I don't know the combination and even if I did, would I really want to put it back in the hands of a crazed pyromaniac? Instead, I grab a roll of large, reinforced gardening bags from the shop floor.

"Hey, that's £4.99," calls out the checkout girl as I walk past.

"Here," I slap some coins down in front of her.

"This is too much."

"Keep the change."

My heart thumps noisily as I pull the can of petrol out of my locker and shove it into the bag. I could not feel more guilty if there were a body in the bag. A body, which I'm about to haul through the store.

I feel like all eyes are on me as I heave my burden out through the shop, but if anybody wonders what I've got in the huge sack, they keep it to themselves. I am almost out the door, when the bloody checkout girl waves for my attention again.

"I need the loo."

"You'll have to wait a minute."

"But I'm bursting."

"I'll be right back."

I drag the bag outside, silently cursing myself for parking so far away from the building. I stagger to my car and dump the petrol can in the boot. Once it's done, I slump down, exhausted. It is only then that I consider the real significance of the petrol.

What does it mean?

Is this just another of Alicia and Jody's sick jokes or are they planning a real fire this time? The thought builds and builds in my head. What if they are? Shouldn't I warn someone? But how can I without incriminating myself? If I go to the police, after everything that's happened, they'll either laugh in my face, or else lock me up.

There must be some way to stop them!

I choose the public pay phone at the shabby precinct just behind the store. Three of the phones have been vandalised beyond repair, but luckily, the fourth is working. I pull DS Penney's business card out of my wallet and check the number. My hand trembles as I dial. I don't use Penney's direct line in case he recognises my voice, but even going through the switchboard is nerve wracking. The words tumble from my mouth the moment someone answers:

"I think someone might be planning to start a fire at Robertson's tonight…"

I hang up before anyone can ask me for my name or address.

"Cigarette?" Jon, the security guard, offers a little later, when I walk outside on my break.

"Um, better not."

Even after washing my hands about twelve times, I'm a little nervous there may still be a trace of petrol on them.

"You giving up?"

"Sort of." I take a sip of my coffee. "So you're on the night shift now?" I ask, keen to change the subject. "I thought I hadn't seen you for a while."

"I switched to nights a few weeks ago," he tells me. "It's an easy gig most of the time. Not many customers to deal with, just a few drunks. Although…" he looks out at the road behind the car park. "I think something's up tonight."

"What makes you say that?"

"That's the third time I've seen a police patrol drive through here."

"Really?"

"Yeah, and there were a couple of community support officers in here just a minute ago."

"Maybe they were on their break."

"Maybe, but I still think something's up."

The police presence makes me feel simultaneously nervous and reassured. *Just have to get through the next few hours,* I keep telling myself. *Then this awful night will be over.*

"Hey, is your phone ringing?"

"So it is."

I'd forgotten I'd set it to vibrate.

I glance at the screen. "Holly, how's it going?"

"You'll never believe this," she says, in a low voice, "but I'm outside Jody's house!"

"You are?" I nearly drop my coffee. "How did you find her?"

"She turned up for the reunion! Turns out, she's still in contact with one of the other girls who went to the camp."

"Oh my god! So tell me - what's she like?"

"Quiet, really quiet. She just sat in the corner all evening, hugging a coke. I'm not really sure why she came. Everyone else seemed to be having a good time, though – they all went on to Archie's."

"But Jody wasn't up for it?"

"No."

"So, what – you followed her home?"

"That's what I do, isn't it? Not that she seems to be doing much. I'm just waiting for the lights to go out, then I'll probably head home myself. I can always come back, now that I know where she lives. But listen, Isabel. There was another unexpected… development."

"What?"

"Julio's ex showed up!"

"You'll have to be more specific."

"His ex-wife, Kate! I couldn't think where I knew her from at first, I mean, I've never actually met her before. But I've seen photos, so she looked kind of familiar."

"Oh god! How did she even find out about the reunion? I was so careful not to say anything."

"Someone else must have told her. She seemed quite friendly with a couple of the other play leaders. One of them must have invited her. But when Jody walked in, she looked like she'd seen a ghost She'd obviously noticed that she looks just like Alicia. I had to go up and warn her, to make sure she wasn't going to give the game away."

"So what did you say?"

"I told her I was a private detective you'd hired. I figured that was close enough to the truth to keep her happy. I warned her to stay away from Jody and said that you'd fill her in on the rest of the details."

I exhale. "So she didn't even realise who you are?"

"No, I don't think so."

Poor Kate. Maybe I should have clued her in about Alicia and Jody before, but I'm not sure she would have believed me, if she hadn't seen Jody for herself.

As I say goodnight to Holly, another thought occurs to me. If Jody is at home, then that means she's not here. If only I could check on Alicia's whereabouts too, but it's a bit late to be calling the Beach House. I could drop Deacon a text though, couldn't I? See if he's awake. He might be. He is a bit of a night owl.

My fingers move quickly over the touch-pad.

- Are you still up?

The phone beeps instantly with his reply:

- Now I am:)

- Sorry, did I wake you?

- Not really. I was reading. It's nice to hear from you.

- I was just wondering if Alicia's still up?
- She's just gone to bed. Did you want to speak to her?
- No, it's OK. It can wait till tomorrow.

So Jody and Alicia are both safely at home, I think with satisfaction, and there are only a couple more hours left on the night shift. Maybe there isn't going to be any trouble tonight, after all.

As an extra precaution, I turn back to Jon, who is still at his post by the door and show him the pictures of Alicia and Jody that I've saved to my phone.

"Are they twins or something?" he asks, flicking from one to the next.

"Just sisters, I think," I say, glancing at my watch. "Look, just ring me immediately if either one of them turns up at the store tonight, OK?"

He raises an eyebrow a little at the request, but doesn't ask any awkward questions.

❄

ONCE I GO BACK INSIDE, things start to get busy. People wander in on their way home from nightclubs, looking for frozen pizzas, sandwiches, drinks and snacks. A handful of shift workers come and do their weekly shop, eager to avoid the crowds. Time passes quickly as I pace through the store, multitasking between the checkouts, shelving staff and the warehouse, where the fresh consignment of baked beans has finally arrived. Then, just as the queues are starting to die down again, one of the new boys waves to get my attention.

"Isabel, call for you in the office."

"Oh, thanks."

I walk in and close the door behind me. It's got to be Sonya, calling to check up on me. I sit down at the computer and pick up the receiver. Might as well get those rosters printed while I take her call.

"Isabel Anderson," I say, in a tone intended to inspire confidence.

"Hello, Isabel."

Not Sonya.

"Hello. Who is this?" I glance at the display, but it just reads 'out of area.'

"I think you know who this is." Her voice is hoarse and emotionless.

My breath comes fast and ragged.

"Jody?"

"We don't have much time," she says, briskly. "If you want to help your friend, you must do as I say."

"Who…what are you talking about?"

"You know very well. That woman you sent to spy on me."

"You've got Holly?" My body jerks to life. "Let me speak to her!"

"There's no time for that. I was hoping it wasn't going to come to this, but you've given me no choice."

I feel my panic rising. "What have you done with her?"

With my right hand, I pull out my mobile and force my shaking fingers to bring up Holly's number.

It rings.

"Hello," I almost gasp with relief as I hear her voice, but to my dismay, it's just a prerecorded message.

Oh, why doesn't she pick up?

Jody is still speaking. "You need to listen very carefully, Isabel. I'm about to give you a set of instructions. If you want to help your friend, you must follow everything to the letter."

Oh god, please let this be a bad dream.

I listen in dismay as she rattles off her instructions, but struggle to take it all in as my anxiety for Holly mounts. Where is she? What have they done with her?

Has she met the same fate as Fluffy?

It's only once Jody hangs up that I'm able to take in the

full force of her words. What am I going to do? If I don't comply with her wishes, there is a real chance that something terrible will happen. Holly's life rests in my hands.

Why me? What did I do to deserve this?

Another person in my situation would march straight out to the police car outside the store. But that door is closed to me, shut some time ago. I'm damned if I do, and damned if I don't. My conscience won't give me a moment's peace. Probably never will.

As I drag myself towards the warehouse, I can't help but marvel that I can still place one foot in front of the other, that my knees don't buckle from the effort. I push open the door with purpose and begin to riffle around, assembling the things I need. Nobody questions my presence there, they just see me with my fancy suit and supervisor's badge and go on with their work, loading and unloading their pallets and crates.

I play my part slowly, waiting for the right moment. Finally, a whistle blows, signalling that it's time for the lads to take their tea break. I watch them file out the door, then take a quick look around, anxious that no one has been left behind. Only then do I set my phone down on the shelf and nod to the camera. I am just about to begin when the door swings open and Deacon barges in.

I have never been so angry to see anyone in my entire life.

"What the are you doing here?"

"I got your message," he gasps, slightly out of breath. "What's going on?"

"I didn't send you any message!"

"Yes, you did! You said it was urgent!"

"I didn't send you any message!" I repeat, furiously. "Now get out of here, quick, quick!"

He stares at me in horror, suddenly seems to realise why I'm so desperate to get rid of him.

"Isabel? What's that in your hand? What…what the hell are you doing?"

But I can't explain it.

The day I met Alicia, an inexorable chain of events was set in motion. Events, which led me, unwillingly, unwittingly to this point. To my left, drips a giant can of petrol, and in my right hand, the lighter is already aflame.

19

I suppose the blood must continue to pump around my body, because if it doesn't, if my heart has actually stopped, then I should have dropped with a thud to the floor. But in this instant, it seems to me that the earth and everything on it, just stops, like someone has pressed the pause button on a giant cosmic remote control. Thoughts freeze mid sentence in my brain. I am stuck in some strange kind of limbo. I don't dare think or even breathe.

Then just as abruptly, someone hits 'play' and we're off again. Deacon dives upon me, grabbing my wrist with one hand and the lighter with the other.

"No, you don't understand!"

I fight as hard as I can, but he is too strong for me. In a matter of seconds, he has wrestled the lighter from me and flung it out of harm's way. Even so, he does not let me go. He starts patting me down, turning out my pockets, checking to see if I have any other means of ignition.

"Get off!" I yell, in indignation, but he does not relent.

I blink my eyes at the camera and try to communicate that none of this is my fault. What will happen to Holly now that Deacon has interfered? Now that I have been forced to disobey Jody's sinister instructions? Will I get a second chance, or is it already too late? I try to free myself from his grasp, but Deacon holds me fast. He seems to sense that it is not yet safe to let me go.

Then, all at once, there is a shrieking in my ears. Screeching, blaring - sirens go off all around us.

"That's the fire alarm!"

But how? Our heads jerk in the direction of the petrol can, but it remains untouched, dripping silently onto the floor. And that's when I hear the most sickening sound I've ever heard, as on either side of us, the doors slam shut. In a flash, Deacon releases his pincer-like grip and we race towards the nearest exit, but it's too late, the door holds fast. We try the other one, but that one holds too. They both appear to be locked and bolted. And then smoke starts to fill the room.

Deacon stares at me in absolute shock. His face has turned completely white, his lips almost purple with horror. I don't think I've ever seen him so scared before. It frightens me almost as much as the terrifying situation.

"What's going on? What have you done?"

"It wasn't me, godammit!"

But this is no time for blame or retribution. We both look around, desperate for another door, a window, some other means of getting out. But there are no windows in the warehouse. There's only the goods entrance at the back and the door leading through to the store at the front. And neither will budge.

"Help, we're trapped in the warehouse!"

I smack my fists against the door that leads through to the store.

"Let us out!"

But my words are drowned out by the screaming of the fire alarms.

I try banging on the other door, the one that leads outside, but that one is even stronger, recently reinforced.

I can't believe this is happening. Is this really how it all ends?

Deacon charges at the inner door, hitting it hard with his powerful shoulders. It must hurt like crazy, but he doesn't cry out, just keeps at it, over and over. And when that doesn't work, he grabs some kind of tool from a nearby workbench and starts hacking away at it, as hard as he can go.

"It's no use," he finally pants. "The door's too strong!"

And that's when the lights flicker and go out. A scream rises in my throat, but I swallow it down, determined to keep it together.

We have to do something! We have to get out of here!

I think hard, trying desperately to remember the layout of the room. There must be something here we can use, something that will help us. But I must think fast. All the time, the room is filling up with smoke, making it harder and harder to breathe.

"Isabel! Where are you?"

"Over here."

I feel my way across the room, past the endless rows of crates and boxes. My eyes are still adjusting to the darkness, but I think I can see what I'm looking for.

Yes, found it!

I touch the cold, hard metal.

"Stand away from the door!"

I climb into the cab of the fork-lift truck. Incredibly, the keys are still in the ignition. I don't know what I would do if they weren't. This is our last chance, our last hope. I've seen the drivers operate these things often enough. Even watched Stu have a crafty go on his lunch break. How hard can it be?

"What are you doing?"

"I'm going to ram the door with the fork-lift!"

"Do you know how to drive that thing?"

I ignore his question and fumble for the controls.

"Get out of the way!"

"Please be careful!"

But he knows that I will not. We don't have time to be anything but frenzied and panicked. And this is not like driving a car. I have no idea which of the knobs and levers control the movement of the vehicle and which move the forks up and down or control the speed. I am, quite literally driving in the dark here. All I can do is hope for the best. The smoke is getting thicker and thicker all the time. If we don't get out soon, that will be it. Game over.

The fork-lift is already loaded with crates of some kind. I don't know what's in them, but as I start to propel the vehicle forward, I just hope it's something strong and heavy. I shunt forwards and back, trying to figure out what I'm doing.

The fork-lift wobbles as I attempt to pick up speed. I can't look as I plough headlong into the door.

"Godammit!"

I hit it with a crunch and still, it isn't enough to break it.

"You've made a dent!"

"Good. I'm going to back up and try again."

"Let me have a go! You'll hurt yourself!"

"Just stay back!"

I don't have time for his macho posturing. I got us into this, I need to get us out. It's just a question of which will hold out longest – the door, the fork-lift or me. I repeat the exercise, fly forwards and back, the vehicle wobbling precariously, unused to this kind of abuse. Finally, finally, there is a loud crash, and a large plume of smoke gushes in through the door.

"You've made a hole," he calls out excitedly. "But it's not quite big enough for us to get through. Give it one more try."

"Nearly there!" I shout down to him, but my words come out as a series of coughs. In fact, it takes three tries, and with each one, more smoke is released into the room.

On my last attempt, I feel the fork-lift listing badly. As I ram into the door, I lose my grip and the next thing I know, I'm flying out of the cab and hitting the wall with a thump.

"Ow!"

I feel Deacon pull me to my feet.

"You've done it, Isabel! Let's get out of here!"

He pulls me through the gap, out of our warehouse prison and into the main store. And the source of all the smoke.

"Stay low to the ground," he coughs. "It'll be easier to breathe."

I'm a little dizzy and confused from the crash and I wouldn't blame him if he left me here for dead. If it were me, I'd think twice about trusting someone I'd just caught trying to start a fire in a warehouse. But he clenches my wrist so tight, it feels like we are handcuffed together.

"You know this place better than I do. Which way?"

"There should be a fire exit to the left," I manage, but the smoke is disorientating. What the hell happened here? How did the place fill with smoke so quickly? And where is everyone? Did they all get out?

My legs are still a little shaky from my exploits with the forklift, but Deacon drags me along and refuses to let me stop or fall behind.

"It should be just along here…"

"Get back!"

"Ahh!"

An involuntary scream erupts from my lungs as a giant ball of fire roars towards us. I scream and scream, and just can't seem to stop. Flames gallop across the paper thin walls, before leaping up to the ceiling and spreading out in an angry sea of orange, right above our heads.

"Quick, where to?"

"This way!"

Neither of us glance back at the fire, but I feel its prickly heat on my back as we race to get out of its deadly path.

Can't. Breathe.

We half-run, half-fall onto the automatic doors at the front of the store.

"It's locked!" Deacon gasps. "Why is it locked? Where is everyone?"

We pound and kick at the glass, but the doors don't show any signs of breaking.

"Let us out!" I scream. "For god's sake, let us out!"

But I can't see a soul. Nobody's out there. Nobody's going to help us.

"There's another way out," I pant. "Up on the roof. Come on, quickly!"

We charge up the static escalators. The smoke seems thicker here, but there's an exit just by the stairs.

"Yes, here! Here it is!"

I push at the door. I'm almost surprised when it gives way at my touch.

"It's opening!"

Deep down, I didn't really think it would. I didn't think there was any way we were getting out. I thought Alicia had seen to that. Pushing all our weight against it, we fall out onto the roof and take greedy great gulps of the night air. The door slams behind us.

We're out!

"I didn't think we were going to make it!" I gasp.

"Me neither!"

"How are we going to get down from here?"

I hadn't realised how high up we are. Everything looks tiny down below. There is a crowd of people milling around, down in the car park, but where's the help? Where's the fire brigade?

"Help!" I yell at the top of my lungs. "Up here! We're trapped."

"They can't hear you."

"Up here!" I yell even louder. "Help!"

Deacon shouts too. We both yell and wave our arms, like we're trying to land a helicopter. But nobody seems to hear us.

Nobody looks up. Instead, the crowd starts to move away. Someone is shepherding them down to the evacuation point at the lower end of the car park. They don't even know we're here.

Deacon's face has lost the deathly white look, and he seems to be back to his usual self; strong, reliable Deacon.

"Don't worry," he says. "It's just a matter of time till the emergency services come and get us. Hey, you're shivering!"

"I can't help it."

I feel his arms fold around me and I don't resist. My legs are like jelly, and I sink down into a sitting position. He sits down with me and keeps his arms wrapped around me, like he's afraid I'll blow away.

"We nearly died in there!"

"I know."

He doesn't ask for explanations, not yet at least, just holds me tight. And despite the fire, despite everything, I feel strangely safe, wrapped in his arms. My eyelids start to flutter, but I don't fight it, just let the sleepy haze wash over me.

"Isabel? Isabel! Wake up!"

I feel myself being shaken, but for a moment, I can't remember where I am.

"Isabel, you have to wake up! The roof's filling with smoke!"

My eyes snap open. Suddenly, I'm alert.

"Fire!"

Toxic fumes stink up the air, billowing out across the night sky. I try to take a breath, but instead my lungs fill with smoke. We are swaddled in a big, grey cloud. And it's hot, unbelievably hot. I don't think I can bear it much longer. I shuffle further forwards, towards the edge of the roof.

"Be careful! You'll fall!"

"I don't think we've got much choice," I say, looking down at all the little ant people below.

"We have to jump!"

20

I hold onto the edge and let my legs dangle precariously over the car park below.

"Don't jump! It's too high."

"But what choice do we have? It's getting so hot."

The panic is returning. The same terrible panic I felt when we were trapped inside. I can't just sit here. I have to do something. *Anything.*

"Please - the fire brigade will be here any moment. There's no way they could miss all this smoke."

But what if they don't get to us in time?

I feel the bile rise in my throat as I edge closer to the brink. I'm not going to die up here. I have to be prepared to do this.

And that's when the bright whirling lights flash through the night, accompanied by the very best sound I've ever heard:

Nee-Naw, Nee-Naw, Nee-Naw.

"Oh god, oh god! They're here!"

We wave our arms in the air, shout with renewed vigour.

"Up here! We're up here!"

"They can't see us!"

Tears steam down my face, not just from the smoke, but also from sheer frustration.

"Why can't they see us?"

Deacon cups his hands over his mouth and shouts for all he's worth:

"Help! We're up on the roof! Heeeeeelp!"

There is a loud cracking sound and Deacon grabs my hand again, as the whole roof shakes.

"What's that? What's happening?"

Then, completely without warning, a ladder reels into sight, and a big brawny fireman reaches out his hand to me.

"It's OK, love. You're going to be fine. You're both going to be fine."

"Oh thank god!"

I cling to him for dear life as he plucks me from the rooftop and helps me onto the ladder. But as I start to make my descent, there is another loud crack from above.

"Deacon?"

"You just get yourself down," the fireman says. "I'll help your friend."

I do as I'm told and climb safely down to the bottom, but all the time, I'm very aware that there are no footsteps above me. I don't look up until I reach the bottom rung. I can't see anything but a cloud of billowing smoke. No Deacon, no fireman.

I barely notice as someone comes up to me and slips a foil blanket around my shoulders.

"Can you move? Good. Please come this way. This area is unsafe."

I step back as loose tiles and other building materials rain down from the roof.

What's happening? Where's Deacon?

"Quick! The roof is collapsing!" One of the firemen shouts. "They'll never get out alive!"

"No!"

I have to do something!

I spring to my feet, hauling myself back up onto the first rung of the ladder, but strong arms pull me back.

"No, it's too dangerous!"

I turn to find myself looking into the disapproving eyes of a fireman.

"Come on, out of the way. We need to make the area safe."

"Is there anything I can do to help?"

"Just stay out of the way. We're doing everything we can."

Instead of helping Deacon, I'm just getting in the way.

I hunch over, seized by another coughing fit. But I am conscious of every second that ticks by.

Where are you?

Suddenly, a cheer goes up around the car park. I look up to see a pair of feet emerging from the cloud. It's the fireman! I hold back my tears as he starts climbing down. For a moment I don't see Deacon, but then he comes into view. His face is black with soot, his hair singed, but he smiles and waves as if he's just been elected mayor. The crowd cheers again, but Deacon looks only at me.

"It's OK now," he whispers, when he reaches me. "We're safe now."

If only it were that simple…

"I need to speak to the police!" I cough, as we are herded away from the burning building. "Please, it's urgent!"

"No, don't try to talk. We have to get you to the hospital."

I open my mouth to speak again, but a paramedic pulls an oxygen mask over my head and it's as much I can do to breathe.

"I need to speak to the police," I say again, as soon as we arrive at the hospital, but nobody seems to be listening. I have trouble keeping my eyes open as Deacon and I are subjected to various tests and x-rays. Amazingly, neither of us is badly burnt, but we are both suffering from the effects of smoke inhalation. I try desperately to stay awake, but there's only so long I can fight the deep sleep my body yearns for.

※

Some hours later, a nurse wakes me.

"You didn't like your lunch?"

"What?" I sit up and rub my eyes. I appear to be on a ward – a private room even? I glance down at the table beside me, where a plate of macaroni sits congealing.

How long has that been there? How long have I been here?

I lean forward and cough. Not my usual smoker's cough, but a really nasty, long, mucousy one.

"Don't worry, that should clear up in a day or two."

"Good." I try to focus my mind. Visions of the fire flash before my eyes. I picture Alicia, sneering, laughing and glance nervously around. Is she here? Or has she gone to ground after her latest stunt? Either way, I'm not going to hang around to find out. Gingerly, I get to my feet and walk down the hall to the communal bathroom. I take a long hot shower, but no matter how much I scrub, I can't get rid of the noxious smell of smoke.

"You're looking much better," the doctor says, once she's examined me. "That sleep must have done you the world of good. I'm happy for you to go home, though you might want to take it easy for a couple of days."

"Thanks."

"Oh, and you've got a visitor waiting outside."

Deacon?

I rush to the door.

But no, it's Kate. I forgot she works at the hospital.

"Oh, Isabel, I just heard! Are you alright?" She rushes over to me and gives me a huge hug.

"I'm fine - I've just been discharged. Have you seen Deacon?"

"I just came from his room. He looks tired, but otherwise OK. He's hoping the doctor's going to discharge him too."

"Thank goodness."

I couldn't live with myself if anything happened to him.

Kate perches on the end of my bed.

"Do you want to talk about it, the fire?"

I look down at my hands. "Oh Kate, it was awful. All the doors were locked and we couldn't get out. I thought we were going to die."

She leans in closer. "But what on earth were you trying to do?"

"What do you mean?"

"Deacon said you were trying to set light to the warehouse. Why on earth would you do such a thing?"

My pulse races at the memory. "I didn't have much choice."

"Why not?"

"Because…because they've got Holly. Oh hell, I have to tell the police!"

I leap up and look around for some clothes, other than the white hospital gown I'm wearing.

"Wait – who's Holly?" Then a flash of recognition crosses her face. "You don't mean the private detective?"

"She's not just a private detective, Kate. I mean, she *is* a private detective, but she's also…" I swallow. "She's also Julio's fiancée and she's been trying to help me. She rang me last night to say she was outside Jody's house, then the next thing I knew, I got a call from Jody herself."

"Jody? You mean the woman who looks like Alicia?"

"I think she's her sister."

"What did she say?"

I remember the conversation word for word. It is as vivid in my memory now, as if it happened just a minute ago. I don't think I will ever forget it. It was the most terrifying conversation of my life…

Jody's voice is cold and flat - completely devoid of human emotion.

"You need to listen very carefully, Isabel. I'm about to give you a set of instructions. If you want to help your friend, you must follow everything to the letter."

"What…what are you talking about?"

"You're going to start a fire at Robertson's tonight."

"You can't expect me to do that! People could get hurt!"

"You'll do it!" she barks. "You'll find a big can of petrol in your locker. Use that. And I need you to transmit live pictures onto the Internet, over your phone, as proof."

"I…I don't even know how to stream live pictures."

"You'll be sent a link, explaining how. Just check your email."

There is no prospect of compromise in her voice. "You have until four AM, or Holly burns."

"But I…"

Before I can say another word, I hear the most sickening scream on the other end of the phone. A sound filled with total terror. It's Holly.

"No! What are you doing to her? Leave her alone!"

But the screams just get louder, more anguished.

"OK, I'll do it!" I say, frantically. "I'll do it! Just let her go."

"As soon as you start the fire."

"Wait - how do I know you'll really let her go?"

"You have my word."

"No, I want proof. I want a picture of her driving away in her car."

"You'll get it. Just as soon as you start the fire."

Kate stares at me, totally open-mouthed. I'm not sure if she believes me, or if she just thinks I'm crazy. Either way, she is kind and sympathetic.

"Do you want me to take you home?"

"No! Take me to the police station."

"Are you sure that's a good idea?"

"I don't have a choice. I have to tell them about Holly."

"OK, just wait a second – I'll grab you some clothes."

She disappears out the door and comes back a couple of minutes later with an old pair of jeans and a jumper. I don't ask her where she got them. I just throw them on and grab my watch from the bedside table.

I am just pulling on my shoes when there is a knock at the door.

"Isabel Anderson?"

"Who is it?"

"It's the police!"

The door swings open as two police officers enter. DS Penney places a firm hand on my shoulder.

"Isabel Anderson, I'm arresting you on suspicion of committing arson at Robertson's Superstore."

"No!"

"You do not have to say anything but it may harm your defence if you do not mention…"

"It's not me you want! You've got the wrong person!" I try to wriggle free, but I feel my arms being pulled behind my back. All the while, Penney continues to rattle off his spiel.

"You've got the wrong person! Tell them, Kate! Holly is in terrible danger. You have to listen to me!"

Penney's partner pushes me forcefully towards the door.

"You can tell us everything down at the station."

I barely notice the stares of other patients as the police frogmarch me out of the hospital. Deep down, I am too consumed with guilt about Holly to care what happens to me. How could I have slept, when I don't even know if she's dead or alive? Vital hours have been lost, hours the police could have used to find her.

❄

The custody sergeant takes my details and we weave our way through the long corridors of Queensbeach Police Station. They lead me to an interview room – the very same one I was in the last time I was here. That same dark, dingy room with no windows and no natural light. All the time we're waiting for the duty solicitor, I am begging them to look for Holly. But I don't think they believe me. I'm not sure they're even listening. They've got their own agenda. I don't get to ask the questions, least of all make any demands.

I am given a cup of water, which I drink in a single gulp - my throat is still raw from the fire. I long for a cigarette to calm my nerves, though I know that's the last thing my body needs. My head aches. Everything aches and oh, how I long to be curled up in bed with Fluffy beside me.

My lawyer arrives - not the woman I had last time, but a bald, freckly man with a ginger beard and glasses. We talk in private for a few minutes and I give him an abridged version of what happened. The more detail I go into, the madder it sounds. He raises his eyebrows but nods and acts like he hears this kind of thing every day.

"I think your best course of action is just to tell the truth," he advises.

I nod my head in agreement. Nervous as I am, I am keen to get it all off my chest.

Penney's colleague presses the record button, and the interview begins.

"I'm DCI Millrose," she introduces herself. "And I think you know DS Penney?"

"Yes."

She waits for me to finish coughing before she continues.

"You have been arrested because you were caught on camera trying to set light to Robertson's Superstore."

I shake my head. "You don't understand. It's not how it looks."

"Isn't it? We pulled this off Ustream."

She places a laptop in front of me and clicks on a video. It's a clip of me about to set light to the warehouse - the clip I filmed myself. I glance at my lawyer. He's doesn't say anything, but I can see he's biting his lip. This does not look good.

Millrose leans forward and presses her point. "If it wasn't for the arrival of your friend at the crucial moment, you would have done it, wouldn't you?"

"But I didn't do it, did I? You can see for yourself. And I didn't have a choice. I told you, they've got Holly."

"And who's Holly?"

"My brother's fiancée. I already told you all this in the car."

"Well, once again for the tape, please. Who is it you say has taken her?"

"Alicia McBride and her sister, Jody."

Penney screws up his forehead. "Your friend Alicia? The same one who recently gave you an alibi?"

I colour at the memory. How stupid was I, accepting Alicia's help?

"She's not my friend. She just pretends to be. She's got some strange vendetta against me - she and her sister."

"And why would that be?"

"I don't know exactly. I think it might have something to do with my brother Julio. Jody used to go out with him – a long time ago. I think…I think she might be the one who started the fire at Rose Cottage. It happened just after Julio broke up with her."

"Let's just stick with the fire at Robertson's for now. Are you saying that you were blackmailed into starting that fire?"

"Yes, except I didn't succeed, as you saw on the tape."

"Why did the place catch fire then? You can't expect us to believe that was a coincidence?"

"No, Alicia must have done it. She must have known I might not go through with it. She might even have sent Deacon the text message that made him come rushing over and catch me in the act."

"So you're saying they blackmailed you into starting a fire, then sabotaged your attempt to do so?"

"Yes. I know it sounds strange, but that's exactly how it happened. It wasn't just about starting a fire. It was about tormenting me."

Millrose shakes her head. "Congratulations, Isabel. I think that's just about the most convoluted story I've ever heard and I've heard a few in my time. Couldn't you come up with anything simpler?"

"But it's the truth! You've got to believe me! I didn't want to hurt anyone. I made sure the place was empty first. And I was going to put it out straight away – as soon as I'd filmed it. But I didn't even get that far. I certainly didn't set any more fires. Why would I? Deacon and I were trapped in the warehouse!" My voice wobbles a little. "We nearly died in there, and I think Alicia and Jody planned it that way. I think they meant to kill us. Or rather, I don't think they cared if we lived or died. It's all the same to them."

Millrose folds her arms in front of her. "I'll tell you why this is so difficult for me to believe, Isabel. First, you made threats, then you were caught on camera trying to set a fire, with the strangest of explanations I've ever heard."

"Threats?" I say, in confusion. "I don't know what you're talking about. I never made any threats!"

"Didn't you? Well, someone rang the police station yesterday to say that there would be a fire at Robertson's. The call was traced to a phone box in the precinct next to the supermarket. We are just checking the CCTV pictures now, but I'm betting we're going to find that it was you."

"But it wasn't a threat! I was trying to warn you!"

"How did you know?" she challenges. "This happened some hours before you were supposedly blackmailed."

"They left a huge can of petrol in my locker. I knew it had to mean something."

"The same can of petrol you were going to use to set fire to the warehouse? How did they know to put it there? How did they know Holly was going to follow Jody home that night? I thought you said it was a spontaneous decision?"

"It was…I…I don't know exactly how they planned it. If it hadn't been Holly they'd kidnapped, maybe it would have been someone else. Julio, or my friend Kate or Rhett… or Deacon. I don't know how their warped minds work."

Penney clears his throat. "There were quite a few fires in Queensbeach last night. Shame you didn't try to warn us about any of the others."

I look at him blankly. "There were?"

Is that why the fire brigade took so long to get to us?

"Yes, in fact, we've had more than our fair share of them over the last few months, wouldn't you say?"

"Well, yes, there do seem to have been quite a number."

"Does the word 'FRY' mean anything to you, Isabel?" Millrose cuts in.

"What?" I sit up sharply.

"You heard me. FRY. F.R.Y. Does it mean anything to you?"

"It…yes. That's the word Alicia has branded onto her back. The word she uses to taunt me. I see it everywhere I go but I have no idea what it actually means."

"Really?"

She places a piece of paper in front of me.

"What's this?"

"Read it."

Puzzled, my eyes scan the page.

I shake my head. "I don't understand."

Millrose leans closer, as though she's about to share an

important secret with me. "This is from the bank statement of a local businessman called Dan Jones. It shows a money transfer from Mr Jones to an organisation called FRY."

She looks me right in the eye as she continues. "For a while, we've suspected that this organisation, FRY, is involved with illegal activities – arson, money laundering and racketeering."

What? Is that why they set the fires? For money?

"But what has all this got to do with me?"

"We've obtained a document from Companies House registry, which names you, Isabel, as the legal owner of FRY."

"What? But I never even knew FRY existed! How could I possibly be the legal owner?"

"Then what's that at the bottom, Isabel?"

"It looks like a signature." I do a double take.

My signature.

"No! That's not my signature. I've never seen this thing before in my life! And besides, if I were really the head of a criminal organisation, I doubt I'd be stupid enough to get it registered in my own name! If anything, I'd open up a secret bank account in the Seychelles or something."

"So you've thought about it then?"

"This is ridiculous!"

"Is it? I bet if we search your house we'll find more evidence. Insurance scams, competition, revenge. Whatever the motive, you'll set the fire for a fee. Isn't that right, Miss Anderson?"

"No!"

21

I glance nervously at my lawyer.

"I don't know any Dan Jones, either. I've never heard of him."

"Dan Jones is the owner of Queensbeach Caravan Park," Millrose says, folding her arms. "But you know that, don't you? You were seen talking to him the day after the caravan park caught fire. I've got witnesses to prove it."

"That was the only time I ever met him! I just went with Alicia to check the damage to her caravan. I felt sorry for her at the time."

Millrose looks sceptical.

"Look - can't you see I'm being set up here? I mean, really. What kind of criminal organisation takes money transfers to start fires?"

"A very profitable one, by the looks of it."

I sigh with frustration. "Why would I want anything to do with this? I've got a proper job."

"Yes, that's right – you're a junior manager at Robertson's, aren't you? How much does that pay? Eighteen - twenty grand?"

"Yes, about that."

"I hear you also have a penchant for expensive designer clothing."

"Well, yes, I like nice clothes. Who doesn't?"

"How are your finances? Have you ever been in debt?"

"No. I mean, not really. I've run up a few credit card bills before but..."

"Do you currently have any credit card debts, Isabel?"

"No."

"How come?"

"I've cut back on my spending recently."

All this stress has been quite good for my bank balance, actually. I haven't had the heart to do much shopping much since Alicia and Jody started to take over my life. In fact, I've managed to save up a surprising amount over the last couple of months – enough to pay off my huge Visa bill, and a bit left over which I've transferred into my savings account.

Penney tries a different tack.

"What does FRY stand for?"

"I really don't know. I told you – I'm being set up!"

Millrose is losing her patience. "Look, this would all go a lot smoother if you'd just cooperate."

I grit my teeth. "That's what I'm trying to do!"

My lawyer clears his throat. "I'd like to speak to Isabel in private, please."

"Go ahead. I think we could all do with a break."

Millrose stops the tape, and she and Penney leave the room, closing the door behind them.

I look at him anxiously. "It looks bad, doesn't it?"

"That depends. You know they're going to search your house?"

"Can they really do that?"

"Yes, they've got a warrant. So if there's any chance they could find something incriminating, you need to tell me now."

"I've already told you – I'm innocent!"

"Then why do you look so worried?"

I twist a loose strand of hair around my finger.

What will they find at my house?

"I wouldn't put it past Alicia to plant something. I've caught her in my house before."

"She broke in?"

"No – my friend gave her a key. I've changed the locks since, but that doesn't mean she hasn't found another way in. Or she could have planted something the last time. That girl's really got it in for me."

He raises his eyebrows.

"I've dealt with these grudge cases before, though none quite as complex as this one. But in my experience, the source of the conflict is usually a man," he glances at me uncertainly – "or a woman. Is there someone the two of you are fighting over?"

"Well, there *is* Deacon," I say slowly, trying not to picture the two of them together. "But I don't think he's the source of the conflict. He's just another pawn in her sick little game. I think this goes way back, to when Julio dumped Jody all those years ago. I can't imagine why she would still want to get revenge, though. Or why she would be taking it out on me."

Penney and Millrose return with cups of tea. I sip mine slowly and try to gauge how much trouble I'm really in.

Millrose looks me straight in the eye. "I'm going to give you one more chance, Isabel. Why don't you tell us what really happened last night? Did you set fire to Robertson's Superstore?"

"No!"

"What about the fire at Queensbeach Caravan Park, or the one at the Waterfront Gym last month?"

"I told you, I didn't start any fires! And anyway - I thought the fire at the gym wasn't started deliberately?"

I look to Penney for confirmation.

"New evidence has come to light. It looks like it might have been arson after all."

Oh hell!

"Look, you have to believe me – none of this has anything to do with me. I haven't started any fires, I swear!"

Millrose crinkles up her plastic cup and tosses it into the bin.

"Perhaps a few hours in the holding cells will change your mind about that?"

"No!" I look at her in horror.

"Unless there's something you want to say?"

"Just that I'm innocent."

"Penney, do you have any more questions?"

"No." He looks at me with disdain. "Let her stew."

Small, dark and disgusting, the cell still reeks of its last inhabitant. It is completely empty, bar for a mattress with a thin blanket on it and a toilet. All those stories you hear about prisoners living in the lap of luxury with PlayStations and televisions must be a load of rubbish. This is the scummiest place I've ever been.

I struggle to calm my nerves.

Instantly, I'm transported back to the scene of the fire. My heart pounds, my chest closes up. I remember the terrifying sensation of smoke seeping into the room, closing my airways.

I've got to get out of here!

I claw desperately at the bars.

"I shouldn't be in here! You've got to let me out!"

A uniformed police officer peers in at me. "Are you OK, love?"

I can't reply. My breaths are coming in slow, desperate gasps.

"First time is it?" he asks, not unsympathetically. "Here, drink some water."

I take the paper cup he offers me and tip the liquid down my throat. It doesn't help. I watch in horror as the word 'FRY' forms in blood-red letters on the wall in front of me. But the police officer's expression remains the same, as if nothing is happening.

I'm the only one who can see it.

I watch with morbid fascination as the blood drips down the walls.

Drip!

Drip!

Drip!

Can't you see that? Can't you smell it?

"Here, have a paper bag."

"What am I supposed to do with this?"

"You breathe into it. It helps you to regulate your breathing."

I do as instructed, for all the good it does. My brain is in overdrive. I'm living and breathing a full-blooded nightmare. I've had too much to take in, too much to process. Alicia is not in my cell. She can't be. And yet the writing is on the wall all the same. I lick my lips. My mouth has that slightly metallic taste - the taste of blood.

This isn't real.

I suck in a bloodcurdling scream, as without warning, the bloody letters burst into flames.

Fire! Fire!

But the police officer, who continues to watch me with interest, doesn't appear to see a thing.

I am not going mad. I'm in shock, I'm tired, and I've been through a traumatic experience.

So why is it so hot?

I feel the warm glow against my body, feel it scorch my skin.

"Please! You've got to let me out!"

"Just keep breathing in and out."

I concentrate on breathing into the bag, inflating and deflating it as I try to stem the panic. To my surprise, it actually helps. The sickness in the pit of my stomach eases and the flaming letters stop dancing around in front of me. I watch as they slide, one by one, to the floor, disappearing in a grey puff of smoke.

"Better?"

"Yes, thanks." I shiver, cold now the flames have gone out. "I think I'd better go and lie down for a bit."

"OK - there's a call button if you need anything."

He turns to leave, presumably to deal with another inmate further down the hall who's been shouting obscenities all the while.

"Don't worry, love – it won't be forever. They can only detain you for 24 hours, then they'll either have to charge you, or let you go."

These words bring little comfort. What if they charge me? What then? Will I have to go to court? And then – the thought explodes in my head – prison?

Is this how I'm going to spend the rest of my life - stuck in a stinking cell, blamed for a crime I didn't commit, for a reason I don't even understand?

I lie down and let my eyelids droop as the world whizzes around me. How did Alicia and Jody plan something so complex, so elaborate? Did they set up a criminal organisation just to frame me? Why go to so much trouble, when I could so easily have died in the fire? Was this their back-up plan, just in case I survived? How could they be so evil, so calculating? What terrible thing did I do to them to make them hate me so much?

❄

I CAST MY MIND BACK, as I've done so many times over the last few months, to that summer at Camp Windylake. I try to remember Alicia and Jody, but there were so many young campers and so many play leaders. I remember there was a group of little girls who were particularly keen on the arts and crafts tent, which I ran. They would hang on every word I said. Some of them even tried to dress like me, clonking around in their big sisters' high heels and carrying little handbags. Kate and I thought it was hilarious at the time. But what if Alicia was one of those little girls? And if so, how did childish adoration turn to such deadly hate?

I try to remember Jody, but I really can't. Julio has had so many girlfriends, each one completely different from the last. At first, I used to try to make friends with them, but after a while I learned not to grow too attached. It would all be over in a matter of weeks, if not days and then he'd be on to the next. It was different with Kate, of course – she was my best friend first and still is – no thanks to my brother.

My thoughts return to my overwhelming guilt about Holly. Despite Kate, despite everything, I can't help liking her. Can't help hoping that against all the odds, things might work out between her and Julio. But how terribly I've failed her! Why couldn't I convince the police she's in trouble? They have the resources to find her. They could trace her car and her phone. They could arrest Alicia and Jody and take them in for questioning. This would all go so differently, if only I had the police on my side.

As my breathing becomes more steady and rhythmic, I am transported back to a time when everything was so much simpler. When I was eighteen and carefree and I worked as a play leader at Camp Windylake.

❄

I AM in the arts and crafts tent, clearing up after a messy day's play, washing down paint-splattered tables and picking dried glue out of my hair, when a small child appears at my side.

"Oh, I didn't see you there!" *I exclaim. I find her sudden presence a little unnerving.*

"Did you want something?" *I prompt, when she says nothing.*

"Are you going to put those in the kiln now?" she asks, pointing at the day's assorted pottery creations.

"Yes, but shouldn't you be getting to dinner?"

"I want to watch."

She looks up at me with eyes as round as saucers as I load the clay into the hot oven. Her face is pallid and ghostly. No wonder the other kids call her Wednesday Adams. In fact, if I'm honest, so do most of the play leaders – just not to her face.

She's a very odd little girl, full of strange ways and tall stories. One time I heard her boasting to the others that she can drink any of them under the table, including the boys. Not a claim that she'd be likely to have to put to the test – she's only ten, after all.

Towards the end of the summer, I ask the children to paint pictures of their families - a task they take up with relish. Wednesday's initial outline is really rather good. She draws her dad, her big brother, her big sister and herself, all smiling and standing in front of a large square house. No mum, I notice - rumour has it, she died in a house fire when Wednesday was just a baby.

But the next time I look, the painting is streaked with red paint – they're all still smiling, but they have red in their hair and on their faces, even their clothes are streaked with red. At first I think she's had an accident with the red paint, but as I watch, she dips the brush in again and adds red streaks to the roof and the windows. This strikes me as rather peculiar but then, the little boy opposite has painted a robotic dog, and his family car appears to be a space rocket. So I just put it down to the children's over active imaginations and tuck it to the back of my mind.

On the last day of camp, Wednesday approaches me with a rather solemn expression on her face.

"Isabel, can I ask you something?"

"Of course," I say, patting the stool next to me for her to sit down. She does not do so. Instead, she fiddles awkwardly with her plastic apron. So I sit there expectantly, waiting to hear what she's got to say. Wondering what kind of yarn she's going to spin.

❄

I am distracted by the sound of keys in the lock. A female police officer throws back the cell door.

"Please come with me."

I try to tune her out, fight to stay in the dream. Except, it doesn't feel like a dream anymore. I'm on the verge of remembering something - something crucial. But it's no use, the police officer's voice cuts right through to my consciousness. I sit up and blink.

Alicia is little Wednesday Adams!

That's why I didn't remember her. I didn't know her as Alicia. Nobody called her by her real name. But what was it she wanted to talk to me about that day at camp? It was something important, I know it was. Oh, why can't I remember?

I get up and follow the police officer.

"Why have I been sent for?" I ask, as she leads me through the maze of corridors. "Have they made a decision?"

"I don't know," she says, striding so fast I struggle to keep up with her. "They just asked me to come and get you."

"Do you think they're going to charge me?"

"I really don't know - I don't know the details of your case."

"You haven't heard anything?"

"No."

Maybe, suggests a tiny voice at the back of my mind, maybe they've realised their mistake? Maybe they're going to let me go?

But the minute I see Penney, any hope I had evaporates. He has a look I can't quite place - self-righteous, smug. He knows something. He thinks he's solved the whole crime. Never mind that the truth doesn't fit.

"It seems your brother reported Holly missing first thing this morning," he tells me.

"So she's still missing?"

Those awful words still ring in my ears,

"You have till four AM, or Holly burns."

"No – we found her half an hour ago."

"You found her!" I resist the urge to throw my arms around him.

"Oh, thank you! Thank you!"

I look round at the sombre faces at the table, troubled that no one appears to share my elation. "Is she…OK?"

Penney looks me straight in the eye.

"You tell me. She was found in your garage."

22

"Is she all right? You have to tell me!"

"She's in a critical condition in hospital."

"Oh god! What…"

"The garage was locked and there were no signs of a break-in. Whoever did this had a key."

"It wasn't me!"

My garage is just a repository for all my junk. I hardly ever go in there. I never even park the car in there. Alicia – or Jody, must have taken the key from my key ring. Is that what Jody was doing on the night of the concert, when she stole my bag and gave it back to me?

I turn to my lawyer for help, but he is busily scribbling notes on the pad in front of him.

"It must have been Jody and Alicia," I insist. "Just ask Holly – she'll tell you."

DCI Millrose folds her arms in front of her.

"Holly's in no position to tell us anything right now. She's sustained a severe head injury."

"Oh, poor Holly!"

"Poor Holly, indeed. We're looking at a very serious assault here, Isabel. Maybe even attempted murder."

I shake my head. "I can't believe they did this just to get at me!"

"So you're saying you had nothing to do with it?"

I stare at Millrose.

"Why would I hurt Holly, let alone try to kill her? She was trying to help me! And she's my brother's fiancée, for heaven's sake."

Millrose curls her lip. "Didn't your brother used to be married to your best friend, Kate?"

"Yes, but…you can't think Kate has anything to do with this!"

"How did you feel when he left Kate for Holly?"

"Well…I…"

"Were you happy about it?"

"Of course not!"

"So how did you feel – annoyed, let down?"

"I felt…sad, for Kate."

And maybe a little guilty, too. He's my brother, after all. I should have known that he's incapable of being faithful and that it was never going to last.

"And what were your feelings towards your brother?"

"Well, of course I was angry, at first."

"Isn't it true you refused to speak to him for several months?"

"Well…yes, but I forgave him eventually. I couldn't stay angry with him forever."

"What made you change your mind?"

"I don't know – he came to see me and I just couldn't stay angry with him anymore. Not when I was faced with him in person. It was one thing to ignore his texts and emails, but I couldn't ignore him when he turned up on my doorstep. I missed him."

"Would you say you get on well with Holly?"

I colour slightly, thinking of the recent past. "I really like Holly. She's great."

"Hmm. But isn't it true that with Holly out of the way, there'd be a chance your brother might get back with Kate?"

"I don't think so."

"But there's a chance?"

"I really don't…"

"Did Kate help you, or were you acting alone?"

"Kate had nothing to do with this!"

"So you were acting alone?"

"No! I wasn't acting…I wasn't…didn't do anything."

I cling to the edge of the table like a limpet.

How do I stop all this craziness?

They're twisting everything I say, everything I've done.

"Please…just talk to Julio. He'll tell you all this is nonsense. He knows I've got no reason to hurt Holly. And he knows what's been happening with Alicia and Jody. He'll back me up."

"Are you OK, Isabel?" My lawyer butts in. "You're awfully pale."

He looks pointedly at Millrose. "I think my client needs a break."

Millrose looks a bit irritated, but she doesn't refuse.

Penney and Millrose get up. As the door shuts behind them, I stare at the cold, blank walls.

"What happens next? When will all this be over?"

My lawyer scratches his beard. "In all likelihood, they'll have to interview Alicia and Jody to get their side of the story."

This news should cheer me up but it doesn't. Alicia is a very, very convincing liar. What if she implicates me further?

My lawyer has no such qualms.

"If they're lying, Millrose will get to the bottom of it. That's what she's trained to do."

I wish I had his confidence.

"In the meantime, it would really help if you could try to

figure out why they started this vendetta. Without motive, it's hard to prove."

"I'm trying." I drain the rest of my drink and scrunch up my paper cup.

I'm sure there's something – stuck in the recesses of my mind, just waiting to be dislodged. If only I could remember. I stare blankly at the wall but it doesn't come to me. My mind's all clogged up with worry and anger and fear.

※

SOME TIME LATER, the door opens to admit Penney and Millrose.

"Are you ready?"

Reluctantly, I nod.

Millrose switches the tape back on.

"We've just spoken to your brother. He says you've been harassing Holly for weeks now. Ringing in the middle of the night and showing up at their house uninvited."

"What?"

"He thinks you need help."

"I don't believe you."

"Here's his statement. Read it for yourself."

I scan the document, reading with disbelief how my own brother has disowned and renounced me. One particular sentence jumps out at me:

'In my opinion, my sister, Isabel Anderson is the one responsible for Holly's assault. Her recent actions have been both bizarre and incongruous. She is clearly in desperate need of professional help.'

"Incongruous?" I snort. "My brother doesn't talk like that! I bet he doesn't even know what it means! Someone's put words in his mouth."

Millrose sits back in her chair. "I can assure you the only people present at his interview were DS Penney and myself."

This makes no sense…

Julio should be on my side. When he saw that picture of Jody, he took me seriously. He and Holly were going to help me figure all this out. They believed me. They both believed me. What changed his mind? *Or should I say, who?*

"He's been coached," I insist. "Blackmailed. They've got to him."

Millrose opens a brown envelope and pulls out two glossy photographs, which she sets on the table in front of me.

"Take a look at these pictures. Take a good look."

It's Holly. Her eyes are closed, her face ashen. She is covered in bandages and hooked up to all kinds of machines. I can't believe how awful she looks, how tortured.

Oh Holly, what have they done to you?

"She was hit over the head with a heavy object – probably the stone statue we found in your garage."

Stone statue? They must be talking about that awful monstrosity Mum sent me for Christmas. I shoved it to the back of the garage so I wouldn't have to look at it. If I had only known it would be used in such an awful way, I would never have taken delivery.

"She also has burns on her feet and legs, as if someone set light to her. See the burn marks here…and here?"

A single tear slides down my cheek.

"It's not pretty, is it?"

I stare at the horrible images.

"How could I possibly have done this?" I ask, trying to pull myself together.

"I was at work when Holly went missing. You can check with my colleagues."

"We have. You were seen leaving the building on several occasions. Where did you go?"

"I…I went to my car a couple of times. And I had a couple of coffee breaks with Jon the security guard. You can ask him."

Except for that one time, when he went to speak to the police patrol car to see if he could find out what was going on.

"And then…well, I was in the warehouse for a while as you know. But surely you have all this on CCTV?"

Penney sits up sharply. "We would," he says and looks at me accusingly. "If *someone* hadn't tampered with the footage."

"You can't possibly think that was me! Why would I do that? That footage would have exonerated me!"

"If you're innocent."

"I *am* innocent." And starting to sound like a broken record.

"What we want to know, Isabel, is who you're working with. You can't have done everything yourself. Not all those fires on the same night."

"No, I couldn't."

"Look, we might be able to offer you a deal here. Just tell us who you're working with. Who else is in your organisation? We need names."

She glances at my lawyer and he looks at me.

"Do you need time to confer?"

"No! I didn't attack anyone. I didn't set any fires, and I'm not 'working' with anyone!"

"Very well then."

Millrose produces a second envelope and pulls out another picture.

"Do you know this man?"

"No." I'm almost afraid to ask. "Who is he?"

"Ben Palmer, local firefighter. He was badly injured three weeks ago, tackling a fire at the Be Beautiful beauty salon just outside Queensbeach. Do you know it?"

I nod, numbly.

That's where I get my hair and nails done.

"We suspect that fire was started on purpose."

She shows me another picture. "And this is Jill Seymour. She and her elderly mother, Ruth, suffered burns in a fire at a greengrocer's in Sandford Dunes last year. That one was also started deliberately. They were lucky to get out alive."

She sets down the photos. "And these might just be the tip of the iceberg. How many fires has FRY started over the years, Isabel?"

"I don't know."

"Take a good, long look at the photos."

"It wasn't me!" I insist. "Can't you see how ludicrous this all is? Check my record – I've never even had so much as a parking ticket! And I hadn't even heard of FRY until I met Alicia. I still don't even know what it stands for!"

I look at Millrose and she looks at me. As adamant as I am that I have done nothing wrong, she is equally convinced of my guilt.

Just when I don't think I can bear any more of these riddles, I am dismissed, banished with my lawyer to another room.

"What do you think they're doing?" I ask, thankful for the reprieve.

"They could be interviewing another witness," he guesses.

"Alicia!" I gasp. The thought of her being just across the hall makes me want to vomit. But she doesn't know I'm in here, does she?

❄

Two hours later, Millrose confirms my worst fear.

"We've just spoken to Alicia McBride."

"Have you let her go? She's a psychopath! She tried to kill me!"

I can feel myself getting hysterical.

Millrose is oblivious to my anxiety. "Alicia had some very interesting things to say. For one, now that she knows the seriousness of the allegations against you, she's retracted the false alibi she gave you before Christmas. She also said that it's you who's been waging a vendetta against her – because you're jealous of her relationship with Deacon Frost."

"But that's not true!"

"Are you jealous, Isabel?"

The colour creeps into my cheeks before I can do anything about it.

"Alicia's only with him to get at me."

"She said she's tried to be your friend, but you've been acting increasingly irrationally. She said she's been avoiding you lately because you've been behaving so oddly."

"Avoiding me!" I burst out. "She hounds me day and night! Lurks outside my house with her sister, watching my every move! And…and…she's the one with the word 'FRY' branded into her back!"

Explain that one, Alicia.

"Yes, that came up. She said you did it."

"What?"

"She said you assaulted her with a branding iron, years back, when she was just a kid at Camp Windylake."

"That's just not true! Why would I do that?"

"She said you tried to recruit her to work for you, and you didn't like it when she said no."

"Recruit her to do what? She was only ten!"

"To break into houses and set light to them. She said you needed a child, someone who could fit through small windows."

"What? That's complete fiction, a fairytale! She always was full of crap!"

And yet, there's something distinctly familiar about this story. I feel like I've heard it before. I think hard, trying to catch the disjointed bits of memory before they go up in smoke. I know there's something in there, hidden away. I feel like Alicia's just given me a clue.

"This was ten years ago, Isabel. Just how long have you been taking money to set fires?"

I shake my head.

"I haven't."

At least, I don't think I have.

What is wrong with me? Am I starting to doubt myself?

A little later, some kind of meal is served, but I can barely look at what's put in front of me. The image of Holly, badly injured and burned sits heavy on my conscience and in my stomach. And what about those other people – the ones who were hurt? They can't possibly have any connection to me. Can they? I have this incredible crushing sensation in my chest, like my insides are caving in. It's not just fear anymore, it's something else. But what? Guilt?

Can I have done this? Can I have broken into houses and set them alight for money? Is it possible I'm so crazy, that I've been leading a double life all along?

No, that's ridiculous!

But if I'm so innocent, then why do I feel so guilty?

A spark of something blazes a trail through my mind. I don't know what it is. The room turns red. I feel as if I am seeing everything through a red-tinted lens, as though I am trapped in Alicia's painting - the one she did when she was ten. Everything looks ghoulish, blood-splattered. Tainted with death and destruction.

This is not real. It can't be…

I squeeze my eyes shut, and when I open them, all the red has gone.

I'm sitting in a different seat now, and there's a custody officer standing in front of me. I realise that something important is happening and yet I struggle to focus. Penney starts speaking, but I hear his words as if I'm not really there, but floating high above them, my brain completely disconnected from my body.

"Isabel Victoria Anderson, you are charged with the abduction and attempted murder of Holly Handsworth, plus multiple counts of arson."

23

And so I languish in prison. Due to the seriousness of the charges against me, I am denied bail and transferred to the notorious Gillmore women's prison; a place I had previously only heard of from newspapers and TV. A place synonymous with riots and serial killers. And if I had imagined myself waiting it out in solitude, maybe getting a little reading done, I'd have been horribly mistaken.

Setting foot in Gillmore is one of the worst things I've ever had to do. Every fibre of my body screams at me to turn around and run, but the place is too heavily guarded. There is no way out.

"I'll be watching you, fire-starter!" jeers one of the prison guards, as I'm herded into the admissions area – a small, confined room with a number of other prisoners. A huge lump builds up in my throat as I realise what's coming:

"We're going to be strip searched!" the woman in front of me hisses. I get the feeling most of them have been here before.

Salt tingles on my tongue.

I will not cry.

The prison guard watches impatiently as I wriggle out of my jumper, T-shirt, jeans and socks.

"And the rest! Come on, don't be shy."

Warily, I undo my bra and fold my arms over my chest.

"We haven't got all day, Princess!"

I let my knickers drop to the floor.

The prison guards have already made up their minds about me. I am every bit a criminal. I do not have the luxury of a cell all to myself as I did at the police station. I have to share. And the truth is, I am terrified of my fellow prisoners, even though most of the ones I come into contact with have yet to be convicted. But they wouldn't be here if they hadn't been accused of some terrible crime, would they? And a little part of me thinks there must be some grain of truth to the allegations against them. There's no smoke without fire – isn't that what they say? And yet, I find myself in the same position, counting down the days until my trial. Wondering if I will ever be vindicated, or if this is just the beginning of a terrible new life.

Gillmore is four hours from Queensbeach – far from everyone I know and love. My heart aches for my home, my friends, for my old comfortable routine, for Fluffy. For much of the time, I am cooped up in my cell, forced to perform the daily rituals of washing, dressing and even using the toilet, in front of a constantly changing stream of cellmates and the ever-watchful eyes of the prison guards, who peep blatantly through the Judas hole. I am allowed out for a short spell in the exercise yard each day, but even this is high risk. I am terrified of who I might encounter.

You see, I am surrounded by broken, damaged people; many of them drug addicts, hungry as vampires for their next fix. Volatile and unstable, these are not the type of people I want to be around. I suppose I make a few friends, but I have no intention of seeing any of them again – if I ever get out, that is. Fights break out daily, usually over the distribution of drugs, but anything can set them off; the slightest gesture, a comment, even an ill-advised glance. A packet of cigarettes is swiped off me the first time I set foot in the yard, but I move on, act like it never happened.

The first few nights, I find it impossible to sleep, but after that I get used to it – the constant banging on the bars, the yells, the shrieks and the moans. It all seems to blend into the background. It becomes almost…normal. Prison cures my insomnia. I suppose that's the one good thing to come out of all this.

❄

One day, I'm standing in the lunch queue, waiting for pudding to be slopped onto my tray, when the inmate next to me suddenly turns on the woman serving:

"What are you looking at, bitch?"

I jump back quickly as she flings scorching hot coffee in her face. My reflexes are sharp these days. They have to be. The woman screams in agony. I feel sorry for her, but I leave it to the prison officers to cart her off to the healthcare wing. I do not want to get involved.

"Hey, Princess!" calls Patty, the prison officer who singled me out when I arrived. "Did you see what happened?"

"No."

Patty is always on my back, wanting me to tell her who did what to whom. But I'm no snitch. I keep myself to myself and keep my nose out of other people's business.

"You think you're better than everyone else, don't you, Princess?"

"No."

But deep down, maybe I do.

The only time I can really relax is when I'm with my lawyer, churning over the facts of my case. But in my third week at Gillmore, the man who comes to see me is not the lawyer I was assigned.

"Isabel?"

"Yes. Who are you?"

"Brian Crawford. I'm your new lawyer."

"I can't afford a new lawyer!"

Not one who wears this season's Gucci suits, anyway.

Actually, he looks kind of familiar. I think I saw him on TV a few weeks ago, defending a politician who everyone said was guilty as sin. If I remember rightly, I think he won.

"You're not to worry about the cost," Brian says, opening his briefcase.

"Your friend's going to take care of that."

"What friend?"

I only have one friend who could possibly afford a swanky new lawyer - Deacon.

Can I let him do this?

I swallow. I've always prided myself on my independence. I'm not the sort of woman who likes to think of herself as 'kept' in any way. I'm not even comfortable with letting a man pay for my dinner, unless I'm planning on returning the favour. And yet…

Can I afford not to?

With the odds stacked against me as they are, there's a very strong chance I will go to jail for a long time. The man sitting opposite me is probably my only chance of freedom, or, at the very least, a lighter sentence. Like it or not, I don't have much choice but to accept.

Brian is meticulous in his search for the facts. It's quite exhausting, going over everything, again and again.

"I already explained all this to the other lawyer," I say, as he quizzes me about the fire at Robertson's again. "Didn't he give you his notes?"

"I know it's a pain, but I need to hear it from you. I need to be sure he asked all the right questions. There might be something he missed. I need every little detail, no matter how tiny. In a case like this, we need to be extremely thorough."

Throughout it all, my main hope is that Holly will come round and tell everyone that this has all been a terrible mistake - that I'm innocent and they should let me go. But poor Holly lies in a coma, stuck in the passageway between life and death. The more time passes, the more unlikely it becomes that she will ever recover.

"Is there any news of Holly?" I ask, each time I see Brian.

But the answer is always the same.

"Sorry, no change."

❄

I STEEL myself as a prison officer walks up to me at the end of lunch one afternoon.

"You've got a visitor."

A visitor?

I've been so alone, so disconnected that I was beginning to think the whole world had forgotten about me. I'm sure my friends would have liked to come and see me, but it's such a long drive from Queensbeach and they'd have to take a day off work.

The prison officer escorts me down to the visitor's area, leaving me with Patty, who lingers longer than strictly necessary over the mandatory checks and searches. I glance anxiously at the clock on the wall.

Come on! Visiting time is almost over…

But Patty takes a sadistic delight in holding me up. By the time I am allowed to step into the visitor's room, there are only 20 minutes left. Still, I can't wait to find out who's waiting for me:

"Deacon!"

It's the first time I've seen him since the night of the fire. It seems unnatural not to run up and hug him, but the prison rules keep us at a platonic distance. He returns my smile but looks distracted, like his mind is on many other things. His demeanour betrays little emotion. He is brisk and businesslike as he goes over my case, my options, and my chances. He doesn't talk about us and he certainly doesn't talk about Alicia. I'm going to have to be the one to ask.

"Have you seen her?"

"No. She was gone when I came home from the hospital. Rhett didn't even see her leave."

"Do you think she'll come back?"

"Don't worry about that right now. We have to concentrate on getting you out of here."

"But what if she comes back? She could set light to the house, or…or…anything!"

I must have raised my voice a bit too much, because the people at the next table turn round to stare.

"Don't worry about me, Isabel. I can look after myself."

You can't fool me. I know you're scared. We both are. Alicia could come back any time.

I long to reach out and squeeze his hand, but I'm not sure I'm allowed. I'm also not sure how he'd respond. I couldn't bear it if he rejected me. Not here. Not now. Not when I need every ounce of my strength just to survive.

After Deacon's visit, I begin to get a few more. Kate, Rhett and Sonya all visit over the next few months. They barely mention the case at all but I find it hard to relate to their idle gossip. I suppose they are trying to keep my spirits up, but never once do they say: "I know you're innocent." Never once do they imply Alicia's guilt. And if my friends think I'm guilty, how on earth can I expect anyone else to believe me?

I sink into a deep despair, don't even care when a nasty prison officer pours gravy in my yoghurt, or when other inmates nick all my chocolate and cigarettes.

Then, just as I'm beginning to think all hope is lost, I

receive a phone call from Brian and finally get the news I've been waiting for.

"Holly's awake!"

I nearly drop the phone.

"Is she going to be OK?"

"Too soon to tell."

❄

As the days pass, news filters through that she's getting better. Not her memory though, apparently. She still doesn't remember what happened.

Or doesn't want to remember.

"But her memory could come back at any time, couldn't it?" I ask Brian, hopefully.

"It's possible. We'll just have to wait and see."

He sounds just like my Mum did when I wanted something when I was a kid. Never an outright 'no', always a vague, indistinct answer — as if she hoped I'd just forget it.

I'm screwed, aren't I?

Even if Holly does remember, that doesn't mean she's going to tell. If Alicia and Jody can turn my own brother against me, they can easily turn Holly. She is not going to be my ticket out of here. No one is.

My cellmate, Rachel, is undergoing a harsh process of detoxification. It's not fun for anyone. There's a lot of moaning and vomiting. The smell is enough to make me want to be sick too, so I keep right out of her way. I spend most of my time lying on my bed, staring up at the ceiling, trying to work out how my life took such a rapid nosedive.

But it's not just the other inmates I'm scared of. It's her… Alicia. I get glimpses of her every now and then — a curly head at the other end of the exercise yard; dark, smouldering eyes in the queue for breakfast. Even the little doe-eyed girl in the visitor room. She is everywhere. I never get a moment's peace. Not even here.

And although I sleep more deeply these days, I dream badly. My dreams are littered with cryptic memories:

I turn around urgently, looking for Wednesday Adams.

"You were going to tell me something," I beg her. "Something important."

She looks at me, derision in her face. Suddenly, she is not little Wednesday anymore. She is grown-up Alicia. And her eyes blaze with fire.

"You had your chance and you blew it. Now I'm taking matters into my own hands."

"No, don't! Come back and talk to me. I promise this time I'll take you seriously. I promise I'll listen."

She fixes me with a terrible scowl. "It's too late now. The damage is already done."

And she spins on her heel and storms off.

❋

THE LONG MONTHS I spend at Gillmore might as well be years, or decades even. I have gone from outright panic to gloomy acceptance of my fate. This is where I belong now. This is my home.

The night before my trial, Rachel is carted off to the healthcare wing so I have the whole place to myself for once. A little quiet before the storm. Before I climb into bed, I do something I can't really explain. I get down on my hands and knees and pray to a god I don't believe in. Pray that I will be spared from this life of misery and torment. Pray for a sign that everything will be all right. My prayers are met with the banging of cell bars and the abrupt descent of darkness - lights out.

I lie down but I can't get comfortable. I fumble under my

pillow. It feels like there's a rock under there. My hands close around something cold and hard.

A mobile phone.

Mobiles are strictly forbidden in Gillmore. Either someone is trying to get me in trouble or they want to get in touch with me. I stare, stupefied, as the display lights up. It's ringing.

"Hello?" I whisper, grateful for the nosy wailings of my neighbours in the next cell. I really can't get caught doing this. Not on the eve of my trial. And yet something compels me to continue.

"You really don't remember, do you?" says the voice in the darkness.

"No."

I hear an elongated sigh.

"I had hoped you would by now. Lord knows I've done my best to jog your memory."

"I know you have."

"I came to you in confidence and told you my deepest, darkest secret. I risked everything to tell you. I looked up to you. I thought you would help me."

"You were ten years old. Just a kid…"

"Yes, I was just a kid. But you were an adult. You were supposed to do the right thing."

"I…"

"Instead, you laughed in my face. Told me not to be so dramatic. Then you repeated everything to my dad, as an amusing story on Parents' Day."

"That's all I thought it was."

"You could have looked into it. You could have checked the facts. He burned me that night, you know. Branded that word into me as punishment for telling you. Burned it into me."

"I… I didn't know…"

"You didn't try. It's a terrible thing, to not be believed, Isabel."

"I know. I know that now."

"And I'm never going to let you forget."

I flush the phone down the toilet. The hours tick slowly by till morning, a long, arduous journey into my personal day of reckoning. The day I've waited for, for so long now. My chance to prove my innocence - to finally get out. But it doesn't feel as I thought it would. There is no sudden burst of adrenaline. No flicker of hope. Just resignation and reconciliation to my fate.

❄

"Ah, Isabel. How are you feeling?" asks Brian, at our final meeting before the trial. His breath smells faintly of the espresso he had at breakfast. "I hope you managed to get some sleep? I just wanted to go over a few things before we go in."

Without thinking, I put my hand up to stop him.

"Brian, wait. I've changed my mind. I want to plead guilty."

24

Brian looks absolutely stunned. "What are you talking about? You can't plead guilty. You didn't do it!"

I look down at the ground. "I'm just not sure it's worth the fight."

"What?"

His face turns a peculiar shade of purple.

It isn't me he's concerned about. It's his track record – his career. Am I supposed to feel sorry for him?

"I just don't have the energy. What's the point when I'm going to be found guilty anyway? Because I will. She'll see to that."

Brian grits his teeth. "I don't take cases I can't win," he says vehemently. "I told you that at the start."

"Yeah, but I don't think you fully appreciate what you're up against."

"We've been over and over this. I get the picture."

I shake my head. "I'm not sure you do. Don't you understand? Alicia can get to anyone. If my own brother won't even back me up then what hope have I got? I might as well admit defeat. Get a lighter sentence."

Brian looks like he's about to explode. "Will you let me do my job?" he spits. "I *can* do this Isabel. We don't have to prove you're innocent. We just have to cast a shadow of doubt. No jury will convict you if they're not convinced."

He makes it sound so easy.

"But what about Alicia and Jody?"

"Just trust me. I know what I'm doing."

I rest my head in my hands.

What if he's right?

If anyone can defeat them, it's Brian. He's one of the top lawyers in the country.

But what if that's not enough?

"It's worth a try, isn't it?"

"OK," I finally submit. "Let's see what you can do."

❆

IN MY DREAMS, I pictured this moment many times. I imagined the crowd of waiting paparazzi. I felt my muscles tense as they zeroed in on me with their telephoto lenses and thrust their microphones in my face. But in reality, the security guards escort me through the back entrance and lead me quietly inside. I am almost disappointed.

This is the most important day of my life! Doesn't anybody care?

The courtroom itself seems smaller than they look on TV. I had assumed I was going to be sitting with Brian, but instead, I am seated in a semi-partitioned area at the back, with a custody officer for company. I spot Millrose, sitting importantly beside the prosecution lawyer. It takes me a moment to place her. It seems so long ago since I sat in her interview room, watching my life unravel.

I sense people watching me from the public viewing area behind. It is an uncomfortable feeling – one that's grown all too familiar. Nervously, I glance round to see who's there.

Kate and Rhett smile back broadly - a little too broadly while Deacon sits like a stone beside them, his shoulders stiff as boards. Our eyes meet, but his expression is grim. He's under no illusions – this is going to be tough.

During the long, agonising wait, I worry incessantly about the safety procedures for the building. Visitors have to go through a metal detector, but what about matches? Flints? Sticks? Alicia can start a fire from anything. Anywhere. I've seen her.

"Court rise."

A deferential hush falls over the courtroom as the door opens. Judge Bagshott is a walking skeleton. His feet barely touch the floor as he sweeps into the courtroom, tall and imposing in his wig and gown. He barely even looks my way as he sits down and begins to wade through the proceedings.

This is all so surreal.

I bite my lip as the prosecution lawyer begins to set out his case. He paints me as this awful, callous person who sets fires for both pleasure and profit and says that I attacked Holly because she's not the girlfriend I wanted for my brother. I glance nervously at the jury and twelve suspicious pairs of eyes meet mine.

They've already made up their minds.

I know I should be listening intently to the proceedings, hanging on every word that will decide my fate, but instead I find myself thinking of ten-year-old Alicia again. Now that she has jogged my memory, it is all coming back to me in big, nauseous waves. I remember a teenage Jody, sullen and weak-willed. She was a bit of a weirdo. A loner - with a suspected drug and alcohol problem. But no one reported her, or asked if she was OK. We didn't think it was our place. In fact, the only person who noticed her at all was Julio, and he soon lost interest once the next pretty girl caught his eye.

But what about Alicia, disturbed little Alicia? Looking back, of course there were signs, clues that something wasn't right; the strange little scorch marks on her clothing, the smoky smell that permeated her hair. No one ever saw her play with fire, but we all knew she did.

※

"They make me climb into people's houses in the middle of the night," she told me, that fateful day.

"To rob them?"

"No, to burn them down."

"Really?" I raised my eyebrows sceptically. She could tell I didn't believe her.

You see, I'd met Alicia's father and older brother when she and Jody arrived at camp. They'd seemed warm and friendly, full of amusing banter. I quite fancied the brother, actually. He had curly black hair and smelled of musky aftershave. So it was for his benefit, rather than the dad's, that I recounted Alicia's tall tale at Parents' Day, but both laughed it up a storm. I had no reason to believe they were not who they seemed to be. No reason to think anything sinister.

※

As I sit, trembling in the dock, Alicia's pitiful little voice rings in my ears:

"Please don't make me go home, Isabel. I can't – I just can't!"

But I just thought she was making excuses. Everybody loved Camp Windylake. No one wanted the summer to be over.

Why go after me? I wonder. Why not the father? The brother? My crime seems so small by comparison.

A familiar figure slips into the public gallery.

It's Julio. He came.

I force myself to focus on what's happening. The first witness is making her way to the stand.

Oh god, it's Holly.

She looks awful – thin and pale, with a long scar that runs all the way down her temple. I plead with my eyes, but she looks away. Flinches when she accidentally glances in my direction, as if I'm too painful to look at. I look back at Julio again, but he has eyes only for Holly.

He's not here for me.

And with this crushing realisation, I sink a little lower.

The prosecution lawyer asks Holly what kind of relationship she had with me, prior to the assault.

I watch as she takes a deep breath.

"She never liked me. I could tell."

That's not true!

"She would act friendly when Julio was around, but as soon as he left the room, it was another story."

"What?"

The whole courtroom turns round to stare at me. I hadn't meant to speak out loud; I was just so shocked by Holly's deceit. The judge transfixes me with his glare and puts his twiggy finger to his lips. He might as well put a gun to my head. I am mute, gagged, unable to say anything as Holly continues to run down my character.

"Can you give me an example?"

"Yes, when Isabel came for Christmas, I thought we were all having a lovely time, but when Julio left the room, she leaned over to me and said:

'You need to break it off with Julio…before you get hurt.' It was the way she said it that got to me. Her voice sounded really chilling. It sounded like…a threat."

It wasn't like that at all – those weren't even the words I used. I only asked her if she was sure she knew what she was doing. There was nothing sinister about it at all. I was only looking out for Holly!

How can she do this to me?

"Can you tell us what happened on the night you were attacked?"

"Yes – I finished work late and I was just about to go home when I got an abusive phone call from Isabel. I'd been getting a lot of those in the weeks before the attack. Usually, I just ignored them, but I'd had enough. I decided to go over to her house and have it out with her once and for all."

"Do you remember what happened next?"

"Yes – I arrived at her house about midnight, but I didn't go in straight away. I started to have second thoughts. I wasn't even sure she would still be up, although I could see a light on."

"But you did go in?"

"Yes. The curtain twitched and I realised she must have seen me. It's all a bit of a blur after that. I remember sitting in her living room, talking and drinking coffee, and it was all quite civilised, except I was getting awfully sleepy. Then Isabel said she had a box of Julio's things in the garage, and could I give them to him? I said I'd go with her to get it, but that's all I can remember."

I cover my mouth with my hand. Why not finish the job? Why not go all out and say that I was the one who attacked her? That's clearly what she's implying. But Holly hasn't done that. She's left that little, niggling room for doubt. That's the way Alicia likes it. She knows it's the not knowing that drives me crazy.

But worse is still to come. Julio is called to the stand.

"Isabel Anderson is your sister?"

Julio wrinkles up his face, as if he's just swallowed a spider.

"Half-sister, yes."

It's like he's ashamed of me!

"How did she react when you started going out with her best friend, Kate?"

"Delighted – she was over the moon."

"And when you married her?"

"So excited. She helped organise the whole thing. You'd think she was the one getting married."

"So how did she take it when you broke up?"

"Not well at all. She didn't speak to me for several months."

"Would you say it affected her badly?"

He clears his throat. "She was devastated."

"And when did she start speaking to you again?"

"When I invited her over for Christmas. I wanted her to meet Holly and see that I was serious about her."

"How did Isabel react when she met Holly?"

Julio shifts uncomfortably. "I thought she liked her at first but…"

"Go on."

"Then she started hounding her, ringing her up at all times of the day and night. She wanted Holly out of my life," he pauses dramatically. "At any cost."

My jaw drops open. *The lying toad!*

"How far do you think she was willing to go to achieve this?"

Julio gestures towards poor, damaged Holly.

"See for yourself."

❋

As time goes by, the audience in the public gallery dwindles. Most days it's just me, slumped, semi-comatose in my chair as the lawyers argue over the finer details. And each night I return to my cramped, squalid, little cell, the events of the day replaying in my head, as my cellmates snore.

Kate is cross-examined about the prosecution's theory that I did this to get her back with Julio. To me, the theory seems ludicrous, and yet, when I look over at the jury, they all look thoughtful and solemn-faced. But Kate is the only person who will admit to seeing Holly at the reunion. None of the other ex-campers will testify, and the bar staff all claim not to remember. How on earth can Brian prove my innocence when so many people are willing to lie?

"I'd like to call my next witness – Alicia McBride."

Just hearing her name makes me quiver. I watch nervously as she places her hand over the Holy Bible. This is the first time I've seen her in months.

My hands make involuntary fists. I don't know how to hold in my hatred. I long to leap over the dock and pummel her to a pulp.

You don't know how close I've come to losing my mind.

I stare at her with intense hatred, revulsion even.

I hate you Alicia McBride! I wish you were dead.

I've built her up to be so much bigger in my mind, but here she is, looking sweet and innocuous as she stumbles her way through the oath. The prosecution lawyer begins to question her and her high-pitched voice breaks as she says the very words I ought to be saying:

"I don't know why she's saying these things about me. I don't know what I did wrong."

She glances fearfully in my direction and tears trickle down her cheeks.

"Take your time," he tells her, softly.

I squirm in my seat. The prosecution must think Christmas has come early. Alicia is too convincing, too conniving. The entire courtroom is under her spell. I see one of the jurors reach up and pat her eye with a hanky.

I don't believe it. Is that a tear?

I try to catch Brian's eye, but he is focused on the next witness, who is already making her way to the stand. My heart beats a little faster as I catch my first proper glimpse of her. The likeness is uncanny. So much like Alicia, only more weather-beaten and wrinkled. She pauses a moment and looks guiltily in my direction. I look deep into her eyes, but it's not there, the wickedness that lurks beneath. Finally, I know for certain. She isn't the one. It really is Alicia who is behind all this. Jody is just too weak, too pathetic to refuse to do her bidding.

The prosecution lawyer questions Jody about her whereabouts on the night of Holly's attack but she lies through her teeth. She admits going to the reunion, but as an ex-camper, there is nothing really incriminating about this. She denies seeing Holly there, denies ever having met her. The way she tells it, she just finished her lemonade and went home to bed.

But she isn't Alicia. Is there a chance the jury won't believe her?

Finally it's Brian's turn to speak up for me. He puts on a good show, but I can tell he's lost some of his usual confidence. After questioning me in detail, he calls Deacon to the stand. I hadn't even known he was going to testify. If Deacon is feeling nervous, he shows no sign of it. His tone is confident and straightforward as he answers Brian's questions:

"Where was Alicia McBride staying on the night in question?"

"At my house."

"And do you know what time she went to bed?"

"Yes – around half past midnight."

"And do you know if she remained in her room for the rest of the night?"

"She did not."

I sit up straight.

What?

"How do you know?"

"Because I looked in on her later and she was gone."

"Do you know what time that was?"

"Yes – it was a quarter past two in the morning. I know because I'd just got a text which I thought was from Isabel, asking me to meet her at Robertson's."

Why has he never mentioned this before? Unless...unless he's made it up. I watch him closely.

He has! He's lying under oath!

My heart swells.

I can't believe he lied for me!

The prosecution lawyer is quick to jump on him, though.

"Could she have been elsewhere in the house?"

"I don't think so – she wasn't in the en suite and there was no one in the lounge or kitchen when I left the house."

"But it is a big house, isn't it? Is it possible you missed her?"

"It's possible, but I don't think so."

I brace myself as Brian calls his final witness – my neighbour, Mr Krinkle. Neville, apparently. Funny, I had never thought of him as having a first name before. I chew on a jagged thumbnail. My previously manicured hands are now rough and calloused, my nails brittle and broken. I work intently on the nail. I can't watch. Everything hinges on his testimony.

"Did you see anything unusual in the early hours of February 27th, the night Holly was attacked?"

"Yes, I did."

"What did you see?"

Mr Krinkle straightens his tie.

"I saw a blue Honda pull up outside Isabel's house, just after midnight."

"Did you see who was driving?"

"No."

"Did you see anyone get out?"

"No, he – or she - just sat there."

"How long were they there?"

"Quite a while, at least quarter of an hour."

"And then what happened?"

"I don't know. I fell asleep."

"What time did you wake up?"

"About two in the morning. There was a noise."

"What sort of noise?"

"A terrible moan. It didn't sound human. I thought it was a fox."

"Did you see anything else?"

"Yes. I saw someone leaving Isabel's house."

"And was it your neighbour, Isabel Anderson?"

"No, it was not."

"Did you see where this person went?"

"Yes. They got into a car and drove off. Not the Honda, but another car parked further up the street. A white one. I didn't see what make."

"Did you notice anything else?"

"Yes. They drove off at quite a speed, as if they were in a hurry to get somewhere."

"Or away from somewhere?"

"Yes."

The prosecution lawyer steps up. "You said you couldn't see this person clearly?"

"No, it was dark."

"Then what makes you so sure it wasn't Miss Anderson?"

Mr Krinkle frowns. "Isabel is tall, with an average build. This person was small and slight – almost like a child. And she had a different walk. It was…I don't know – daintier."

It was Jody, I know it was. If only the police had been able to find her DNA at my house.

I still struggle to get my head around what must have happened. Holly had never been to my house before, so when she thought she was following Jody home from the reunion, she must have actually been following her to my house. Jody must have had a key to the front door. She walked right in, as if she owned the place. She led Holly into a trap. I don't know exactly what happened next. Maybe Holly decided to get out of the car and have a snoop, or maybe Jody went and got her, but somehow, Holly ended up injured and unconscious in my garage.

※

AND SO THE proceedings draw to a close. As Judge Bagshott sums up the case, I struggle to take in what he's saying. Despite sitting through the entire trial, day in, day out, I feel like I'm hearing it all for the first time.

"I think we've done enough," Brian says, as the jury goes to deliberate.

But I've come to know him well enough to know when he's putting on a brave face. Outwardly, his confidence has increased as the days have gone by, but there have been telltale signs to the contrary – the sweat he keeps mopping from his brow, the heavy bags that have appeared under his eyes. These are not the signs of a confident man.

Waiting is the worst kind of torture. The jury does not reach a verdict that afternoon, or the next. I take a deep breath and let the air gush through my lungs. When will it all be over? Will it ever be over?

Then, finally, just when I think I can't bear it another minute, the court reconvenes.

"Has the jury reached its verdict?"

"It has."

25

"On the count of the abduction and attempted murder of Holly Handsworth, we find the defendant, Isabel Anderson, not guilty."

I jerk my head up. Have I heard right?

"On multiple counts of arson, we find the defendant not guilty."

Somebody gasps. I think it might be me.

Not guilty, not guilty, not guilty.

"I'm…free to leave?"

I can't believe it.

Judge Bagshott is still talking but I don't hear a single word. It's over. It's all over. I just want to get out. I try to step out of the dock, but the ground below me tilts 90 degrees. I half-walk, half-stumble towards the door.

"Isabel?"

Strong arms reach out to steady me.

"I'm free. I'm finally free!" I bury myself in Deacon's chest.

He looks as shocked as I feel.

"You really didn't think this was going to happen, did you?" I whisper.

"No. I was all set to appeal."

But for once, God is smiling on me.

For no reason at all, I laugh. People turn to stare, probably wonder if I'm crazy after all, but I can't help it. This is the first time I've laughed in months. The first time I've had something to laugh about.

"What's so funny?" Deacon asks, as I catch my breath.

"I think it's just the immense relief," I gasp.

"You OK now?"

I nod. "Get me out of here!"

The need to get out is suddenly overwhelming. I am terrified that if I don't get out immediately, the decision will somehow be reversed and I'll be thrown back into prison. Deacon understands my urgency. Taking me by the arm, he leads me through the open doorway.

Not a second too soon. A line of fire soars through the air and a loud bang echoes around the chamber. Order descends into chaos as people scream and panic to get out.

"Keep going," Deacon hisses.

"What's happening?"

"Someone's let off a load of fireworks."

I look back, alarmed to see a rocket erupt from under the very seat where I was just sitting. It explodes in a hissing shower of sparks that would be very pretty in the cool, night sky, but here, in this enclosed space, is downright dangerous.

"Come on, let's get out of here. Let the police handle it."

He pulls me towards the exit and we both shake the sparks from our hair and clothes.

"You alright?"

"I think so."

I can't help but take one more look back into the chamber. Amidst all the chaos, someone is being handcuffed, I can't make out who. Alicia wouldn't be stupid enough to do it herself, would she? No, she'd have a lackey. She always has a lackey.

❄

Cameras flash in my face as Deacon guides me past the waiting press. I shield my face, not wanting to look at them, let alone talk to them. Moments later, Brian appears and jubilantly announces that he'll be making a short statement on my behalf. I smile slightly as the crowd diverts its gaze to him. Let him enjoy his moment in the spotlight. He deserves it.

Deacon's car is parked round the corner. I heave a huge sigh as I climb in and shut the door behind me.

"Congratulations!" Rhett and Kate yell, as they clamber into the backseat. I know I should be pleased to see them, but I haven't got the energy to respond. I smile weakly.

Deacon starts the car. "You OK?"

I nod, but I'm not really. Now that the initial burst of elation has died down, I feel deflated. My life as I knew it is over. It can never be the same - not after so many months in prison. I have lost so much time – an entire spring and summer that I will never get back. More than that, I've lost a part of me.

Deacon wakes me as we approach the lights of Queensbeach.

"Where to? You want to go home?"

"Can we go back to yours?" I ask, sleepily.

"I'll cook something special to celebrate," Rhett offers from the back. "What do you fancy? Toad-in-the-hole? Lancashire hotpot?"

"Anything," I smile sleepily. "Just as long as you make it."

Another person in my situation might have indulged in elaborate fantasies of what they'd do when they got out. Where they would go, what they would do, who they would spend that first special evening with. But not me. When I was in jail, I couldn't allow my mind to wander that far – to believe I could actually be set free. And there is still Alicia to think about. Where is she now? And what is she planning next?

As we drive past Robertson's, I can't help noticing that the place has been completely repainted. And in place of the giant 'R' on the roof, there is now a happy squirrel.

"Robertson's changed hands?" I say, in disbelief. "Sonya never said a thing!"

"Yeah, Filbert's bought it after the fire. Apparently Robertson's wasn't properly covered by their insurance."

So someone did benefit from the fire! Does that mean someone paid Alicia to start it? Was it Bernie? A slight prickle runs down my spine. Did he also pay her to set fire to his car? Bile builds in my mouth, and I turn my head in the other direction, just in time to see the sea, glimmering and green.

I watch as the last fishing boat of the day chugs in. The sea tosses it this way and that before allowing it into the safety of the harbour. But it could just as easily have dashed it against the rocks. The sea is unpredictable like that.

Rhett is as good as his word and cooks up a storm. I sit round the table with my friends, eating chicken and potatoes and glugging wine, just like the old days. We talk about all the things I've missed while I've been away. Apparently, the police swarmed on Mustafa a few weeks ago and tried to deport him, but he was back at work a couple of days later.

"The man must have a really good lawyer," Deacon says, serving me another helping of potatoes.

I don't bring up my own strange history with Mustafa. I haven't got the strength. And we don't discuss where I've been, either. I'm not ready to, not yet. You could be forgiven for thinking I'd been on an extended holiday as we all adjourn to the lounge to watch Eastenders.

Or you would, if it weren't for that damn knock at the door.

Rhett answers it.

"Isabel, it's for you."

I sit up in alarm.

Who knows I'm here?

"Relax, it's just Julio."

"Oh."

Reluctantly, I make my way to the door.

"I thought I'd find you here. I wanted to tell you... I wanted to apologise..."

I fold my arms. "I'm not interested."

"But if you'd just give me a moment to explain…"

"I don't have a moment," I spit. "I have just spent 8 months in prison. I can't stand here and listen to your bullshit. I don't have time."

I try to shut the door, but he sticks his foot in the way.

"Alicia threatened to kill you," he blurts out. "That's why I…we said what we said. You've seen what they did to Holly. I couldn't let them do that to you too."

I bite my lip. My anger is a rabid dog. I am in no mood for reconciliation.

"I think you'd better come in," says a voice from behind me.

I look round in astonishment. Deacon, who has never liked my brother and never tried to hide it, ushers him inside.

Julio sticks his hands in his pockets as he follows him down the hall. We go into the lounge and sit down. I am too numb to think straight. It is not the time for explanations and forgiveness, not on the night of my release. And yet, here is Julio, desperate to get this off his chest.

Just when I think things couldn't get more uncomfortable, Kate appears.

"Hi Julio."

"Er…hi…"

I look from one to the other and realise that this is the first time they've met since the divorce.

"Would you like a cup of coffee?" Kate offers. "Rhett's just made some."

"Um…OK. Thanks."

"You still take it with two sugars?"

"Yeah."

Julio's hand shakes slightly as he holds his coffee, causing it to drip down his arm and onto his jeans. There is a box of tissues on the table but I say nothing.

I've heard that his wedding has been postponed. The official story is that Holly needs more time to recover, but I can't help wondering if she's having second thoughts. I wouldn't blame her if she wanted to put as much distance between herself and our family as possible.

Julio is here to unburden himself. He tells of his panic when Holly failed to come home that night and his horror, when the police called to say they had found her.

"How is Holly now?"

"Physically, she's on the mend, but it will take her a while to get over the trauma. Especially after Alicia paid us a visit and told us what to say in court. Holly thought we should go to the police, but I wouldn't let her risk it. We both knew she meant business."

I know he's expecting my sympathy, but I'm not sure I can give it. It's not that I don't care about what happened to Holly – of course, I do but I wouldn't have got through the last 8 months if I hadn't hardened my heart just a bit and it's not that easy to undo. Not overnight, anyway.

Deacon excuses himself to take a phone call, and Rhett and Kate busy themselves, clearing the table, leaving Julio to my mercy.

"Why didn't you warn me, tell me what was going on?"

"I was scared of what she might do."

"Don't you think I was scared, locked up in a cell all that time, not knowing if I was ever going to get out?"

"I said I was sorry."

"Well, sorry isn't good enough. Not by a long way."

"Isabel…"

"You're not going to believe this!" Deacon bursts in, before I can release the full torrent of my anger.

"What?"

"That was Brian on the phone. He reckons she's been arrested."

"Who?"

"Alicia."

All time stands still.

"What? What happened? Tell me! Quick!"

"They got her on that firework stunt."

"That was her?"

"No, she got some poor exchange student to do it, but a witness saw her giving the kid the fireworks."

I can't believe this. Alicia arrested, on the very day I've gained my freedom. How is this possible?

It can't be this easy.

I let out a strange, strangled whistle. I don't know whether to laugh or cry.

"They've got her!"

Julio reaches over and squeezes my hand, but even in my elation, I can't return the gesture.

"Knowing Alicia, she'll probably wriggle out of it. They won't be able to hold her for long."

I'm not that lucky.

"Maybe, but if they start digging around, they might just find a few skeletons."

"Let's hope so."

"Anyway, I think it's about time we opened this, don't you?"

He holds up a bottle of my favourite champagne.

"Oh Deacon, you've already spent so much. I don't know how I'm ever going to repay you."

"Well, then - one glass of champagne is hardly going to make any difference, is it?"

I laugh at his logic. "Go on then."

"Julio, would you like a glass?"

"No thanks - I really should get home to Holly." He turns to me. "I'm so glad you're out, Isabel and I really am sorry."

"Thanks."

I let him show himself out.

I try not to think about him as I enjoy the first champagne I've had in a very long time.

"You OK?" I ask Kate, who is unnaturally quiet.

"Yeah, why?"

I narrow my eyes. "You know – Julio."

Because he broke your heart into a thousand tiny pieces.

"Oh, him!"

"I never thought I'd see the two of you in the same room again."

"Yeah, well things are different now."

"You're over him?"

"Absolutely – have been for a while. Besides, I have more important things to worry about."

She smiles mysteriously.

"What does that mean?"

She pulls a picture out of her wallet and hands it to me.

"What's this?"

"What does it look like?"

"A scan picture." I stare at her in amazement. "Are you…pregnant?"

She nods. "Thirteen weeks and counting."

"What? I didn't even know you were seeing anyone!"

She smiles ruefully. "Well, it wasn't exactly planned, but I'm happy. We're happy."

"So who's the mystery man? Anyone I know?"

"Well, actually…"

She looks up as Rhett walks over with a glass of orange juice in his hand. He sets it down on the table and slips his arm around her waist.

"You told her then?"

"You're…the father?"

"Is it that hard to believe?"

"No, no, of course not. It's just… taken me a bit by surprise, that's all!"

I leave them to it and go and find Deacon, who's using the computer in his study.

The desk is stacked precariously high with papers and legal books.

You really tried to get me out, didn't you?

"Ah, I take it they've told you their news?"

"You knew about this? Why didn't you tell me?"

"Kate wanted to tell you herself – in person. Not in some manky visitor's room. Aren't you happy for them?"

"Of course I am – I just…didn't see it coming, that's all."

"You didn't?" He laughs. "Rhett's had a thing for Kate ever since I can remember. The only thing I'm surprised about is that it's taken them this long to get together."

So that's why I've never seen him with another girl! Poor Rhett. He must have been devastated when she married Julio.

He looks at me closely. "You thought he was on the other bus didn't you?"

"Well, what was I supposed to think? He *is* rather fond of shopping. And cooking." I pause, thoughtfully. "Perfect boyfriend material, really. But I just can't believe he's liked her for all these years! How could she not notice?"

"People can be a bit blind, when it comes to love."

"Like you and Alicia?" I blush – I hadn't meant to utter these words aloud.

"No."

"I'm sorry, I shouldn't have said anything."

Are you still in love with her? Even after everything she's done to me?

"No, I meant – that's not what happened,"

"What *did* happen?" I try to keep my tone casual, but every nerve in my body jangles.

245

"I wanted to make you jealous."

"Yeah, right."

"I know it was stupid, but you always looked at me as your friend. And I wanted to be more than that."

I blink. "Why didn't you say something?"

"I did! Don't you remember? At the ball, the Christmas before last."

I look down at the ground. "I thought you were joking. We'd both had a bit too much to drink that night."

"That's the trouble. You never took me seriously."

He hangs his head. "And the thing with Alicia – that was her idea. She said if you saw me with someone else, you might realise what you were missing. I know it was stupid and juvenile, but I thought it might just work. I didn't know what she was then, or I would never have gone along with it."

"So you were never… in love with her?"

"No, never. I only have eyes for you, Isabel."

I melt into him.

The first kiss is soft and sweet and tender. Soon his hands are on my back and in my hair. His body presses against mine as he kisses me more deeply, more urgently. I'm tempted, oh how I'm tempted. *But how can I even consider this?* His cruel words, spoken so many months ago, still sting in my ears: "Fluffy's disappearance is probably her own doing."

"No!" I pull back sharply.

He looks at me in confusion.

"Isabel? What's wrong?"

"I was there that night, when you were talking to Kate about me. When you told her Fluffy ran away because of me."

"Ohhh…" Deacon's face changes. "No, Isabel – it wasn't like that."

"I heard everything."

I look at him expectantly, waiting for him to deny it, to apologise, anything.

"I know that's what I said…"

So it's true.

I spin on my heel.

"Isabel!"

"Leave me alone, Deacon. I really appreciate everything you've done for me, but there's really nothing more you can say."

I do a lot of thinking on the long walk home. It's strange, picking my way through the familiar streets. This is the first time I've been on my own, truly on my own, for months. As much as it hurts, I have to accept this. If Deacon doesn't believe in me, then there's no future for us and no point in pretending.

My wind battered car waits for me on my driveway, the windows muddied with leaves and cobwebs. I find the front door slightly dented. The police must have broken it down to get in when they were looking for Holly. It's been fixed, but you can still tell something happened here.

Inside, the place is a lot tidier than I left it. Kate and Rhett have been round to clean. There are fresh flowers on the windowsill and not a single dish left in the sink or on the draining board. Even Fluffy's bowl has been washed and neatly put away. I sniff the air. Rhett has put in one of those plug-in air fresheners. It smells lovely and lemony, and yet it makes me feel incredibly sad, as if the citrus smell has wiped out the last vestige of Fluffy. I take his bowl out of the cupboard, fill it with water and place it back on the ground. Then I go upstairs to pack. If I set off now, I should be in Scotland by the morning.

26

The gentle motion of the train must have lulled me to sleep. I slide open the window and enjoy the cool breeze on my face, as sheep patterned fields whiz by. Am I really here, hundreds of miles away from Alicia, Jody and all the craziness of the last year?

As the train pulls into the station, I glance furtively around but no one takes the slightest bit of notice as I set off into the picturesque Fenley village. I don't know how long the police will detain Alicia, but I'm betting it won't be long. That's why I had to get away when I did. It's best for everyone that they don't know where I am. I try not to think of the friends I've left behind. I try not to think of Deacon and my unresolved feelings for him. If my friends can't find me, then nor can my enemies.

I walk into the village shop and linger in front of the display of cigarettes at the counter. I had to cut back on them while I was in prison, but now they are freely available, I'm not sure I really want them anymore. Instead, I fill a basket with groceries; bread, butter, eggs, milk, cheese, wine, coffee and chocolate - everything I need to sustain myself for the next few days plus a bottle of water for the long walk up the hill. And I know it's a long walk, because I've been here before.

My friends and I rented Tumbledown Cottage last summer, after Kate and Julio broke up. We thought it would help Kate take her mind off things. I'm hoping it will do the same for me now. Quaint, scenic and secluded – it's the perfect place to hide.

Tumbledown Cottage, Northwest Highlands

The cottage is just as I remember; that faint smell of oak and heather, low ceilings supported by solid black beams, walls painted in various shades of peach, lemon and pistachio. Despite the short notice, Marjorie, the owner, has left me a homemade Victoria sponge and turned up the heating, so the cottage is warm and snug when I arrive. There is no need for me to light the open fireplace - not that I had any intention of doing so.

I take a long, hot soak in the bath and change into my pyjamas. I am tempted to open a bottle of wine, but then what would I do tonight? Instead, I brew some coffee and flip through a magazine, marvelling at how the fashions have changed since I've been inside. My eyelids grow heavy and I allow myself to fall asleep in front of the TV. I am faintly aware it's still on as I'm drifting off, but I do not make any move to turn it off. I have become too accustomed to noise.

I dream of my purple moon again that night; A moon with a fantastic halo and sherberty-orange stars that pulse brightly in the night sky. I haven't had that dream for so many years, and yet here it is again, as if to mark the start of my new life.

I wake at first light and watch the sun break over the mountains as I eat my eggs. The weather is grey and bleak most of the time, and the only person I see is Marjorie, the white-haired landlady, who drives up on Friday to collect her rent. She is curious about my situation, especially when I tell her that I would like to stay on for a few more weeks, but I don't let her lure me into conversation. I doubt anyone's heard about the trial in these parts and I'd like to keep it that way.

I only go down to the village when I run out of fresh food and even then I don't go anywhere but the village shop. I gaze wistfully through the windows of the little boutique Kate and I found the last time we were here, but I don't go in. It's crucial that I keep a low profile. Besides, what use do I have for beautiful dresses now?

※

By Saturday, though, cabin fever has crept in. I need to get out, even if just to go down to the village. I promise myself I'll be careful, that I won't get caught in conversation by the shop assistant, or linger too long outside the boutique. I just need to taste my freedom for a bit, to remind myself that I can come and go as I please now. That I'm no one's prisoner.

But as I open the door, something flies past me, into the cottage. I jump back, startled, till I see that it's just a little robin. He's very friendly - hops right up to me and accepts crumbs from the table. He's such a sweet little thing, I would love to keep him but I could never do that. I could never put him in a cage. Instead, I let him eat his fill and then show him the way out.

It's raining hard as I return from my shopping expedition, laden with a rucksack full of groceries and wine. I towel off and put everything away. In addition to the usual sundries, I've treated myself to a face-mask and a French manicure kit. These, along with a box of macaroons and a Coronation Street DVD, ought to keep me occupied for the rest of the day.

I am just about to apply the first coat of nail polish when there is a knock at the door.

Who's that?

My hair stands on end a little as I go to the door. I cannot let go of the fear that Alicia will come after me. That she'll go to the ends of the earth to find me. That I'll never truly be free of her.

I spot Marjorie's pink umbrella through the spy-hole and start to unbolt the door. But it isn't Marjorie who stands, dripping from head to toe, in the doorway.

"You didn't let me explain…"

"Deacon!"

Water drips from his body and pools on the bristly doormat.

I thought I'd never see you again!

"Can I come in?"

"I think you'd better," I say, quick to recover my composure.

I pull him inside and help peel off his sopping wet raincoat.

"How on earth did you find me?"

"Your neighbour."

"Mr Krinkle? Doesn't that man ever learn?"

"Apparently not. He was at his window the night the minicab picked you up. He overheard the driver yelling 'taxi for the station'."

"He couldn't be bothered to ring the doorbell, the lazy sod. But how did you know I was coming here?"

"The overnight train was the only one running at that time of night and I knew you'd only been to Scotland once before and that was with me."

My mouth drops open. "So you came all this way - on the off-chance?"

"Not quite. I rang Marjorie to see if you'd booked the cottage."

"Oh. I hadn't thought of that."

I feel a slightly heady sensation as he reaches for me and grips my shoulders.

"I can't believe you just left like that. Were you ever coming back?"

He sounds…angry, no, more than that – hurt, upset.

"I didn't think I was ever going to see you again!"

"Me neither." I pull away, before I do something reckless. I'm so torn and confused. Too shocked to think clearly. I hadn't expected him to come after me like this. Hadn't prepared myself for the possibility that he'd find me.

"I'll make us some coffee," I say. "Then we can talk properly."

"Fine. I'll go and change into some dry clothes."

I try to collect my thoughts as I boil the kettle. Part of me is giddy with excitement, but another part wonders if this can ever work.

"You really should let me explain about those things I said," he says, accepting a cup.

I look down at my palms. "I don't think there's anything you can say."

"Just hear me out, OK?"

"OK."

Because I'm not quite ready to let you go yet.

"Those things I said – they were all for Alicia's benefit. I knew she was listening at the door that night. I needed her to believe that I was still taken in by her. I didn't want her to know that I was onto her. "

His face is flushed and earnest. Is it possible he's telling the truth?

"Come on, Isabel. You know me."

I thought I did.

"You sounded so…convincing…"

He presses his lips together. "I have to admit – there was a moment when I did wonder about you. You were acting so strangely that I was genuinely worried, but it wasn't for very long. The more time I spent with Alicia, the more I could see that she was the sick one, not you. I never really thought you could harm Fluffy. I could never think that."

My body's in shock. I feel like I'm floating on air.

"So you don't think I'm crazy?"

"Well, not in a clinical sense…"

"I still find it hard to believe that you weren't really in love with Alicia."

I saw the way you looked at her. You never looked at me like that.

"Isabel, I don't know what I have to say to convince you. Except that you're the one I want. The only one."

He reaches over to me and I'm afraid he's going to touch me, afraid I won't be able to control myself if he does, so I set down my coffee and walk over to the window, from where I can steer the conversation back to safer waters.

"How is everyone? Is Kate OK?"

"She's fine. She doesn't understand why you left in such a rush, though, or why you won't answer her calls. She was threatening to come and find you herself."

"So that's why you came?"

"You know why I came." He takes a deep breath. "I do have some news, though. I don't really know how to tell you this – I don't want to scare you."

"What? What is it?"

"The police found the bodies of Alicia's father and brother at their holiday home in France. Apparently, the bodies had been there some time."

"They'd been…murdered?"

"The French police thought the deaths were accidental, but considering what we already know, I doubt that's true."

So that's why Alicia came after me. She'd already got revenge on her family. I was just next on her list.

"Brian made a few calls for me and it sounds like Penney

and Millrose are going over there to speak to the French police. They want to launch an investigation."

"Let's hope they get it right this time."

"That's the thing. Brian reckons that if they do press charges, then Jody's going to take the rap for it all. She'll do anything Alicia tells her, and she's got a history of psychiatric illness. She can play the insanity card if she has to."

"So Alicia won't go to prison?"

"I don't know, but it sounds like Jody has already confessed to some of the lesser charges. They're sending her to Gillmore."

"Gillmore?" I relish the very idea of Jody being sent to the place where I was wrongly incarcerated. The taste is quite delicious on my tongue. If only Alicia were going too. How poetic that would be.

"But I didn't come here to talk about them, Isabel. I came here so that we could talk about us."

He takes my hand in his, and electricity flows between us.

"Will you come home with me?"

"I don't think I can. Not if the police release Alicia."

"But what about us?"

"I don't know – we'll have to work something out."

"We have to."

He finishes the last of his coffee and looks at me with strangely bloodshot eyes. "Something's wrong…"

His hand slips through my fingers. There is a sickening thump as he hits the floor.

"Deacon!"

His skin is cold and clammy, but I feel queasy even as I rush to his side. I retch as I roll him into the recovery position, then double over as the nausea hits me.

Where is my phone?

My ears buzz and tingle and black dots dance in front of my eyes. This is the last thing I remember.

27

A thick fog weighs me down. I try to make sense of what's happening but my brain can't seem to process it and my body refuses to help.

I try to lick my lips, but my mouth feels heavy and my lips taste slightly sugary, like when you lick an envelope. Or when someone sticks a strip of parcel tape over your mouth.

As the fog lifts, I look down and see that my arms and legs are also bound with tape, making it impossible to move from the cold, hard surface I'm lying on. To my left, I can see an old oak dresser, stacked with willow-patterned cups and plates.

I'm still in Tumbledown Cottage. Tied to the kitchen table.

Panic grips me. I don't understand what's happened. One minute we were talking, the next we were dropping like flies.

"Deacon?"

But my words are muffled.

"Deacon!"

There is no reply. Desperately, I look around.

Where are you?

Finally, I spot him – tied to a chair, his head slumped forward in his lap.

"Deacon!"

There is no response, but I can tell by the rise and fall of his stomach that he is breathing.

High heels clack on the wooden floorboards. I close my eyes and try to pretend that I'm still unconscious. The footsteps stop. Hair tickles my neck. She is standing right over me, her breath like fire.

"I know you're awake, Isabel. You might as well open your eyes."

I shiver uncontrollably as her slim fingers trace my neck.

"Are you cold? Maybe I should light a fire?"

My eyes snap open and she nods with satisfaction.

"What did you do to us? Poison our coffee?"

But my words are stifled by the tape.

"We'll just wait for Deacon before we begin," she says, as though we're about to conduct a seminar.

"Begin what?"

Deacon's eyes flicker open and shut.

Oh god. I'm so sorry I got you into this.

I watch his face go from confusion, to alarm, to anger, all in the space of about thirty seconds. He looks at me and I look at him, desperate to communicate. Desperate to escape.

"This conversation is getting a bit one-sided."

Alicia leans over and rips the tape from my face. It stings, but I refuse to show any emotion.

"Are you at least going to tell me why?" I say, stalling for time. I'm very aware of Deacon, straining to get free.

"Why? You know why!"

"But why now, after so many years?"

She looks at me cautiously, as if deciding whether I deserve to hear the truth.

"I found you by chance," she finally says. "I had a job to do in Queensbeach and I popped into Robertson's for some supplies. That was where I saw you. I recognised you straight away." Her voice drops slightly. "I remembered you, as if it was yesterday, but you didn't even give me a second glance."

"Maybe I didn't see you…"

"You served me at the till! We had a conversation. I even asked you about places to stay and you told me about the caravan park."

I shake my head. "I'm sorry I didn't recognise you. I meet a lot of people at Robertson's."

"My life was hell when I met you at camp, but clearly, my pain meant nothing to you. I told you my deepest, darkest secret and instead of helping me, you made it a thousand times worse. So yeah, when I saw you again, I saw my chance to get my own back. I wasn't that innocent, little ten-year-old anymore. I knew I could destroy you. So I watched you for a while, found out where you lived, who your friends were. And then, when I was ready, I arranged for us to meet."

She looks around for something, I'm not sure what. I glance at Deacon, who is struggling for all he's worth but his binds hold tight.

"What does FRY stand for?" I ask, desperately. Anything to keep her talking.

"You still don't know?"

I shake my head.

"Fire Releases You. My dad was right about that. It *does* release you."

Her wicked eyes sparkle. "There's something incredibly wild about starting a fire from scratch. It's like giving birth to a brand new life. I can make fire from the most basic ingredients. I don't even need matches."

"I know. I saw you at Deacon's barbecue. You made a fire out of practically nothing – just a couple of flints rubbed together."

"Yes, I did, didn't I? It's such a beautiful thing, fire." She smiles thoughtfully, before snapping back to attention. "And now, you're going to burn, bitch!"

She storms over to the stove and there is a click as she ignites the flame. Then she picks something up and places it on the hob. The resulting smell reminds me of the soldering iron we had in the tech lab at school.

"What are you doing?"

She doesn't answer.

"What *is* that?"

I'm not even sure she hears me. She is too enchanted by the flickering blue flame, the crazy witch.

I glance at Deacon, but he is squirming too intently to catch my eye.

Shit! How do I get her talking again?

"How did you start that fire, that day at Deacon's?" I ask.

But the conversation is over. After a couple of minutes, she picks up whatever it is by the handle and brings it over to the table. It looks hot. Really hot. The bottom is smouldering.

It's a branding iron.

"Nooo!"

She brings it down on my stomach and I scream as I have never screamed before.

The branding iron burns straight through my shirt, onto the tender flesh of my tummy.

"Get it off! Get it off!"

The pain! I wiggle and writhe with all my might, but I can't shift it. Can't shift her.

"Somebody! Help!"

And just like that it stops. I watch in amazement as Deacon rips through his bonds with the aid of a penknife he must have had in his pocket. He flings her across the room, the branding iron clattering down to the floor beside her.

"You OK?"

I nod, but Alicia is as quick and agile as a cat. She hits the ground running and takes off at quite a speed.

"Quick, catch her!" I shriek, as she bolts for the door.

Deacon runs after her. He has to, because as long as Alicia is free, we will never be safe.

My eyes stream as I look down at the scorched skin on my stomach. A freezer full of ice stands just a metre away, but I am still bound to the table and can't move an inch towards it. It feels like eternity until Deacon returns, but it is probably only a couple of minutes. He drags Alicia with him, kicking and yowling like an animal, tearing at his flesh with her teeth.

"Quick, tie her up!"

I ache to be set free, but I know he must deal with her first. I'm still in agony, as he shoves her into the very chair he himself was tied to and binds her tightly with her own tape, which she left conveniently by the sink.

Finally, he rushes over to me and places a bag of frozen peas on my stomach, before slashing the tape from my arms and legs.

"Are you sure she's secure?" I ask, glancing nervously in Alicia's direction.

"For the time being. Now, let me see that wound."

"It hurts!" I whimper.

"I know," he says. "Let me help you over to the sofa. You'll be more comfortable there."

"How did she find us?" I ask, once I'm settled.

"She must have followed me up here. I'm so sorry, Isabel. I just had to see you."

"I know." I squeeze his hand. "I'm so glad you did."

My voice drops to a whisper. "But what are we going to do with her?"

His eyes meet mine, and I'm not sure I like what either of us is thinking.

Fate has twisted the knife once again, leaving us with a cruel dilemma.

"We have to let her go sometime."

"If we do, she'll kill us both."

"Then what are we going to do – go to the police?"

"But what if the police let her go again?" I bite my lip. "We don't have to decide right now, do we?"

"I suppose not."

I get up and walk over to Alicia. It feels strange to finally have all the power.

"Don't get too close," Deacon warns.

"I need to ask her something."

I pull the tape from her mouth and hope it stings her as much as it stung me.

"What did you do with Fluffy?"

"You'll never know."

She spits in my face.

I seal the tape back over her mouth and walk away. Any sympathy I ever felt for her has gone. She doesn't have a human bone in her body.

❄

The evening passes almost pleasantly. Deacon cooks sausages and mash for supper and it tastes bloody good - the best meal I've had all week. He offers some to Alicia but she refuses to eat or drink anything, even water.

See? You're killing me.

She thinks by doing this, we'll have to let her go, but she's wrong.

We don't have to do anything.

Her little girl voice is soft and pitiful but it has no effect on me anymore.

"I need to go to the toilet!"

"Then I'll take you."

Deacon looks up sharply. "We'll both take you."

"How can I sleep?" she whines as the day becomes darker. "Tied to a chair like this? It's not right."

"You'll live."

There can be no opportunity to escape.

"If you don't let me go, my sister will go after Rhett."
"She's bluffing."
"And Kate."
Neither of us even look up.
"And the baby."
"How does she know about the baby?" Deacon whispers. "They haven't even gone public yet."
"I don't know."
It's like she has hidden knowledge.
"Have you been spying on us?"
"Spying on you? I could still be living in the Beach House for all you know! It's so ridiculously big, you'd never notice!"
I shudder at the thought.
"Did you really start all those fires?" I can't help asking. "At the caravan park? And Bernie's car and the gym? Oh and Rose Cottage?"
"Rose Cottage?" she laughs. "That one was Jody!"
So Rose Cottage was Julio's fault – in a way.

❆

I NEVER THOUGHT I'd be able to sleep with Alicia so close to me, but somehow, curled up in Deacon's arms, I do. There are perfectly good beds upstairs but we choose to sleep on the threadbare sofa. It's vital we all stay together, in the one room. That way we know where everybody is. There's no chance Alicia can escape.

In the morning, Deacon examines my stomach again.
"It's looking much better," he says with satisfaction. "Maybe it won't scar after all."
It will scar. I know it will.
In fact, I'll probably be scarred for life, but at least now my outside will reflect my inside.
"Do you think she meant it about Jody going after Kate and Rhett?" I whisper, as we eat our breakfast.

"I don't think she'll have much chance as long as she's locked up in prison, being someone else's bitch."

My cheeks burn, as I remember what it was like, being locked up with criminals, not knowing if I would ever get out. But I won't allow myself to feel pity for Jody. She might not be as bad as Alicia, but she's guilty nonetheless.

We try to ignore Alicia, snarling and moaning in the corner all day while we play cards and watch TV.

Rat-a-tat-tat!

"Shit, who's that?"

As fast as lightning, Deacon flies over to Alicia and plants his hands over her mouth, warning her to be quiet. Then she starts shouting and screaming as loud as she can. I grab a strip of tape and plaster it over her mouth, but her cries are still faintly audible.

I go to the peephole.

"It's Marjorie! What does she want? The rent isn't due till the end of the week."

"She probably wants her umbrella back. I was supposed to return it this morning."

"What shall we do, pretend we're not in?"

"No, she'll only come back. Quick, let's hide Alicia in the bathroom. She won't be able to hear her there."

We pick her up in the chair she's tied to and carry her through the utility room to the back of the house.

Even with tape over her mouth, it is impossible to make her completely quiet.

"Shut up!" I hiss, terrified that Marjorie will hear.

But the harder I try to silence her, the more she yells.

"If you don't shut up, I'll have to knock you out!" I threaten, looking around for a heavy object. My eye rests on the big, red fire extinguisher in the corner.

How appropriate that would be!

I pick it up and walk towards her with it, but Alicia just laughs.

She thinks I don't have it in me. That may have been true once, but I'm not so sure anymore.

"I'll deal with her," Deacon says, taking the fire extinguisher out of my shamed hands. "You get rid of Marjorie. Just for heaven's sake, don't let her in."

I hurry to the door, grabbing the umbrella from the coat stand on the way.

"Hi Marjorie," I call, trying to drown out Alicia's cries. "Here's your umbrella."

"Thank you, dear. Here, I made you a casserole. I know how you young things don't have time to cook."

She hands me a cloth-wrapped Pyrex dish.

"Oh, how lovely of you!"

The old lady peers past me into the cottage. "Shall I pop it in the oven?"

"No!" I say, a little too sharply. "I mean, we've just had afternoon tea. We'll have it a little later."

"As you wish, dear."

But she still doesn't make any move to leave.

What does she want?

"So, I understand you've got your friend Deacon staying with you?"

"Yes. I hope that's all right?"

"Only, you arrived in such an awful hurry. I thought maybe you'd had a falling out?"

"Me and Deacon?"

What is she getting at? God, how do I get rid of her?

"Isabel?"

I turn round to find Deacon standing behind me. He has stripped down to his boxers, his hands placed confidently on his broad hips, so little is left to the imagination.

"Oh, I'm so sorry! I didn't realise we had company!"

Nicely done!

The old lady blushes.

"Oh, I see, I'm interrupting! Please excuse me. I'll leave you to it."

But she is smiling as she hands over the casserole and instructs me to heat it at 180 degrees for fifteen minutes.

Gossip! That's it. She was just after was a bit of gossip.

She wanted to know if Deacon and I were together, because the last time she saw us, we definitely weren't. Well, the spectacle Deacon just treated her to seems to have satisfied her curiosity. I watch as she clambers back into her Land Rover and pets the little dog who is waiting for her in the passenger seat.

"Do you think we got away with it?" I ask, as she drives away. I set the casserole down on the kitchen counter, and try not to stare as Deacon slides back into his jeans.

"I think so. I don't think she would have hung around otherwise. Besides, she's a little hard of hearing if I remember correctly. I don't think she would have heard Alicia unless she'd come inside."

"I just hope you're right."

"Hmm…hmmm," comes Alicia's muffled cry from the bathroom. She still has the tape over her mouth.

"We'd better go and get her."

"Do we have to?"

"Afraid so."

"I need to stretch my legs," she whines, when Deacon removes the tape. "My legs ache. My ribs ache. Everything aches. I'll get deep vein thrombosis."

"Come on then. We'll walk you around the living room for a bit. No funny business though, or you'll go right back in the chair."

❄

MARJORIE'S CASSEROLE IS DELICIOUS. There's plenty left over but Alicia refuses to even taste it. She's still on hunger strike.

Hasn't drunk a drop of water all day. I wonder how much longer she's going to keep this up for. How much longer we can hold her.

"Would you like a glass of wine?" Deacon asks me, as we finish washing and drying the dishes.

"We probably shouldn't."

"Yeah, I suppose you're right."

But I have just got out of prison. Don't I deserve to relax?

"Perhaps one glass won't kill us?"

He grins. "I'll get it."

We snuggle on the sofa and watch old movies, back to back. We don't really notice when one glass of wine becomes two but soon, we've finished the entire bottle.

"Shall we open another?" he asks, but I'm already up and reaching for the corkscrew.

"What are we going to do about her?" he murmurs, coming over to take his glass. "We can't keep her tied up like this forever. It isn't right."

"Why isn't it right? After everything she's done to us."

"You know we'll have to let her go sometime. We'll just have to figure out how we're going to do it."

"But we can't!"

"There's no other option. We'll have to go to the police. Ask for their protection."

"You think I'm going to put my life in the hands of the police, after everything that's happened to me?"

I feel the heat rising inside of me.

"Isabel…"

"No, don't touch me. You obviously don't understand a thing I've been through."

"I do understand! I just want what's best."

"That's the problem with you, Deacon Frost. You always think you know best!"

My eyes blaze with fury. But instead of rising to my anger, a smile tugs at the corner of his mouth.

"You're so sexy when you're angry."

"Shut up! This is hardly the time. I could throw a chair at you!"

But my anger only fuels the flame.

"That's it. I have to have you right now!"

"What, here? Pressed up against the kitchen sink? With her watching?"

"She's asleep."

"Are you sure?"

I can never figure out if her snores are real.

"Quite sure."

He tugs at the tie at the side of my wrap dress and it falls wide open.

I try to look outraged and indignant, but I make no move to cover up. He does not touch me. Not yet. Instead, he takes a step back, his eyes drinking in the first glimpse of me in my underwear. My nipples harden under the intensity of his gaze and he licks his lips in anticipation. His fingers trace the soft straps of my bra, toy with the clasp at the back. I am not even aware that he has unhooked it until my breasts spill out and they are in his hands. I kiss his lips, his shoulders, stroke the muscles that define his chest. if Alicia were to wake up right now, I would not, could not stop.

"Do you…want to go upstairs?" he asks tentatively. "Unless…you want to wait?"

Wait? Wait for what? Alicia? She doesn't deserve our consideration. She doesn't deserve anything.

"Let's go."

I glance at her as we pass, but Deacon has tied her securely to the chair. Even if she does wake up, there's no way she can escape.

We make it to the hallway before we start kissing again, tugging at each other's clothes. We start our way up the stairs but fall into a heap on the second step.

"Your legs are so smooth."

"Hmm…"

"What are you thinking?"

"I'm thinking how glad I am that I shaved them yesterday."

He smiles, and his hand disappears between my legs.

Clothes go flying; shirt, dress, trousers and underwear litter the staircase and the hall. By the time we reach the bedroom we are both naked. He takes my hand in his and kisses it tenderly, before leading me over to the king-size bed. The warmth of our bodies contrast with the unexpected coldness of the room. I pull back the cover and lie down, waiting expectantly as he crawls on top of me, careful to avoid pressing on my bandages.

"You don't know how long I've waited for this."

"Shh!" I press my finger to his lips.

But he is insistent. "I've wanted to do this since the first night we met, when I threw you out of Millennium. You were so brazen, so stubborn."

"And you were such a pig!"

He refuses to take offence. We laugh like idiots and the duvet forms an envelope around us, like the warm embrace of invisible hands.

"Is this OK?" he asks softly.

"It's wonderful."

My stomach smarts a little, but I kind of like it.

"I don't ever want this to end. You're so beautiful."

"I know."

He smiles with amusement as I roll him off me and climb on top. I sit astride him, look deep into his warm, intelligent eyes and rock gently back and forth. The bed creaks with each motion. I don't know if Alicia can hear us downstairs, but a voyeuristic part of me hopes she can.

"Oh, that's so good…"

I grip the headboard with both hands, as my pleasure

grows more and more intense. I can't speak. His touch sends a shiver through my soul.

We tremble together.

It's…unbelievable. And yet, I am filled with an overwhelming sense of foreboding, like the evil outside is waiting to be let in. That, by this very act, I've let it in. I lie down by his side; feel his big strong arms around me, protecting me.

"I wish we could stay here forever."

"Me too, but we have to go back down before Alicia wakes up."

"Just a few more minutes?"

I close my eyes.

As I start to drift off, I picture the little robin who visited me yesterday morning. He hops up onto the kitchen table, looking for more crumbs, but the table is sticky and he gets his feet stuck. The poor little thing is unable to fly away, and the more he struggles, the more the goo sticks to his feathers. I've no idea what to make of this image.

Maybe it's just the residue of whatever Alicia used to drug us.

I wake up with a jolt.

"Deacon!"

"What?"

"I thought I heard something."

He rubs his eyes. "I can't hear anything."

"I'll just go downstairs and check."

I am already out of bed.

"Wait. We'll both go."

We pick our way down the stairs, pulling on our clothes as we go. To my relief, the living room is just as we left it. Alicia still curled up in her chair in the corner.

"See? She's still sound aslee…"

And that's when a hand reaches out of the shadows and grabs me. I feel a metal blade, cold against my skin. Its jagged edges nibble at my throat.

28

"Help!" I splutter.

The figure in the chair sits up and opens her eyes. But it isn't Alicia at all.

"Jody!"

I thought you were in prison!

She must have arrived while we were upstairs and set Alicia free. The door was bolted, but it would take more than a lock to keep her out. Even a prison couldn't keep her in. I should have known that.

And they switched places just to mess with me.

Oh how could we be so stupid? We should never have let Alicia out of our sight. Not for a minute.

"Let her go, Alicia!"

Deacon draws himself up to his fullest height, but he doesn't come any closer. Not while she holds the blade so close to my neck.

Alicia laughs her irritating little laugh. "So – the lovebirds return. Though you took a lot longer when you were with me, Deacon."

Deacon goes red in the face. Is that anger, or is he hiding something?

After all, she is young and beautiful – would he really have been able to resist if she'd thrown herself at him?

Maybe.

Maybe not.

But this is hardly the time to be thinking about that - I don't dare swallow, the blade is so close to my throat.

"I told you to let her go!" Deacon says, moving closer.

"Shut up!" Alicia snaps. "You're going to do exactly as I say."

She turns to Jody. "Don't just stand there gaping. Go and bring the car round."

She must have parked further up the road, so we wouldn't hear the sound of the engine. She trots off obediently. You'd think she was the younger sister, not the older one.

Alicia wastes no time.

"Deacon, there's some lighter fluid in the cupboard under the sink. Go and get it."

Deacon does.

"Good, now empty it all round the room. More vigorously, Deacon. You're not watering the garden."

She doesn't move the blade an inch from my neck while she barks out these instructions. Alicia was always dangerous, but now she's doubly so. Holding her hostage has both heightened her anger and wounded her pride. She's got more to prove now, a new score to settle. Instead of saving ourselves, we've only succeeded in poking the bear.

I've got to do something - quickly, before Jody returns.

I take a deep breath and jab Alicia hard in the ribs. She yelps in surprise. Before she has a chance to recover, I stamp down hard on her foot, and twist round, pulling myself out of her hold. It's a dangerous move, but it works. The blade clatters noisily to the floor and I kick it safely under the TV cabinet.

"Give me that!" she says angrily, snatching the lighter fluid from Deacon's hand.

"Isabel, watch out!" Deacon cries, as she aims straight for my face.

But I am fast as lightning these days. I dart deftly out of her way, and she gets lighter fluid all down her skirt.

Just at that moment, Jody walks back in, seemingly oblivious to the change in dynamics. Before anyone can do anything, she produces a pack of cigarettes from her top pocket.

"Here, you want one?"

In one fluid motion, she lights it and tosses it to her sister. The cigarette floats like a feather through the air. Then womf! The flame ignites, right at Alicia's feet.

I don't quite know how I get away. One moment I'm by the window, the next I'm crashing through the open doorway, Deacon and Jody and I all landing in a heap at the door.

Alicia lumbers after us. She is a ball of flames.

"Help me!" she shrieks.

I watch in horror as Deacon reaches out to her, pulling her out of the now burning Tumbledown Cottage.

"Deacon - it's too dangerous! You'll catch fire!"

"We can't just leave her!"

The doctor in him takes over. He throws her to the ground and rolls her over and over in the damp grass, quenching the flames.

"Release me!" she croaks, her words barely audible.

We all watch to see what happens next. For a moment, she lies limp as a doll. Then, all at once, she starts coughing, then vomiting. Molten ash spews from her lips like hundreds of tiny insects. Her eyes are yellow marbles as her whole body convulses. Her arms and legs jerk wildly, and she froths at the mouth. Deacon waits until the seizure abates and then places her in the recovery position. She lets out one last horrific roar and then there is complete silence. Not even the birds in the trees make a sound.

He leans over her prostrate body, feeling for a pulse.

"Anything?"

He shakes his head.

"There's no way an ambulance will get here in time," says Jody, standing behind him.

Why doesn't she do something? This is her sister!

Because she doesn't want to, I realise.

She doesn't want Alicia to live any more than I do.

As long as Alicia is alive, she can't be her own person.

The three of us look at each other.

"We can't just…let her die."

It feels like the right thing to say. Not because I want Alicia to live, but because I don't want to be like the monster she's become.

I watch numbly as Deacon goes through the motions of trying to pump life back into her body, but we all know it's too late. Her face is drained of all colour. Even her eyes have lost their darkness.

She lies so still, so tragically beautiful, as Jody leans down and kisses her blue-tinged lips. She brushes away the ash from her sister's kohl-smudged eyes and closes first one and then the other. I'm glad she's done this.

Someone once told me that if a dead person's eyes are left open, they'll find someone to take with them.

I shiver at the thought.

Jody takes Alicia's hands and places them together, as if in prayer. She looks angelic, peaceful even. Ready to move on to the next place, wherever that may be.

I look at Jody. "You saved us."

"She saved herself," Deacon says, his arms folded.

Jody bites her lip. "Go ahead. Call the police. Just give me a head start. They'll never understand what happened."

She takes a Swiss army knife from her pocket. I watch as she hacks off a lock of her sister's hair, so dark and wild - so like her own and slips it into her wallet.

Something to remember her by, I suppose.

She gives Alicia one last glance, then walks way. Her gait is a little unsteady as makes her way to her dirty white escort, registration F-R-Y. I watch as she drives off down the rocky mountain road.

I look at Deacon. "It's over!" I sigh. "It's really over!"

I know I should feel sad and sombre and maybe even a bit guilty for my part in all this, but I don't. I feel…incredible. Invincible, even. This is the best thing that could possibly have happened. Deacon seems to feel it too. He lifts me up and swings me round and round, and when he sets me down again, we share a long, passionate kiss. This isn't the time and it's hardly the place but we just can't help ourselves. For the first time in over a year, I feel free. Much freer than the night I was released from prison. Because this time, the freedom is real. No more running, no more hiding. No more worrying about who's lurking in the bushes, who's waiting in the shadows. Who's planning to torch my house while I sleep.

"I'm sorry. This isn't how it was supposed to be," he says, as he sticks his phone in his pocket. Neither of us can get a signal up here, and even in our excited state, we know we need to get help, before the fire spreads to the forest behind.

"This is exactly how it should be," I contradict him. "A new beginning."

Because from this point on, everything is going to seem wonderful, if only in comparison to what's come before.

"Don't you see? She can't hurt us anymore. We get to live our lives again, as if she never existed. Well, maybe not quite the same…" I reach for his hand and give it a squeeze. He squeezes back tightly, and does not let go as we begin the long descent down to the village, under a strangely purple sky.

29

I'm no stranger to police interviews by now, so I'm not particularly alarmed when we are taken into separate interview rooms at the police station. The long walk down the mountain has given us plenty of time to concoct our story. We've decided we're going to tell the truth – just not the whole truth. We've agreed not to mention the part about keeping Alicia hostage.

You'd be forgiven for thinking that I'd be nervous, after all, I just got out of jail and I've suddenly got a dead body on my hands. A dead body *and* a burning cottage. But now that we're here, I feel a strange confidence that I'd never have thought I'd possess in such a situation. I'm almost casual as I sit in my plastic chair, sipping my watery cup of coffee. Calm enough to ask for more sugar. Calm enough to request a sandwich.

"There are a couple of inconsistencies we'd like to clear up," the DCI says, after he's finished listening to my account.

"Yes?"

Like the fact that we kept Alicia hostage for two days before she died?

I resist the urge to clench my fists. It's imperative that I remain calm, show no outward sign of nerves. Prison has made it easier for me to lie, easier to live with untruth. Being surrounded by thieves and liars all day certainly taught me a thing or two in that department. Even if the DCI suspects what we did, he'll never be able to prove it. Deacon and I are safe, home free. Just as long as he stays as strong as me.

Oh god, what if he's confessed?

The DCI purses his lips. He looks perplexed, as if he's trying to work out a complex mathematical equation.

Come on, out with it!

"Isabel, we're having trouble locating Alicia's body."

My heart skips a beat.

"What? Alicia...the body is right in front of Tumbledown Cottage! You couldn't miss it. Unless it was cremated by the fire?"

The DCI scratches his chin. "No, the fire had virtually fizzled out by the time we got there – in fact, most of the cottage is still standing. But there was no sign of a body. We've got police scouring the mountain, but there doesn't seem to be any sign of it."

I grip the table, trying to stop the world from spinning off its axis.

"I have to ask you again, are you absolutely sure she was dead?"

"Absolutely! I mean, Deacon's a doctor. He ought to know!"

"So where is the body?"

I think fast.

"Jody must have gone back for it!"

It's the only explanation I can think of.

"Why she would do that?"

I shake my head. "I don't know! To hide the evidence? Or maybe she just needed a bit longer to say goodbye? It all happened so quickly, maybe she wasn't in her right mind?"

"Hmm...." He doesn't seem altogether satisfied.

"Excuse me, I have to take this," he says as his phone starts to pulse.

I nod and he steps out of the room, leaving me to stare into space. Even in death, Alicia is taunting me.

What the hell is going on? Are they lying about the body to make me confess?

The DCI returns, looking extremely sombre. I'm no longer feeling casual. I need to know what's happening, and I need to know now.

"What? What is it?"

"They found blood, lots of it, daubed on the walls of the cottage."

"What?"

"It spelt out a word, FRY, all in capitals. Does that mean anything to you?"

"Yes, yes it does, but I don't understand how it got there!"

I think my brain might be splintering in two.

It has to be Jody. But why would she write on the walls in her dead sister's blood? I don't know how, or why, she's done all this but I have to believe she was overcome with guilt and grief. Because if I consider of any of the alternatives, I may never sleep again.

30

"Isabel!"

Sonya embraces me with a big bear hug. I feel like I've aged ten years since I've been away. My face is more lined, and an alarming number of grey hairs have crept onto my head. But Sonya looks younger, somehow. Happier, more at ease with the world.

"You've changed your hair," I say, admiring her glamorous new do. Her hair looks really thick and glossy. I pat my own tangled locks a little self-consciously. My beauty regime went out of the window while I was inside and it's going to take a while to repair the damage.

"I've always wanted to go blonde. Do you like it?" she asks.

"It really suits you. What made you take the plunge?"

"Oh, you know – new job, new look."

"You're like a whole new woman!"

Sonya smiles, looking pleased. "Come on, let me show you around."

I recognise quite a few faces as we walk around the new store. Jon the security man is at his post by the entrance, but instead of just watching the door as he did at Robertson's, he is smiling and joking with the customers, welcoming them in. He even asks one of the checkout boys to come and help a frail old lady carry her shopping to her car. We didn't offer service like that at Robertson's.

The girl at the fish counter smiles as I walk past, as does the lad on the deli. If this had happened at Robertson's, I would have been frantically casting an eye over my outfit, looking to see if I'd left a few buttons undone. I shake my head in amazement as I watch them interact with the customers, politely offering advice on which cut of meat would be best for a dinner party and which fish would taste nice poached.

Filbert's is like the Robertson's we always wanted. The staff are well-trained, friendly and upbeat. Their uniforms are smart and tasteful, no garish green or awful orange. Everyone looks well-groomed and more importantly, hygienic. And best of all, there's no Stu.

"What happened to Stu when Robertson's went under?" I ask, as we peep into the warehouse. I feel a little peculiar setting foot inside, even though both exits are open wide. I can't help remembering that fateful moment when the alarms went off and Deacon and I thought we were going to die.

But this warehouse is quite different from the old one. There's no card-playing here. All the staff are hard at work, and the chap in charge is walking up and down with his clipboard, checking details and calling out instructions. There are no girly calendars in this office. Quite the contrary, pinned to the noticeboard above the desk are framed certificates for teamwork and good management. It bears no resemblance whatsoever to Stu's old office.

"Didn't you hear?" Sonya says, her eyes sparkling with obvious delight. "It was Stu's fault Robertson's didn't get their insurance money. It was recorded as an accidental fire in the end, so they should have been able to make a claim, but that was all irrelevant as far as the insurance company was concerned. Stu let the policy expire. Only by 24 hours, as it happened, but too late for Robertson's to get their hands on any of the money."

"Wow! What incredibly bad luck!"

"Yeah, what a wazzock! If he weren't so lazy, he would have checked that the insurance renewal had gone through on time, instead of just leaving it for a temp to deal with. But you know Stu, he'd rather lark about with his mates than do an honest day's work."

"So what's he doing these days?" I ask curiously. "I take it he's not working here?"

"Hell, no!" Sonya laughs at the thought. "He's working at the greasy burger bar in the precinct. You know, the one with all the lettering peeling off and the tramp sleeping in the doorway."

"You're kidding! Wow, that's quite a come down."

"Yeah, well, his reputation is in tatters. He won't get another management job in a hurry, not when everybody knows that he's the plonker who brought down Robertson's. The local paper ran a headline piece on it. I've kept a copy for you in the office."

I smile. "Have you framed it?"

But I can't help feeling a bit sorry for Stu. I mean, I never really liked him that much, but to think that one little…OK, one huge mistake cost him everything. Well, I suppose I know how that feels.

"It's all turned out for the best, really," says Sonya, brushing the lint from her powder blue suit, a new addition to her wardrobe. "After all, this town really is only big enough for the one supermarket."

"As long as you get to run it!"

"Absolutely! I mean, Bernie's still the boss for now, but he's taking early retirement in a few months, so I'm in a strong position to take over."

"That's great, Sonya!"

As we take the escalator upstairs, I feel a bit like one of the kids in Charlie and the Chocolate Factory. My eyes bulge as I see how large the clothing department is, all the different fabrics and designs. You wouldn't think we were still in a supermarket. This place looks like a department store.

"So, I was wondering - are there any vacancies at the moment?"

I try to keep my tone casual, but I'm hanging on her reply. Despite my innocence, I've heard it could be hard for me to get a job now that I've been in prison, especially here. Queensbeach is a small town and everyone is still talking about the trial. Not to mention Alicia's untimely demise.

Sonya leans over to straighten up a display of T-shirts. "I'm afraid there are no junior management positions at the moment."

"Oh."

I suppose I should have expected as much.

"But how would you feel about working here in the clothing department? We are currently recruiting a trainee buyer."

Me, a fashion buyer?

"You mean I'd get to buy clothes for a living?"

Sonya laughs, "Well, there is a bit more to it than that, but I know you'd be great. Here, let me get you a job description. You can have a look through it at home."

I'm pretty sure I don't need to see the job description but I take a copy anyway so as not to look unprofessional. I need a job as a matter of urgency, and this one sounds ideal.

One Month Later

Ding-Dong!

"I'm coming," I yell, from the landing.

A black and white fur ball bounds past me and down the stairs, his little cowbell jingling loudly.

"Hi Kate."

"Hi Isabel. Hi Fluffy!" She scoops up my cat and strokes his head with affection.

Fluffy purrs, contentedly.

"Mind you don't get cat fur all over your cocktail dress," I warn her, but I lean over and pet him too. It's just so good to have him back.

※

I*t was* Deacon who finally figured out what had become of Fluffy. I was still feeling a bit freaked out when we got back from Scotland, so he offered to stay the night at my house. But once the taxi dropped us off, he took my hand and led me up the path to Mr Krinkle's instead.

"Deacon?"

Mr Krinkle answered the door.

"Hello." It was as though he'd been expecting us. "Just a moment."

He disappeared inside.

I looked at Deacon. "What's going on?"

My neighbour returned, carrying a cardboard box.

"He likes to sleep in here."

I peered inside.

Two large, green eyes met mine.

"Fluffy! Oh my god! Fluffy!"

I scooped my cat up in my arms and held him like a baby.

"I thought you were gone forever!"

I took in his warmth, his smell, the soporific sound of his purr.

Mr Krinkle looked down at the ground.

"It was an honest mistake — at first. I thought he was a stray. His tag must have come off. Then I saw all the posters. I know I should have given him back, but I get so lonely all on my own…"

Poor Mr Krinkle.

I knew I should be angry, but I wasn't really. If it weren't for him, I might still be rotting in jail. And besides, if he hadn't taken Fluffy, it's quite possible Alicia would have. In a way, his actions might have saved him.

"You can visit him whenever you like," I said impulsively. "I'm sure he'll be quite happy to wander between our two houses, pretending he hasn't been fed."

Then I looked at Deacon. "I don't know what to say...."

Deacon smiled.

"You can thank me later."

❄

"Do you realise it's snowing outside?" Kate says now, snapping me out of my reverie.

"Is it?"

I run to the window and look outside. Sure enough, small delicate snowflakes have started to fall, coating the drive with a thin, white blanket. She takes off her coat, her bump clearly visible under the midnight blue dress I helped her buy.

"So come on then. Are you going to do my make-up or what?"

"Of course!" I smile. "Let me just open the bubbly. Non-alcoholic for you, of course!"

Fluffy settles himself on her lap as I apply her mascara and lipstick.

"You don't even need foundation or blusher, you lucky thing," I say, marvelling at how radiant her skin looks. I finish with a touch of lip gloss and hand her a mirror so she can admire the results.

"Thanks, Isabel. Looks great. But hadn't you better hurry up and get yourself ready? Rhett and Deacon will be here any moment."

"That's OK, I'm almost ready."

I skip upstairs to my bedroom. My cocktail dress is hanging on the wardrobe door where I left it. It's the most exquisite shade of green I've ever seen, the bodice decorated with delicate black lace. I shiver with delight as I slip into it. The dress was a little on the expensive side, but that's OK. My new job pays a lot better than the old one. And it's amazing what a visit to the beauty salon can do. For tonight, at least, my skin has lost that tired, frazzled look. My cheeks are almost as rosy as Kate's and my hair looks glossy and styled.

I shall go to the ball!

I smile happily at my reflection.

Knock! Knock!

"Can I come in?"

I open the door for Deacon.

"Want me to zip you up?"

"Yes, please." I pull my hair up out of the way.

"You look stunning," he tells me, as he closes the zip.

I straighten his bowtie. "And you look like a penguin."

Deacon smiles. "I'm going to take that as a compliment. I happen to love penguins."

He reaches into his pocket. "I'm really glad you're wearing green, because I wanted to give you these."

He pulls out a little jewellery box and places it in my hands.

"What's this?"

"Go on, open it."

I do. A tiny pair of emeralds twinkle in the light.

"They're beautiful!" I gasp, holding them up to my ears.

"And so are you."

He leans forward to kiss me and I almost drop the earrings on the floor as I get lost in his embrace.

❄

I FEEL a little lump in my throat as I follow my friends up the steps of the Queensbeach Civic Hall. A glass of champagne is pressed into my hand as soon as I step through the door, and an army of waiters walk around offering dainty canapés.

"Hey, isn't that the guy off Eastenders?" Rhett whispers, as we glance over at the Mayor's table.

I look but I don't really care. This time last year, I would have been thrilled to meet a soap star, but right now all I care about is spending time with my best friends. It's so wonderful to have the four of us back together again, even if we won't remain four for much longer.

"You want to dance?" Deacon asks, as the orchestra starts to play.

"You know what? I don't think you've ever asked me that before," I marvel.

"There's a reason for that!" Rhett winks.

Turns out Rhett's right. Deacon has no sense of rhythm. He steps on my toes, trips over his feet and whirls me into a table. Lord of the dance, he is certainly not.

"Told you," whispers Rhett, as we sit down again.

"I don't know what you're talking about," I lie.

"Oh, come on!"

But I refuse to admit it's the truth. Deacon is probably the worst dancer I've ever known, but he's my boyfriend and I find it kind of endearing.

❄

THE NEXT MORNING I pour myself a strong cup of coffee. It was a late night and I'm glad I had the forethought to book the day off work. Home seems like home again, now I've got Fluffy back. He rubs up against me as I open my desk drawer and pull out the big pile of mail that's been waiting for me since I got out of jail.

Most of it's junk mail, plus tons of bills, which I don't need to worry about because Deacon took care of all that. Then I notice a handwritten envelope, right at the bottom of the pile. I glance at the date on the stamp. It must have been sitting here for several weeks. I don't recognise the writing, so I'm a little curious as I open it and read the childish scrawl:

I*f you are reading this, you have probably already killed me.*

I screw it up tight – and toss it in the bin, but it's too late, I've already seen it. Her voice is in my head:

I want you to know that I forgive you.
  I have prayed for you as you must pray for me.
  Do not mourn me, for I am in a better place now.
  I am with you and I will watch over you always.

Your friend forever,

Alicia

ALSO BY LORNA DOUNAEVA
MCBRIDE VENDETTA SERIES BOOK TWO

Angel Dust

It's every parent's worst nightmare…

When Isabel's daughter, Lauren is snatched from outside her school, she suspects Jody McBride is behind the kidnapping. Yet the detective in charge of Lauren's case seems more interested in picking apart her statement, and investigating members of her family.

Can Isabel persuade the police to take her seriously, or will she have to take matters into her own hands? In order to save Lauren, she must take a stark look at her own relationships, and consider how well she really knows her daughter.

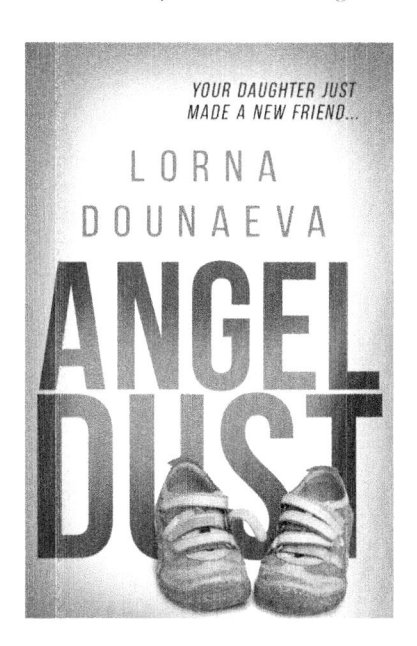

ALSO BY LORNA DOUNAEVA
MCBRIDE VENDETTA SERIES BOOK THREE

Cold Bath Lane

Who will pay the price for her silence?

Nine-year-old Jody is does well in school, despite living in a run-down part of East London.

Then one terrible night, her life changes forever, and Jody is forced to make an impossible choice between telling the truth and keeping her family together.

The police bring her in for questioning, and pressure her to tell them what really happened but is Jody ready to admit it, even to herself? Will the truth win out, or will Jody be sucked into a web of lies in order to protect her family?

This disturbing crime novel is utterly gripping and impossible to put down.

ALSO BY LORNA DOUNAEVA
THE PERFECT GIRL

She was beautiful, popular and successful, the one they all wanted to be. So who, or what, was she running from?

When reclusive writer, Jock falls for vivacious Tea Shop owner, Sapphire, he is amazed that she seems to feel the same way about him. He watches with pride as Sapphire is crowned May Queen at the town's May Day celebrations, but his joy turns to heartbreak when she runs off into the crowd, never to return.

As the days pass, he becomes increasingly desperate. Everyone he speaks to seems to love Sapphire. No one has a bad word to say about her. So why did she run away like that, and what is stopping her from coming back?

The Perfect Girl is a claustrophobic British thriller set on the English/Welsh border.

(The Perfect Girl was previously titled May Queen Killers)

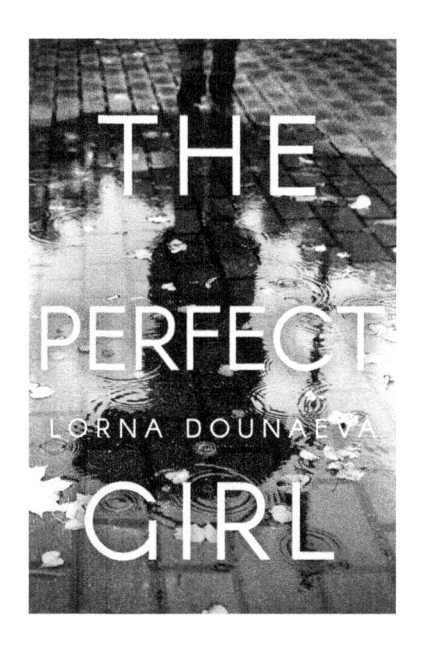

ALSO BY LORNA DOUNAEVA
THE GIRL IN THE WOODS

She finally had the family she had always wanted, so why did she feel as though someone had stepped on her grave?

Suzannah and Noel are desperate for a child so when they get the chance to adopt a young girl called Orchid, they jump at the chance. They have been warned that it will take time for Orchid to settle into their family, but the problems they encounter seem out of the ordinary. Rooms are flooded, mirrors are smashed and Orchid owns up to none of it. Then things take a sinister turn and Suzannah becomes truly frightened. Who is this child they have let into their lives and will they ever be able to tame her?

AFTERWORD

You can now join my readers' club to receive updates on new releases and giveaways at www.lornadounaeva.com

You can also contact me at info@LornaDounaeva.com

ABOUT THE AUTHOR

Lorna Dounaeva is a quirky British crime writer who once challenged a Flamenco troupe to a dance-off. She is a politics graduate, who worked for the British Home Office for a number of years, before turning to crime fiction. She loves books and films with strong female characters and her influences include *Single White Female* and *Sleeping with the Enemy*. She lives in Surrey, England with her husband and their three children, who keep her busy wiping food off the ceiling and removing mints from USB sockets.

facebook.com/LornaDounaevaAuthor
twitter.com/LornaDounaeva
instagram.com/lorna_dounaeva